GUIDE TO FOOD SAFETY
THIRD EDITION

David McSwane, H.S.D. • Richard Linton, Ph.D. • Nancy R. Rue, Ph.D.
Development Services by Learnovation, LLC

Editor-in-Chief: Lawrence R. Kohl
Editorial Assistant: Gwendolyn Lee
Editorial Assistant: Kelsey Anderson
Product Liaison: Dr. Jill Hollingsworth
Production Editor: Anna Graf Williams
Senior Design Coordinator: Karen J. Hall
Copy Editor: Cheryl Pontius
Cover Illustration: John Wise

Copyright © 2010 by Food Marketing Institute, Arlington, VA 22202. All rights reserved. Produced in the United States of America. This publication is protected by copyright and permission must be obtained from the publisher prior to any prohibited reproduction, storage in a retrieval system, or transmission in any form or by any means, electronic, mechanical, photocopying, recording, or likewise. For information regarding rights and permissions, write to: FMI, 2345 Crystal Drive, Arlington, Virginia 22202.

10 9 8 7 6 5 4 3 2 1

ISBN: 978-0-9819903-0-9

NOTE FROM FMI

In recent years, consumer confidence in food safety has grown fragile, the result of many foodborne illness outbreaks and recalls. The single most important measure the industry can take to restore that confidence is to prevent food from becoming contaminated in the first place. Manufacturers are undergoing rigorous audits requested by retailers under the FMI Safe Quality Food Program and other certification systems. Retailers can ensure their managers and employees observe the highest food safety standards by having them trained and certified under the FMI SuperSafeMark® program.

SuperSafeMark® is the only training program designed specifically to teach employees how to control the safety risks in a retail food environment. The industry developed this program with leading food safety experts, scientists and educators, who brought decades of experience in training retail food handlers and managers.

This program is grounded in the fundamentals of food safety science established by the principles of the hazard analysis critical control point (HACCP) system. The training is based on the most current Food and Drug Administration *Food Code*. It teaches employees the skills and knowledge to become certified food safety professionals in the states where their stores are located. In fact, approximately 30,000 retail food workers use SuperSafeMark® to earn certification each year.

We can help instill consumer confidence in the safety of food they buy in retail stores by demonstrating our commitment and professionalism through SuperSafeMark® training and certification. This guide provides you with the essential knowledge you need to apply each time you prepare, handle, display and sell food. These best practices will help ensure your customers remain confident you have the best food safety measures in place.

Leslie G. Sarasin, Esq., CAE
President and CEO
Food Marketing Institute

Contents

Preface xvii

Acknowledgments xxiii

Chapter 1 Retail Food Safety 2

Learn How To 2
Essential Terms 4
New Challenges Present New Opportunities 4
Food Safety—Why All the Fuss? 5
Why Me? 6
Changing Trends in Food Consumption and Choices 7
The Problem: Foodborne Illness 8
    Contamination 9
    Microorganisms (Germs or Microbes) 10
The Food Flow 10
A New Approach to an Old Problem 11
Facility Planning and Design 12
Keeping It Clean and Sanitary 12
Education and Training Are Key to Food Safety 13
The Role of Government in Food Safety 14
    The FDA *Food Code* 14
The Role of the Food Industry in Retail Food Safety 15
Food Protection Manager Certification 15
Summary 17
Discussion Questions (Short Answer) 19
Quiz 1.1 (Multiple Choice) 19
Quiz 1.2 (True/False) 21
References/Suggested Readings 21
Suggested Web Sites 22

Chapter 2 Hazards to Food Safety   24

Learn How To   24

Essential Terms   26

Foodborne Illness   27

Foodborne Hazards   28

    Bacteria   29

    Spoilage and Disease-causing Bacteria   31

    Bacterial Growth   31

What Disease-causing Bacteria Need in Order to Multiply   32

    Food   34

    Acidity   34

    Temperature   35

    Time   35

    Oxygen   36

    Moisture   36

Potentially Hazardous Foods (PHF)   37

Potentially Hazardous Food (Time/Temperature Control for Safety Food)   38

Ready-to-Eat Foods   40

Foodborne Illness Caused by Bacteria   40

    Foodborne Illness Caused by Sporeforming Bacteria   41

    Sporeforming Bacteria   43

    Foodborne Illness Caused by Non-Sporeforming Bacteria   46

    Non-Sporeforming Bacteria   46

Foodborne Illness Caused by Viruses   52

Foodborne Illness Caused by Parasites   55

Problems Caused by Fungi   59

Foodborne Illness Caused by Chemicals   59

    Naturally Occurring Chemicals   60

       Food Allergens   60

Natural Toxins   62

Man-made Chemicals   65

Foodborne Illness Caused by Physical Hazards   66

Summary   67

Discussion Questions (Short Answer)   69

Quiz 2 (Multiple Choice)   69

References/Suggested Readings   71

Suggested Web Sites   72

CHAPTER 3 FACTORS THAT AFFECT FOODBORNE ILLNESS   74

Learn How To   74

Essential Terms   76

Factors That Contribute to Foodborne Illness   76

What Is Time and Temperature Abuse?   78

How to Measure Food Temperatures   79

When and How to Calibrate a Thermometer   82

Boiling Point Method   83

Ice Point Method   83

Measuring Food Temperature   83

Preventing Temperature Abuse   85

Keep Cold Foods Cold and Hot Foods Hot!   87

The Importance of Handwashing and Good Personal Hygiene   90

Using Disposable Gloves   93

Personal Habits   95

Outer Clothing and Apparel   95

Personal Health   96

Cross Contamination   97

Other Sources of Contamination   99

Make Sure the Work Area Is Clean and Sanitary   100

Summary 101

Discussion Questions (Short Answer) 102

Quiz 3 (Multiple Choice) 102

References/Suggested Readings 104

Suggested Web Sites 105

CHAPTER 4 FOLLOWING THE FOOD PRODUCT FLOW 106

Learn How To 106

Essential Terms 108

Buying from Approved Sources 108

    Inspecting Delivery Vehicles 109

Determining Food Quality 109

Measuring Temperatures at Receiving and Storage 110

Following the Flow of Food 110

    Receiving 111

    Packaged Foods 112

    Reduced Oxygen Packaging (ROP) 112

    Red Meat Products 118

    Poultry 119

    Game Animals 120

    Eggs 120

    Fluid and Dry Milk and Milk Products 122

        Fluid Milk 122

        Cheese 122

        Butter 122

    Fish 123

    Fruits and Vegetables 125

    Juice 126

    Frozen Foods 127

    Storage of Food 128

Types of Storage   128
   Refrigerated Storage   129
   Freezer Storage   130
   Dry Storage   131
   Chemical Storage   132
   Storage Conditions for Foods   133
Food Preparation, Handling, and Service   136
Ingredient Substitution   136
Avoiding Temperature Abuse   137
Thawing   137
Cold-Holding   139
   Frozen, Ready-to-Eat Foods   140
   Pre-packaged Foods   140
Cooking   141
Cooling   143
Hot-holding and Reheating   145
Time as a Publich Health Control   146
Food Handling   146
Discarding or Reconditioning Food   147
Refilling Returnable Containers   147
Self-service Bar   148
   Rules for Self-service Bars: 148
   Checkout and Bagging   149
Temporary Facilities and Mobile Food Facilities   150
Vending Machines   151
Home Meal Replacement   152

Summary   153

Discussion Questions (Short Answer)   154

Quiz 4 (Multiple Choice)   154

References/Suggested Readings   157

Suggested Web Sites   157

Chapter 5 Facilities, Equipment, and Utensils 160

Learn How To 160

Essential Terms 162

Design, Layout, and Facilities 162

    Regulatory Considerations 163

Work Center Planning 164

Equipment Selection 165

    Size and Design 165

    Construction Materials 166

        Metals 167

        Stainless Steel 167

        Plastic 167

        Wood 168

Types of Equipment 169

    Cooking Equipment 169

    Ovens 169

    Refrigeration and Low-temperature Storage Equipment 171

    Reach-in Refrigeration 172

    Cook-chill and Rapid-chill Systems 174

    Hot-holding Equipment 175

    Other Types of Food Equipment 176

        Slicers 176

        Mixers, Grinders, Choppers, Tenderizers, and Saws 176

        Ice Machines 177

    Ambient Temperature Display Equipment 178

    Live Seafood Display and Holding Tanks 179

    Single-service and Single-use Articles 180

    Warewashing Equipment 181

    Manual Warewashing 181

    Mechanical Warewashing 182

Installation   183

Maintenance and Replacement   184

Lighting   184

Heating, Ventilation, and Air Conditioning (HVAC)   186

Summary   187

Discussion Questions (Short Answer)   188

Quiz 5 (Multiple Choice)   189

References/Suggested Readings   192

Suggested Web Sites   193

CHAPTER 6 CLEANING AND SANITIZING OPERATIONS   194

Learn How To   194

Essential Terms   196

Principles of Cleaning and Sanitizing   196

Removal of Food Particles   198

Application of Cleaning Agents   198

Soaking   198

Spray Methods   199

Clean-in-place Systems   199

Abrasive Cleaning   199

Rinsing   200

Detergents and Cleaners to Be Used   201

Cleaning Frequency   203

Sanitizing Principles   206

Heat Sanitizing   206

Chemical Sanitizing   208

Factors That Affect the Action of Chemical Sanitizers   210

Chlorine   210

Iodine   211

Quaternary Ammonium Compounds   211

Mechanical Warewashing   213

Mechanical Warewashing Process 213

Manual Warewashing 216

Cleaning Fixed Equipment 218

Cleaning Environmental Areas 222

Ceilings and Walls 223

Floors 223

Equipment and Supplies Used for Cleaning 224

Summary 226

Discussion Questions (Short Answer) 227

Quiz 6 (Multiple Choice) 228

References/Suggested Readings 230

Suggested Web Sites 231

CHAPTER 7 ENVIRONMENTAL SANITATION AND MAINTENANCE 232

Learn How To 232

Essential Terms 234

Condition of the Establishment 234

Proper Water Supply and Sewage Disposal System 235

Condition of Building 236

Floors, Walls, and Ceilings 237

Floors 237

Walls and Ceilings 238

Restroom Sanitation 239

Handwashing Sinks 239

Plumbing Hazards in Retail Food Establishments 241

Cross Connections 241

Backflow 241

Methods and Devices to Prevent Backflow 242

Backflow Prevention Devices on Carbonators 244

Grease Traps   245

Garbage and Refuse Sanitation   245

   Inside Storage   246

   Outside Storage   246

Pest Control   247

   Insects   248

   Rodents   251

      Signs of Rodent Infestation   252

      Rodent Control   254

   Integrated Pest Management (IPM)   255

Summary   256

Discussion Questions (Short Answer)   257

Quiz 7 (Multiple Choice)   258

References/Suggested Reading   260

Suggested Web Sites   260

CHAPTER 8 FOOD SAFETY MANAGEMENT PROGRAMS   262

Learn How To   262

Essential Terms   264

The Problem   264

The Solution   265

Start with a Good Set of Instructions   266

The HACCP Approach to Food Safety   270

The Seven Principles in an HACCP System   270

   Principle 1—Hazard Analysis   271

   Principle 2—Identify Critical Control Points (CCPs)   271

   Principle 3—Establish a Critical Limit for Each CCP   271

   Principle 4—Monitoring CCPs   272

   Principle 5—Take Corrective Action   272

   Principle 6—Establish Procedures to Verify the HACCP System Is Working   272

Principle 7—Establish Effective Record Keeping   272

Retail HACCP: A Process Approach   273

Food Safety Management and HACCP Requirements   277

Other Food Safety Management Programs   278

Coding and Product Identification   281

Food Recall Procedures   282

Challenges of Food Safety Management   283

Summary   283

Discussion Questions (Short Answer)   284

Quiz 8 (Multiple Choice)   285

References/Suggested Readings   286

Suggested Web Sites   287

CHAPTER 9 FOOD SAFETY REGULATIONS AND CRISIS MANAGEMENT   290

Learn How To   290

Essential Terms   292

State and Local Regulations   293

Permit to Operate   293

Federal Agencies   295

Other National Food Safety Related Organizations   297

Inspection for Wholesomeness, Grading, and Generally Recognized as Safe   298

Food Recall   298

Food Labeling   299

Nutrition and Ingredient Labeling   299

Food Allergen Labeling and Consumer Protection Act   300

Safe Food-handling Label   300

Date Marking for Ready-to-Eat, PHF (TCS)   301

Recent Initiatives in Food Safety   303

Contents　　xv

　　　National Food Safety Initiative　303

　　　The FIGHT BAC!™ Campaign　304

　　　Project Chill Campaign　304

　　　Consumer Advisory　305

Crisis Management　306

　　　Water Supply Emergency Procedures　306

Foodborne Illness Incident or Outbreak　308

　　　Check the Product Source　309

　　　Formal Investigations　309

　　　Food Defense　309

Summary　311

Discussion Questions (Short Answer)　312

Quiz 9(Multiple Choice)　312

References/Suggested Readings　314

Suggested Web Sites　315

Glossary　317

Appendix A Answers to End-of-Chapter Quizzes　337

Appendix B The Process for Determining PHF (TCS)　339

Appendix C Summary of Agents That Cause Foodborne Illness　343

Appendix D Multi-Tiered, Risk-Based Employee Health System　349

APPENDIX E CONVERSION TABLE FOR FAHRENHEIT AND CELSIUS FOR COMMON TEMPERATURES USED IN FOOD ESTABLISHMENTS   **361**

APPENDIX F AREAS OF KNOWLEDGE DEEMED IMPORTANT FOR THE PERSON IN CHARGE   **363**

APPENDIX G NEW RISK DESIGNATIONS FOR FOOD CODE PROVISIONS   **365**

INDEX   **367**

PREFACE

Supervisors and managers of retail food establishments take on a great burden of keeping food and food products safe from the moment they enter the establishment. There are many opportunities for food to be contaminated between production and consumption. Food can be contaminated at the farm, ranch, orchard, or in the sea. Food also can be contaminated at food processing plants and during transport to retail food establishments. Finally, food can be contaminated during the last stages of production, at retail establishments, and by patrons in their homes. The importance of keeping food safe cannot be underrated. Retail food supervisors and managers can use the *SuperSafeMark® Guide to Food Safety* to assist them in this daunting task.

Food safety is especially critical in retail food establishments because this may be the last opportunity to control or eliminate the hazards that might contaminate food and cause foodborne illnesses. Even when purchased from inspected and approved sources, ingredients may contain contaminants when they arrive at a retail food establishment. It is important to know how to handle ingredients safely and how to prepare food in a manner that reduces the risk of contaminated food being sold to your patrons.

The Food and Drug Administration (FDA) is one of the federal agencies responsible for protecting our nation's food supply. The FDA recognizes the importance of food safety in retail food establishments.

The agency's *Food Code* recommends that retail food managers be able to demonstrate knowledge in food safety. This knowledge will be helpful to managers as they create and implement food safety management programs within their operations.

Food safety in retail food establishments begins with managers who are knowledgeable about food hazards and who are committed to implementing proper food-handling practices in their facility. It also requires properly trained food workers who understand the essentials of food safety and sanitation and who will not take shortcuts when it comes to food safety.

The authors of this textbook have been training retail food managers and employees for over 30 years. Many excellent resources are available for this type training. However, the authors wanted to create a book that was customized for the retail food industry and would meet the training needs of supermarkets, superstores, food warehouses, limited assortment stores, convenience stores, and other types of traditional and nontraditional stores.

The SuperSafeMark® materials have been proven effective for teaching food safety and sanitation to many different audiences. The authors recommend the textbook and supplemental materials for in-class and home-study courses to prepare retail food establishment managers to take a national food protection manager certification examination.

One of the most important tasks you face is to train and supervise food workers. Your knowledge is useless if you do not teach employees the correct way to handle food. Learn to recognize any break in standard operating procedures that might endanger food safety. Avoid the problems related to embarrassment, loss of reputation, and financial harm that accompany a foodborne disease outbreak.

Some state, local, and tribal governments have passed legislation to require certification of one or more managers in each retail food establishment. Other jurisdictions are considering doing the same. Most certification programs require candidates to pass a written examination to demonstrate knowledge of food safety and sanitation principles and practices. Some jurisdictions require completion of a food safety course before taking the exam.

There is growing support for a nationally recognized examination and credential for retail food protection managers. The Conference for Food Protection (CFP) recognizes food protection manager examinations from several providers. Contact the CFP at www.foodprotect.org for more information about the test recognition process and the various providers who have one or more forms of their examination recognized by the CFP.

This manual was created to provide food safety information that can be used to train food store administrators, managers, and associates so that they can ensure the preparation of safe food and prevent foodborne illnesses from occurring due to their store operations.

This manual will effectively prepare food store employees to sit for a food protection manager certification exam provided by any of the ANSI/CFP accredited test providers.

The team of McSwane, Linton, and Rue wanted to produce a book to accompany the FDA's 2009 *Food Code*. We trust you will find this text accurate, comprehensive, and, most of all, useful.

David Z. McSwane, H.S.D., REHS, CP-FS, is Professor of Public Health at the Indiana University School of Medicine. He has over 25 years experience in food safety and sanitation working in state and local regulatory agencies and as a consultant to the food industry. Dr. McSwane has pub-

published numerous articles and presented papers on a variety of subjects related to food safety.

Dr. McSwane is a nationally recognized trainer in food safety and sanitation. He has taught courses at the university level and for regulatory agencies, retail food establishments, food industry trade associations, vocational schools, and environmental health associations throughout the United States. Dr. McSwane is a recipient of the Walter S. Mangold award, the highest honor bestowed by the National Environmental Health Association. He has been a correspondent for the Food Protection Report and is a member of the Environmental and Public Health Council at Underwriters Laboratories, Inc.

Richard Linton, Ph.D., is Professor of Food Safety and Director of the Center for Food Safety Engineering in the Food Science Department at Purdue University. He has provided research, education, and outreach leadership to the food industry for over 15 years. Dr. Linton is actively involved in developing and teaching food safety programs for the food industry including hazard analysis critical control programs (HACCP), good manufacturing practices, good agricultural practices, the better process control school, sanitation, and safe food-handling practices for retail food establishments. His industry programs have been delivered throughout the United States and in many international countries.

Nancy Roberts Rue, Ph.D., R.N., has a background in teaching in technical education. Her doctorate is in educational leadership and curriculum and instruction from the University of Florida. With 30 years experience in higher education and evaluation at Indiana University and St. Petersburg Junior College, she is dedicated to the task of building educational materials that meet the needs of those who want to learn. She is now an independent writer and consultant on training and development techniques.

Learnovation©, LLC, has provided expert instructional design and developmental editing for the original versions of the *SuperSafeMark*® materials. Recognized for their team of experts with years of experience in instructional design, they assisted in the customization of this book and developed tables, charts, key point boxes, and illustrations that allow for ease of learning.

The *SuperSafeMark*® *Guide to Food Safety* is part of a series of books and training materials that apply directly to retail food establishments, such as supermarkets and convenience stores. This is a quick and easy-to-read, full-color guide including the "must know" information about food safety and sanitation in retail food operations.

In addition to the *SuperSafeMark® Guide to Food Safety,* the food safety series endorsed by FMI, includes:

- The *SuperSafeMark® Trainer's Kit:* an easy-to-follow, bulleted training and teaching guide with a PowerPoint slide presentation full of effective illustrations and photos that help drive food safety points home. The kit also includes an image bank of photos and illustrations for customizable presentations and printable full-color posters that address important food safety principles.

- The *SuperSafeMark® Quick Reference:* an easy-to-read, illustration-rich booklet designed for the line worker. This concise reference focuses on the key areas of personal hygiene, time and temperature abuse, cross contamination, and cleaning and sanitizing practices.

- The *SuperSafeMark® Quick Reference Trainer's Kit:* an easy-to-use tool for teaching line workers about basic food safety concepts. The kit contains a PowerPoint slide presentation that can be used to teach food workers about personal hygiene, preventing time and temperature abuse, avoiding cross contamination, and proper cleaning and sanitizing practices. The kit also includes printable full-color posters that address important food safety principles.

- The SuperSafeMark® Food Safety programs in both Online and CBT format. FMI has partnered with LearnSomething, Inc., to develop training courses for line workers and managers. The line worker course is available in English and Spanish and takes about one hour to complete. This course is an excellent way to teach the basics of safe food handling to employees. The manager course is more comprehensive and takes about 15 hours to complete. This course can be used to prepare individuals to take one of the food protection manager certification examinations required in many state and local jurisdictions.

The authors wish all readers success in their food safety and sanitation activities and in achieving certification if they desire to pursue it. Regardless of where you work, you must always remember—foodborne illness is preventable. Follow the basic rules of food safety and you will enjoy a satisfying career in the retail food industry.

Control Point Icons

Throughout the *SuperSafeMark® Guide to Food Safety* you will encounter control point icons in the margins of the text. Control point icons are placed next to text to indicate moments at which action might be taken by a supervisor or an employee to correct or prevent a possible food safety issue. Control point icons can be found throughout the text for each of the following important food safety areas:

 Proper Cleaning and Sanitizing

 Preventing Cross Contamination

 Avoiding Time and Temperature Abuse

 Proper Personal Hygiene

 Key Concept

Acknowledgements

The authors wish to thank their families and colleagues who, through their support and patience, helped us with the completion of this project.

John Wise was a tremendous asset to this project. His drawings enabled us to present information that is technical and sometimes tedious in an entertaining way that makes it easier to understand.

A grateful thanks goes to the FMI staff and FMI members who contributed to this project. Their collective technical expertise and insight into supermarket operations and food safety programs make this manual second to none.

Finally, the authors wish to thank all those persons who read this manual and implement its recommendations, making food safer every day.

Learn How To:

- Recognize how food safety and sanitation practices prevent foodborne illness in retail food establishments.

- State the problems caused by foodborne illness for individuals who become ill and the retail food establishment blamed for the incident.

- Identify trends in menus and consumer use of food products prepared in retail food establishments.

- Describe the role of government (federal, state, local, and tribal) in retail food safety.

- List the types of retail food establishments identified in this text and the influence of the FDA *Food Code* and state or jurisdictional codes on these operations.

- Define the term *Hazard Analysis Critical Control Point (HACCP)* as applied in food safety management.

- Recognize the need for food protection manager certification.

CHAPTER 1
Retail Food Safety

Peanut Butter Containing Products Cause Nationwide Scare

National, state, and local news outlets have been providing continuous updates about the largest U.S. product recall ever recorded. Over 2,100 different peanut-and peanut butter-containing products were recalled nationwide because of the possible presence of Salmonella *bacteria. Products being recalled include items such as peanut butter, snack bars, breakfast cereals, crackers, and ready-to-eat sandwiches.*

Salmonella is one of the leading causes of foodborne disease in the United States, leading to over one million cases of illness each year. The bacteria cause human infection and common symptoms of diarrhea, fever, and headache. The disease usually begins 24-48 hours after eating a contaminated food and can last up to a week.

To date, over 700 people have become ill, over 50 have been hospitalized, and 9 people have died from eating products that contain peanut butter contaminated with Salmonella. *Retailers are being urged to communicate with customers who might have purchased some of these products and to remove all recalled products from store shelves. Certainly, this outbreak and recall will have significant public health and economic impacts to the peanut industry and the retail food industry.*

What could be done to prevent or minimize this type of problem?

Essential Terms

Cleaning	Foodborne illness
Contamination	Microorganisms
Convenience store	Germs
FDA *Food Code*	Microbes
Food establshments	Retail food establishment
Foodborne disease outbreak	Sanitary

New Challenges Present New Opportunities

The food industry is one of America's largest enterprises. It employs about one-quarter of the nation's work force and produces 20% of America's Gross Domestic Product (GDP). Billions of dollars worth of food are sold each year. Americans have made food a prominent part of their business and recreational activities.

The food industry is made up of businesses that produce, manufacture, transport, and distribute food for people in the United States and throughout the world. Food production involves many activities that occur on farms and ranches, in orchards, and in fishing operations. Food manufacturing takes the raw materials harvested by producers and converts them into forms suitable for distribution and sale. The retail distribution system consists of the many food operations that store, prepare, package, serve, display, vend, or otherwise provide food for human consumption. The term **food establishment** refers to all facilities involved in food distribution.

Supermarkets continue to be the primary destinations for purchasing groceries; 83% of shoppers named at least one supermarket among the list of stores where they shopped within the past 30 days. Additionally, 68% stated one of the most important features they consider when selecting a store is whether it is neat and clean (FMI's *U.S. Grocery Shopper Trends*, 2009). There are 10 different store formats currently operating in the retail food industry. These can include:

- Conventional supermarkets
- Superstores
- Warehouse stores
- Convenience stores.

This book focuses on information related to food safety and sanitation in any retail food establishment. The term **retail food establishment** includes any store selling a line of dry retail food, canned goods, or non-food items plus perishable items. A **convenience store** is a compact drive-to store offering a limited number of high-convenience items. The information would also apply to other types of retail food stores such as supercenters, warehouse stores, and wholesale clubs.

Food Safety–Why All the Fuss?

Everyone knows the United States has one of the safest food supplies in the world. So why all the fuss? The answer is simple. Foodborne illness happens, and it adversely affects the health of millions of Americans every year. **Foodborne illness** is the sickness some people experience when they eat contaminated food. It impairs performance and causes discomfort. Estimates of the number of cases of foodborne illnesses vary greatly. A report issued by the Centers for Disease Control and Prevention (CDC) estimates foodborne diseases cause approximately 76 million illnesses, 325,000 hospitalizations, and 5,000 deaths in the United States each year (Mcad et al., 1999).

The Food Marketing Institute (FMI) reports nearly 83% of shoppers are completely or mostly confident the food they buy in their retail food establishment is safe. However, 53% see contamination from bacteria and germs as a serious health risk (FMI's *U.S. Grocery Shopper Trends*, 2009). That is a compelling reason to keep the food sold in your operation as safe as possible.

Why Me?

You may be asking yourself, "What does all this have to do with me?" The answer is "PLENTY." Customer opinion surveys show cleanliness, price, and food quality are the top three reasons people use when choosing a place to eat and shop for food. Customers expect their food to taste good and not make them sick. It is the responsibility of every retail food establishment owner, manager, and employee to prepare and serve safe and wholesome food and preserve their clients' confidence. **As a retail food manager, you must understand foodborne illness can be prevented if the basic rules of food safety are routinely followed.**

The CDC reports the mishandling that causes most foodborne disease outbreaks occurs within retail food operations (restaurants, retail food establishments, schools, churches, camps, institutions, and vending locations) where foods are prepared, served, and sold to the public. These foods may be eaten at the retail food establishment or sold for preparation and consumption elsewhere.

Foodborne illness costs billions of dollars each year in the form of:
- Medical expenses
- Lost work and reduced productivity by victims of the illness
- Legal fees
- Punitive damages
- Increased insurance premiums
- Lost business
- Loss of reputation for the retail food establishment.

> **Prevention of foodborne illness must be a goal in every retail food establishment.**

Most Cases of Foodborne Illness in Retail Food Establishments Are Caused by Foods That Have Been:

- Improperly cooked and/or held at improper temperatures
- Handled by infected food employees who practice poor personal hygiene
- Exposed to disease-causing agents by cross contamination
- In contact with contaminated equipment not properly cleaned and sanitized
- Obtained from unsafe sources.

Changing Trends in Food Consumption and Choices

Due to changes in our eating habits and more knowledge about food safety hazards, recommendations for safe food handling are always changing. For example, retail food establishments used to cook ground meat to an internal temperature of 140°F (60°C). But that was before Shiga toxin-producing *Escherichia coli* bacteria came on the scene. Now retail food establishments are required to cook ground meat to an internal temperature of 155°F (68°C) for 15 seconds. This higher temperature is needed to destroy the Shiga toxin-producing *E. coli* bacteria that may be present throughout the raw, ground meat. The safety of unpasteurized juices, like apple cider and fresh-squeezed orange juice, was not a concern in the past. Now, we read about outbreaks in these juices involving *Salmonella*, *E. coli*, and parasites. As a result, most juice products are now heat pasteurized to improve their safety.

> More than 50% of the food eaten by Americans is prepared in food-processing plants, restaurants, retail food establishments, delicatessens, cafeterias, institutions, and other sites outside the home.

Some emerging food safety concerns include *Listeria monocytogenes* in ready-to-eat processed foods, Shiga toxin-producing *E. coli* in raw meat and unprocessed fruit juices, Hepatitis A virus in deli sandwich operations and shellfish, and parasites in fresh produce. The future may bring other types of problems.

Technologies used in the food industry are also changing. A lot of research is being done on irradiation and other types of food-processing methods that do not use heat. They may become more common in the future. You need to keep up with this information as it relates to retail food establishment operations.

Customers have less time to prepare food because more of them are working outside the home. As a result, they are buying more ready-to-eat foods or products that require minimal preparation in the home. These foods are produced using a variety of processing, holding, and serving methods that help protect them from contamination.

The Problem: Foodborne Illness

Foodborne illness is a disease caused by the consumption of contaminated food. A **foodborne disease outbreak** is defined as an incident in which two or more people experience a similar illness after eating a common food. Recent outbreaks of foodborne illness have been caused by:

- Shiga toxin-producing *Escherichia coli* bacteria in lettuce, unpasteurized apple cider, and radish sprouts
- *Salmonella* spp. in cut melons, alfalfa sprouts, ice cream, roma tomatoes, raw almonds, and peanut butter
- Hepatitis A virus in raw and lightly cooked oysters and green onions
- *Listeria monocytogenes* in hot dogs, luncheon meats, and cheese.

These Groups of People Are Immunocompromised and At Risk of Foodborne Illness:

- The very young
- The elderly
- Pregnant or lactating women
- People with impaired immune systems due to cancer, AIDS, HIV, diabetes, or medications that suppress response to infection.

Foodborne illness can cause severe reactions, even death, for individuals in these highly susceptible categories. The availability of a safe food supply is critical to these people.

Contamination

Contamination is the presence of substances or conditions in the food that can be harmful to humans. Foods can become contaminated at a variety of points as the food flows from the farm to the table. Raw foods can be contaminated at the farm, ranch, or on board a commercial fishing boat. Contamination can also occur as foods are handled during processing and distribution. Measures to prevent and control contamination must begin when food is harvested and continue until the food is consumed.

Foods can become contaminated at several points between the farm and the table.

Soil, water, air, plants, animals, and humans are some of the more common sources of contamination. Contaminants present an "invisible challenge" because you can't see them with the naked eye. Many types of food contamination can cause illness without changing the appearance, odor, or taste of food.

Contaminants can be transferred from one food item to another by cross contamination. This typically happens when microbes from a raw food are

Sources of contamination

transferred to a cooked or ready-to-eat food by contaminated hands, equipment, or utensils.

Microorganisms (Germs or Microbes)

Microorganisms (also called germs or microbes) cause the most common types of food contamination. Microorganisms include bacteria, viruses, parasites, and fungi that are so small they can only be seen with the aid of a microscope. Bacteria and viruses pose the greatest safety challenges in retail food establishments. Microbes are everywhere around us—in soil, water, air, and in and on plants and animals (including humans).

Most microorganisms are harmless. However, some microbes can cause problems when they get into food. The microbes that must be controlled in a retail food establishment are the ones that cause foodborne illness and food spoilage. It is important to remember the germs that cause foodborne illnesses usually do not alter the taste, odor, and appearance of the food.

Microorganisms–common causes of foodborne illness
(Copyright Dennis Kunkel Microscopy, Inc.)

The Food Flow

The food flow consists of food products and the ingredients used to make them as they flow through a retail food establishment. The food flow begins with the purchase of safe and wholesome ingredients from approved sources. Once the food is delivered, it then flows through receiving into storage. The final stages in the food flow are preparation, display, and sale. Preparation and display include all the activities that occur between storage and consumption of the food by your customers.

Preparation steps frequently involve thawing, cooking, cooling, reheating, hot-holding, cold-holding, handling, and display. Improper food handling and display can lead to foodborne illness. For potentially hazardous foods (those that support bacterial growth), time and temperature must be monitored and controlled. Handling of ready-to-eat foods (those not requiring cooking) can also involve a lot of contact with an employee's hands or with food-contact surfaces. It is always important for food employees to practice good personal hygiene, use proper handwashing techniques, and avoid touching food with their bare hands. However, when handling and displaying ready-to-eat foods, it is crucial!

> **You must learn to recognize foods that could have been contaminated prior to delivery.**

Delivery ➡ Receiving ➡ Displaying

Some of the steps involved in the flow of food

Since handling and display are typically the last steps prior to consumption of the food, efficient monitoring and control of safe food practices are also critical. As products flow through a retail food establishment, they are handled many times and in many different ways. Controlling food safety and quality is of utmost importance.

A New Approach to an Old Problem

Food industry professionals and regulatory officials agree better ways to protect people from foodborne illness must be found. The FDA *Food Code* recommends using the Hazard Analysis Critical Control Point (HACCP) system as an important component of your food safety management program. The Pillsbury Company developed this innovative system in the 1960s for the NASA space program. Officials in the space program realized a foodborne illness in space could present a life-threatening situation. Therefore, it was critical for all food used by the astronauts to be as near 100% safe as possible.

The HACCP system follows the flow of food through the retail food establishment and identifies each step in the process where contamination might cause the food to become unsafe. When a problem step is identified, action is taken to make the product safe or, if that is not feasible, the food may have to be discarded. The HACCP system should be designed to accommodate the types of products served and the production equipment and processes used in the establishment. A more detailed discussion of the HACCP system as a component of your total food safety management program is presented in Chapter 8 of this book.

> **Retail food stores** can control the flow of food by setting up a food safety management program that includes a HACCP system.

Facility Planning and Design

A well-planned facility with a suitable layout is essential for the smooth operation of any retail food establishment. Layout, design, and facilities planning directly influence:

- Employee safety and productivity
- Labor and energy costs
- Customer satisfaction
- Better inspection scores.

Some retail food establishments are located in buildings designed and constructed specifically for a food operation. Others are located in buildings converted to accommodate food preparation, handling, display, and sales. Either way, the better your facility is planned, the easier it will be to achieve your food safety goals and earn a profit.

Keeping It Clean and Sanitary

It is the responsibility of every person working in the food industry to keep things clean and sanitary. Effective cleaning of equipment reduces the chances of food contamination during preparation, storage, display, and service. **Cleaning** involves removal of visible soil from the surfaces of equipment and utensils. **Sanitary** means healthful or hygienic. It involves reducing the number of disease-causing microorganisms on the surface of equipment and utensils to acceptable public health levels. Something that is sanitary poses little or no risk to human health. Good sanitation also minimizes

Sanitary makes sure it's safe.

attraction of pests, increases the length of time equipment is in service, improves employee morale and efficiency, and is important from other aesthetic considerations.

Shopper satisfaction is highest in food establishments that are clean and bright and where quality food products are safely handled and displayed.

Education and Training Are Key to Food Safety

You and your employees must know the correct way to manage food safety and sanitation. The importance of teaching employees about food safety is increased by the global nature of our food supply. Control of factors during growth, harvest, and shipping is not always possible when food is produced in so many different parts of the world. Also, an error in time and temperature management, cross contamination, or personal health and hygiene of food employees can increase the risk of foodborne illness. Storage, preparation, holding, display, and handling procedures are critical in the prevention of foodborne illness. Employees do not typically come to the job knowing this information. They have to be trained.

Good training can prevent foodborne illness.

> The prevention of foodborne illness begins with the knowledge of where contaminants come from, how they get into food, and what can be done to control or eliminate them.

The Role of Government in Food Safety

The purpose of government regulation in food safety is to oversee the food-producing system and protect food intended for human consumption. Governmental agencies enforce laws and regulations to protect food against adulteration and contamination. Regulatory personnel monitor both the process and the product to assure the safety of the food we eat.

There are several U.S. federal regulatory agencies, such as the Food and Drug Administration (FDA) and the U.S. Department of Agriculture (USDA), that set food safety standards to make our food supply safer. The federal agencies are usually involved with assuring the safety of foods that are processed or prepared and then transported in interstate commerce. Most retail food establishments are governed by state, local, or tribal agencies, such as a health department or department of agriculture. These agencies are likely to have the most direct impact on the everyday activities of retail food establishments.

The FDA *Food Code*

In 1993, the FDA published the *Food Code*, which replaced three earlier model codes—*The Food Service Sanitation Manual* including a Model Food Service Sanitation Ordinance of 1976, *The Vending of Food and Beverages* including a Model Sanitation Ordinance of 1978, and *The Retail Food Store Sanitation Code of 1982*—with one code. The FDA has made a commitment to revise the **Food Code** every four years, with the assistance of experts from state and local government, industry, professional associations, and colleges and universities. However, it was determined that a "biennial" revision (supplement) was necessary to keep pace with changes

2009 FDA *Food Code* book

occurring in food safety and the food industry. In this text, the 2009 *Food Code* will serve as the resource from which safe food-handling recommendations are taken and will be referred to as the FDA *Food Code* from this point forward.

The FDA *Food Code* is not a law. Rather, it is a set of recommendations designed for adoption and use as a model by state, local, and tribal jurisdictions when formulating their own rules and regulations. You will need to obtain a copy of the health rules and regulations that apply to the retail food establishments in your jurisdiction.

The Role of the Food Industry in Food Safety

The retail food industry is assuming greater responsibility for overseeing the safety of its own processes and products. Customers expect and deserve food that is safe to eat. If a retail food establishment is involved in a foodborne disease outbreak, customers may retaliate by taking their business elsewhere or by seeking legal action. Financial loss and damaged reputation are some of the outcomes of a foodborne disease outbreak that can cause serious harm to the establishment found responsible for the problem. One means of preventing the harmful effects of a foodborne disease outbreak is to start a food safety management program in the retail food establishment. This helps assure that proper safeguards are used during food production, handling, and display. The ability to prove a food safety system was in place at the time a foodborne disease outbreak occurred is very important. It has been deemed an acceptable defense in court cases in which victims of foodborne illness have sought punitive damages.

Food Protection Manager Certification

Several organizations including the Conference for Food Protection (CFP), the FDA, and the trade associations for food retailers, such as the FMI, have recommended food manager certification as a means of assuring that individuals who are in charge of retail food establishments are knowledgeable about food safety.

Some state and municipal agencies already require certification of food managers, and others are considering it. Most certification programs require managers to pass a food safety examination recognized by the CFP. These examinations are designed to link food safety theory to practice. By passing a certification examination, the retail food manager is able to demonstrate proficiency in food protection management. Information

A Certified Food Protection Manager is a Person Who:

- Is responsible for identifying hazards in the day-to-day operation of a retail food establishment that prepares, packages, serves, vends, or otherwise provides food for human consumption
- Develops or implements specific policies, procedures, or standards aimed at preventing foodborne illness
- Coordinates training, supervises or directs food preparation activities, and takes corrective action as needed to protect the health of the customer
- Conducts in-house, self-inspection of daily operations on a periodic basis to see that policies and procedures concerning food safety are being followed.

A Certified Food Protection Manager Must Demonstrate Knowledge and Skills in Food Protection Management Including the Following Areas:

- Identifying foodborne illness
- Describing the relationship between time and temperature and the growth of microorganisms that cause foodborne illness
- Describing the relationship between employee health and food safety
- Naming the eight major food allergens and the symptoms they produce
- Recognizing problems and potential solutions associated with facility, equipment, and layout in a retail food establishment
- Recognizing problems and solutions associated with temperature control, preventing cross contamination, housekeeping, and maintenance.

A more detailed list of knowledge areas is presented in Appendix F.

about the CFP and its program for recognizing food protection manager certification examinations can be found at the organization's Web site at www.foodprotect.org.

Some managers will voluntarily seek training before they take a certification examination. Some jurisdictions will require training before testing while others will require only the test. Training can involve participating in a formal course, or it could involve using a nontraditional approach such as home study, correspondence, distance learning, or interactive computer programming.

This book is written as a teaching tool to be used in conjunction with traditional and nontraditional food manager certification programs. Like the manager certification examinations, it links theory to practice. The authors of this book and the FMI recognize that knowing about food safety is not enough. You must also be able to apply the principles and practices that enhance food safety during preparation, display, and handling.

Summary

Back to the Story . . . The recall described in the vignette at the beginning of this chapter is, unfortunately, a common challenge for the retail food industry. Food products are being recalled for both safety and quality reasons nearly everyday. The retail food industry provides a very important role during a food recall–perhaps the most vital role.

Since most food products are ultimately purchased by consumers at retail food establishments, retailers provide an essential line of communication to their customers. Retailers help to remove recalled products from their shelves so potentially dangerous products are not sold to the public. They also can communicate to customers that may have already purchased potentially dangerous foods through information provided by "value added cards" or "frequent shopper cards" and by press releases to the local media.

Retailers also provide an essential role in communicating information about recalled food products to other parts of the food industry including food distributors, food manufacturers, and food growing operations. They can let these industries know how much and what types of recalled products have been purchased by their customers.

The key to minimizing public health and economic impacts of food recalls is having a plan in place BEFORE the food recall occurs. Key components of this plan should include an effective and quick mechanism to remove products from retail shelves, an effective system to communicate information to your customers, and an effective system to communicate information to other parts of the food indus-

try that may be involved. It is a good idea to set up a "mock recall" program to test the effectiveness of the program you hav in place.

Elements of food safety

✔ It is the duty of every food establishment operator, manager, and employee to handle foods safely. Failure to do so can have a serious financial impact on your establishment and may cost you your job.

✔ You can protect the health and safety of your customers by developing and implementing effective food safety and sanitation practices within your establishment. In the following chapters, you will learn more about how food is contaminated and what actions are needed to prevent, control, and eliminate the agents that frequently cause foodborne illness and spoilage. This information will provide the dual benefit of helping you prepare for a food protection manager certification examination and to implement a food safety management program in your retail food establishment.

Discussion Questions (Short Answer)

1. Discuss the role of government in food safety programs.
2. Define the terms *sanitary* and *contamination*.
3. List some examples of food establishments.
4. How does news media coverage influence food safety issues?
5. What is a foodborne disease outbreak?
6. What impact do purchasing trends have on food safety?
7. How does food safety affect young children, elderly people, pregnant women, and people with compromised immune systems?
8. Discuss how certification of food managers could affect food safety.
9. Identify some reasons to implement food safety programs in retail food establishments.
10. Discuss some reason(s) you are studying food safety and sanitation.

Quiz 1.1 (Multiple Choice)

Choose the **best** answer for each question.

1. If two or more persons become ill as a result of eating the same food, it is called a foodborne:
   a. a. illness.
   b. b. contamination.
   c. c. hazard.
   d. d. disease outbreak.

2. According to the CDC, the estimated number of deaths due to foodborne illness each year in the United States is:
   a. 5,000.
   b. 25,000.
   c. 1,000,000.
   d. 75,000,000.

3. Sources of contamination for the food we eat include:
   a. insects and rodents.
   b. uncooked poultry and meat.
   c. dirty hands and bacteria.
   d. all of the above.

4. The food safety management system being used to monitor and control contamination in potentially hazardous foods is called:
   a. integrated pest management.
   b. cleaning and sanitizing.
   c. Hazard Analysis Critical Control Point.
   d. *Food Code*.

5. Which of the following groups of people are **not** considered to be highly susceptible to foodborne illness?
   a. Young children.
   b. Elderly people.
   c. People with weakened immune systems.
   d. College students who live in dormitories.

6. The cost of foodborne illness can occur in the form of:
   a. loss of sales.
   b. medical expenses.
   c. legal fees and fines.
   d. all of the above.

7. Reports by the CDC show that in most foodborne illness outbreaks mishandling of the suspect food occurred within which of the following stages?
   a. Transportation.
   b. Retail food establishments (preparation/handling).
   c. Food manufacturing.
   d. Food production (farms, ranches, etc.).

8. If a piece of equipment is sanitary, it:
   a. is free of visible soil.
   b. has been sterilized.
   c. is a single-service item.
   d. has had disease-causing germs reduced to safe levels.

9. How does the *Food Code* affect individual states and jurisdictions?

   a. The *Code* is a federal law that must be enforced by state agencies.
   b. The *Code* regulates food manufacturing facilities (processors) in state jurisdictions.
   c. The *Code* provides a model for new laws and rules in state, local, and tribal jurisdictions.
   d. The *Code* validates current practices.

Quiz 1.2 (True/False)

Answer questions 1–5 with either **True** or **False**.

1. The HACCP system is only used to monitor food processing in manufacturing plants.
2. Certification of food protection managers and employees refers to screening done for health problems.
3. Regulatory agencies are assigned the task of monitoring the production and processing of food from harvest to the consumer.
4. The term *retail food establishment* includes any store selling a line of dry retail food, canned goods, non-food items, and perishable foods.
5. Bacteria and viruses cause most foodborne illnesses.

Answers to the multiple-choice and the true/false questions are provided in Appendix A.

References/Suggested Readings

Centers for Disease Control and Prevention (2000). *Surveillance for Foodborne Disease Outbreaks—United States, 1993–1997*. U.S. Department of Health and Human Services. March 17, 2000. Atlanta, GA.

Food and Drug Administration (2009). 2009 *Food Code*. U.S. Public Health Service. Washington, DC.

Jay, James M., Martin J. Loessner, and David A. Golden (2005). *Modern Food Microbiology, 7th ed.* Springer Publishing Co. New York, NY.

Mead, Paul S., Laurence Slutsker, Vance Dietz, Linda F. McCaig, Joseph S. Bresee, Craig Shapiro, Patricia M. Griffin, and Robert V. Tauxe (1999). "Food-Related Illness and Death in the United States." *Emerging Infectious Diseases,* Vol. 5, September–October. Centers for Disease Control and Prevention. Atlanta, GA.

Potter, N., and J. Hotchkiss (1995). *Food Science 3rd ed.* Aspen Publishers. Gaithersburg, MD.

Suggested Web Sites

Gateway to Government Food Safety Information
  www.foodsafety.gov

United States Department of Agriculture (USDA)
  www.usda.gov

Centers for Disease Control and Prevention (CDC)
  www.cdc.gov

Food and Drug Administration (FDA)
  www.fda.gov

USDA/FDA Food and Nutrition Information Center
  www.nal.usda.gov/fnic

Partnership for Food Safety Education
  www.fightbac.org

The Food Marketing Institute
  www.fmi.org

Conference for Food Protection
  www.foodprotect.org

Notes

Learn How To:

- List the three main categories of foodborne hazards.

- Identify the difference between infections, intoxications, and toxin-mediated infections as classes of foodborne illness.

- List the factors that promote the growth of disease-causing bacteria.

- Explain how temperatures in the danger zone between 41°F (5°C) and 135°F (57°C) can affect growth of disease-causing bacteria.

- List the major types of potentially hazardous foods (time/temperature control for safety foods).

- Identify the characteristics common to potentially hazardous foods (time/temperature control for safety foods).

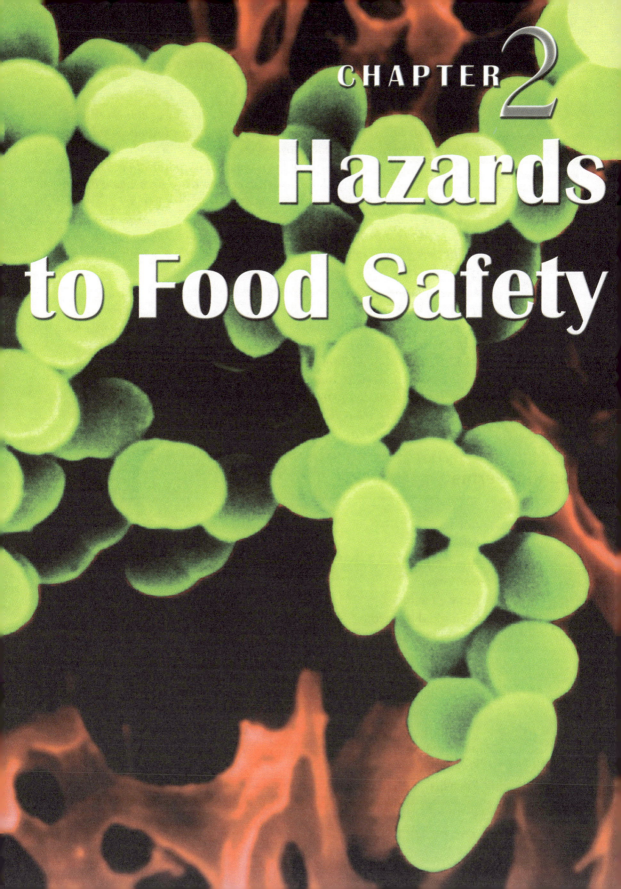

CHAPTER 2
Hazards to Food Safety

Multi-State Outbreak of E. coli O157:H7 Infections Linked to Consumption of Fresh Spinach

In 2006, a large foodborne disease outbreak caused by E. coli *O157:H7 bacteria was linked to the consumption of fresh bagged spinach and products containing fresh spinach. During the outbreak, more than 200 people in 26 states became ill and 102 of them required hospitalization. The most common symptoms of* E. coli *O157:H7 infections are diarrhea and bloody stools. Most healthy adults recover from an infection within a week. However, some people, especially children and older people, can develop a type of serious kidney damage and even death. In the 2006 outbreak, 31 people developed a severe type of kidney disease called hemolytic uremic syndrome (HUS) and three people died as a result.*

An investigation conducted by the US Food and Drug Administration (FDA) and the State of California revealed four spinach fields were the possible source of the E. coli *O157:H7 bacteria that caused the outbreak. Though the exact source of the bacteria was not confirmed,* E. coli *O157:H7 was isolated from animal wastes in the cattle fields nearby the implicated spinach fields and from a wild boar found in one of the fields. There is also a possibility irrigation wells used to grow spinach and surface waterways near the fields could have been contaminated with feces from cattle and wildlife.*

What could be done to prevent this type of problem?

Essential Terms

Acidic	Pathogenic
Aerobic	pH
Alkaline	Physical hazards
Anaerobic	Potentially hazardous foods
Bacteria	[time/temperature control
Binary fission	for safety foods – PHF(TCS)]
Biological hazards	Ready-to-eat (RTE) foods
Chemical hazards	Spoilage
Facultative anaerobic	Spore
FATTOM	Temperature abuse
Food allergen	Toxin
Foodborne hazard	Toxin-mediated infection
Infection	Vegetative cells
Intoxication	Virus
Onset time	Water activity (A_w)
Parasite	

Foodborne Illness

Many people have had foodborne illness and did not even know it. The symptoms of foodborne illness are very similar to those associated with the flu. The type of microbe, how much contamination was in the food, and the general condition of the affected person all contribute to the severity of the symptoms.

Ingredients for foodborne illness

General Symptoms of Foodborne Illness Usually Include One or More of the Following:	
• Headache	• Abdominal pain
• Nausea	• Diarrhea
• Vomiting	• Fatigue
• Dehydration	• Sore throat with fever.

Foodborne illness is generally classified as a foodborne infection, intoxication, or toxin-mediated infection. Your awareness of how different microbes cause foodborne illness will help you understand how they contaminate food.

Classifications of Foodborne Illness	
Infection	Caused by eating food that contains living, disease-causing microorganisms
Intoxication	Caused by eating food that contains a harmful chemical or a toxin produced by microorganisms
Toxin-mediated Infection	Caused by eating a food that contains harmful microorganisms that produce a toxin once inside the human intestinal tract.

Foodborne illnesses have different onset times. The **onset time** is the period between the time a person eats contaminated food and when they show the first symptoms of the disease.

Anyone can become ill from eating contaminated foods. In most cases, healthy adults will have flu-like symptoms and recover in a few days. The risks and dangers associated with foodborne illness are much more serious for people who are immunocompromised. Immunocompromised populations include infants and young children, elderly, pregnant women, individuals with suppressed immune systems due to acquired immune deficiency syndrome (AIDS), cancer, or diabetes, and people taking certain types of medications. For these individuals, the symptoms and duration of foodborne illness can be much more severe—even life-threatening.

> **Onset times** vary depending on factors such as the victim's:
> - Age
> - Health status
> - Body weight
> - Amount of contaminant ingested with the food.

Immunocompromised populations

Foodborne Hazards

A **foodborne hazard** is a biological, chemical, or physical hazard that can cause illness or injury when consumed along with food.

Biological hazards include bacteria, viruses, parasites, and fungi and are:

- Very small and can only be seen with the aid of a microscope
- Commonly associated with animals, humans, plant materials, water, and the environment

- The most common cause of foodborne illness
- The primary target of a retail food safety program.

Chemical hazards are toxic substances that may occur naturally or may be added during the preparation or processing of food. Examples of chemical contaminants include agricultural chemicals (i.e., pesticides, fertilizers, antibiotics), cleaning and sanitizing compounds, heavy metals (lead and mercury) food additives, and food allergens for allergen-sensitive people. Harmful chemicals have been associated with severe poisonings and allergic reactions. Chemicals and other non-food items should be labeled clearly and never placed near food items.

> **Biological hazards are by far the most important foodborne hazard in any type of retail food establishment.**

Physical hazards are hard or soft foreign objects in food that can cause illness and injury. They include items such as fragments of glass, metal, unfrilled toothpicks, jewelry, adhesive bandages, and human hair. These hazards result from accidental contamination and poor food-handling practices that can occur at many points in the food chain from the farm to the customer.

Bacteria

Bacteria are single-celled microorganisms that require food, moisture, and specific temperatures to multiply. Bacteria can cause foodborne infections, intoxications, and toxin-mediated infections. In retail food establishments, most bacteria are destroyed or controlled by:

- Monitoring time and temperature
- Good personal hygiene practices
- An effective cleaning and sanitation program
- Measures that minimize cross contamination

All bacteria exist in a "vegetative state." **Vegetative cells** grow, reproduce, and produce wastes just like other living organisms. Some bacteria have the ability to form structures called "spores." **Spores** help bacteria survive when their environment is too hot, cold, dry, or acidic, or when there is not enough food. Spores are not able to grow or reproduce. Bacteria spores are discussed in greater detail later in this chapter.

Destroy bacterial spores or keep them from changing into the dangerous vegetative state in which they can grow and cause illness.

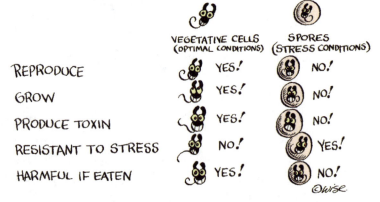

The vegetative and spore states of bacteria cells

However, when conditions become suitable for growth, a spore can germinate much like a seed. The bacterial spore can then return to the vegetative state and begin to grow again. Bacteria can survive for many months as spores, and it is much harder to destroy bacteria when they are in spore form.

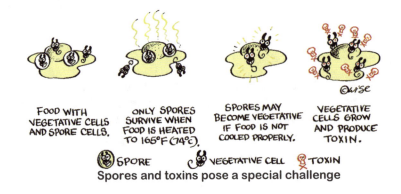

Spores and toxins pose a special challenge

Spoilage and Disease-causing Bacteria

Bacteria are classified as either spoilage or pathogenic (disease-causing) microorganisms.

Spoilage bacteria break down foods so they look, taste, and smell bad. They reduce the quality of food to unacceptable levels. **Pathogenic bacteria** are disease-causing microorganisms that can make people ill if the vegetative bacterial cells or their toxins are consumed with food. Both spoilage and pathogenic bacteria must be controlled in retail food establishments.

Bacterial Growth

Bacteria reproduce when one bacterial cell divides to form two new cells. This process is called **binary fission**. The reproduction of bacteria and an increase in the number of organisms are referred to as bacterial growth. Bacterial growth follows a regular pattern that consists of four phases:

1. **Lag phase**—Bacteria exhibit little or no growth as they adjust to their environment. This phase lasts only a few hours at room temperature but can be increased by keeping foods out of the temperature danger zone.

2. **Log phase**—Bacteria double in number every 15 to 30 minutes under the most optimal conditions.

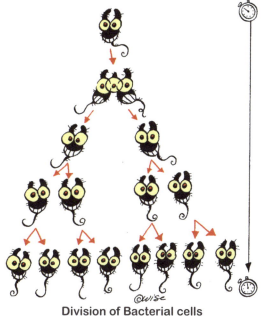
Division of Bacterial cells

3. **Stationary phase**—The number of bacteria is steady as the number of new organisms being produced is equal to the number of organisms that are dying.

4. **Death phase**—Bacteria die off rapidly because they lack nutrients and are poisoned by their own wastes.

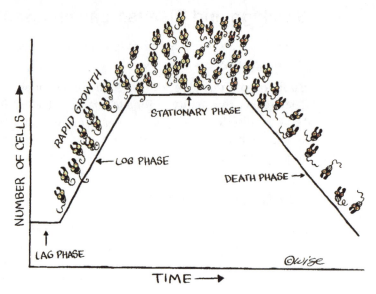

Bacterial growth curve

What Disease-causing Bacteria Need in Order to Multiply

Disease-causing bacteria need six conditions in order to multiply or grow in foods.

1. Food
2. Acid
3. Temperature
4. Time
5. Oxygen
6. Moisture

Microbes eat the same foods we do.

> Since many foods naturally contain microorganisms, it is necessary to control one or more of these six conditions to prevent bacteria from multiplying.

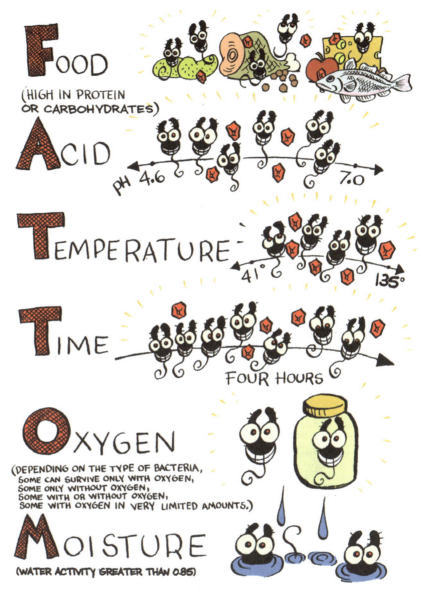

FATTOM

An easy way to remember the requirements for bacterial growth is by using the acronym **FATTOM**.

Food

A suitable food supply is the most important condition needed for bacterial growth. Most bacteria prefer foods high in protein or carbohydrates like meats; poultry; seafood; dairy products; and cooked rice, beans, and potatoes.

Acidity

The **pH** symbol is used to designate the level of acidity or alkalinity of a food. You measure pH on a scale that ranges from 0 to 14.

Most foods are acidic and have a pH less than 7.0. Foods highly **acidic** (pH below 4.6) like lemons and limes will not normally support the growth of disease-causing bacteria. Pickling fruits and vegetables preserves the food by adding acids, such as vinegar. This lowers the pH of the food in order to slow down the rate of bacterial growth.

A pH above 7.0 indicates the food is "**alkaline**." Only a few foods are alkaline. Examples of alkaline foods are olives, egg whites, and soda crackers.

Most bacteria that can cause foodborne illness prefer a neutral environment (pH of 7.0) but are capable of growing in foods that have a pH in the range of 4.6 to 9.0. Since most foods have a pH of less than 7.0, we have identified the range where most harmful bacteria grow as 4.6 to 7.0. Many foods offered for sale in retail food establishments have a pH in this range.

Disease-causing bacteria grow best when the foods they live in and on have a pH of 4.6 to 7.0.

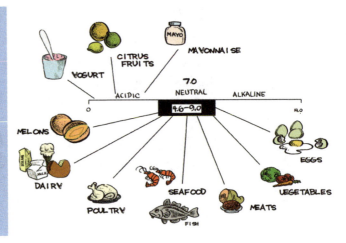

What Disease-causing Bacteria Need in Order to Multiply

Temperature

Most disease-causing bacteria can grow within a temperature range of 41°F (5°C) to 135° F (57°C).

> **Temperature abuse** is the term applied to foods that have not been heated to a safe temperature or kept at the proper temperature to control bacterial growth.

This is commonly referred to as the food "temperature danger zone." A few disease-causing bacteria, such as *Listeria monocytogenes*, can grow at temperatures below 41°F (5°C), but the rate of growth is very slow.

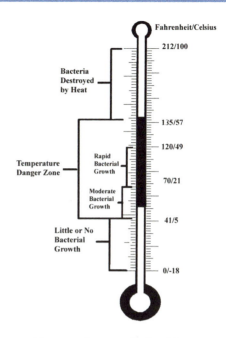

Temperature control guide

Time

For most bacteria, a single cell can generate over one million new cells in just a few hours. Because bacteria have the ability to multiply rapidly, it does not take long before many cells are produced. Bacteria need about four hours to grow to high enough numbers to cause illness. This includes the total time a food is between 41°F (5°C) and 135°F (57°C).

Time	0	15 min.	30 min.	60 min.	3 hrs.	5 hrs.
# of cells	1	2	4	16	> 1000	> 1 million

> **Bacterial cells can double in number every 15 to 30 minutes.**

> **Careful monitoring of time and temperature is the most effective way to control the growth of pathogenic and spoilage organisms.**

Oxygen

Bacteria also differ in their requirements for oxygen. **Aerobic** bacteria must have oxygen in order to grow. **Anaerobic bacteria** cannot survive when oxygen is present because it is toxic to them. Anaerobic bacteria grow well in vacuum-packaged foods or canned foods where oxygen is not available. Anaerobic conditions also exist in the middle of cooked food masses, such as in large stockpots, baked potatoes, or in the middle of a roast or ham. **Facultative anaerobic** forms of bacteria can grow with or without oxygen.

> **Controlling oxygen conditions is not an effective way to prevent foodborne illness. Regardless of available oxygen, some disease-causing bacteria will be able to adapt to the conditions and grow.**

Moisture

Moisture is an important factor in bacterial growth. The amount of water in a food available to support bacterial growth is called **water activity**. It is designated with the symbol A_w. Water activity is measured on a scale from 0.0 to 1.0. Water activity is a measure of the amount of water not bound to the food and is, therefore, available to support bacterial growth. Water activity is really a measurement of relative humidity of a food.

> **Disease-causing bacteria can only grow in foods that have a water activity higher than 0.85.**

For example, fresh chicken has 60% water by volume, and its A_w is approximately 0.98. The same chicken, when frozen, still has 60% water by volume but its A_w is nearly zero. Lowering the water activity of foods to 0.85 or below preserves many foods. Drying foods or adding salt or sugar reduces the amount of available water. For example, jams and jellies that contain a lot of sugar have an A_w much less than 0.85 because the sugar binds tightly to the water, making the water unavailable. This alone prevents the growth of disease-causing microorganisms.

Water activity (A_w) of some foods sold in food establishments

Potentially Hazardous Foods (PHF)

The *Food Code* classifies the following natural and man-made items as **potentially hazardous foods**:

- Foods of animal origin that are raw or heat-treated
- Foods of plant origin that are heat-treated or consist of raw seed sprouts
- Cut melons
- Garlic-in-oil mixtures that are not modified in a way to inhibit the growth of disease-causing microorganisms
- Cut tomatoes including sliced, diced, chopped, and pureed tomatoes.
- Cut leafy greens (lettuce, spinach, and salad mixes).

If potentially hazardous foods are held in the temperature danger zone [between 41°F (5°C) and 135°F (57°C)] for four hours or more, infectious and toxin-producing microbes can grow to dangerous levels. Potentially hazardous foods have been associated with most foodborne disease outbreaks. It is critical to control the handling and storage of potentially hazardous foods to prevent bacterial growth.

Examples of potentially hazardous foods

Potentially Hazardous Food (Time/Temperature Control for Safety Food)

In the 2005 edition of the FDA *Food Code*, a new term and definition for *potentially hazardous foods was created. Potentially hazardous food (time/temperature control for safety food)* or PHF (TCS) is the current term used to refer to a food that requires time and temperature control for safety to limit pathogenic microorganism growth or toxin formation. Some examples of PHF (TCS) foods that require temperature and time control for safety are animal foods that are raw or heat-treated, plant foods that are heat-

Potentially hazardous food (time/temperature control for safety food) [PHF (TCS)] requires time and temperature control to limit pathogenic microorganism growth or toxin formation.

treated or consist of raw seed sprouts, cut melons, garlic-in-oil mixtures, cut tomatoes, and cut leafy greens.

Foods that are not considered PHF (TCS) include: (a) air-cooled hard-boiled eggs with shell intact, pasteurized egg with shell intact treated to destroy all viable *Salmonellae*; (b) commercially sterile shelf-stable foods in unopened hermetically sealed containers; (c) a food that because of its pH or water activity, or interaction of pH and water activity, is designated as a non-PHF (TCS) food; (d) a food that has undergone a product assessment showing that the growth or toxin formation of pathogenic microorganisms is unlikely due to intrinsic factors of the food (i.e., natural or added preservatives or antimicrobials), extrinsic factors of the food (i.e., reduced oxygen packaging), or a combination of these factors.

> **The terms potentially hazardous foods and PHF (TCS) are used interchangeably throughout the book and are intended to mean the same thing.**

The new definition of PHF (TCS) takes into consideration pH, water activity (A_w), pH and water-activity interaction, heat treatment, and packaging for a determination of whether the food requires time/temperature control for safety. In some foods, it is possible neither the pH value nor the water activity value is low enough by itself to control or eliminate pathogen growth; however, the interaction of pH and water activity together may be able to accomplish this. This is an example of "hurdle technology" that food microbiologists use to understand complex interactions in foods. Hurdle technology involves several inhibitory factors being used together to control or eliminate pathogen growth, when they would otherwise be ineffective if used alone.

In order to better describe the interactions of pH and water activity, Tables A and B were included in Annex 3 of the FDA *Food Code*. The same tables are provided in Appendix B of this book. The focus of Table A is to describe the conditions needed for a non-PHF (TCS) food that is prepared, heat-treated, and packaged. Table B describes the conditions needed for a non-PHF (TCS) food for a prepared and heat-treated food that is not packaged. Note in each table, different criteria are established based on the interaction of different levels of pH and water activity.

The PHF (TCS) approach will provide more flexibility to the food industry to establish storage conditions for foods that will not support growth of pathogenic microorganisms or toxin formation. However, for this approach to work effectively, individuals must understand the concepts of pH and water activity in food and know how to measure them accurately.

Food product consistency is also very important as a slight change in pH or water activity could make a big difference in the relative safety of the food. Even a small change in product formulation can have a large impact on bacterial growth. While the new approach provides greater options for food operators, the concept should be used with caution to ensure food conditions do not permit pathogenic microorganism growth or toxin formation.

This original concept was developed by a working group at the Institute of Food Technologists (IFT). More information can be obtained by reviewing the IFT Report, *Evaluation and Definition of Potentially Hazardous Foods*, at http://members.ift.org/NR/rdonlyres/82EEDE0C-51C6-4943-95EF-3E8A95162BAF/0/crfsfssupn2p001109.pdf.

Ready-to-Eat Foods

Ready-to-eat (RTE) foods can become contaminated if not handled properly. The FDA *Food Code* identifies the following types of foods as ready-to-eat:

> **Ready-to-eat foods are food items that are edible without washing, cooking or additional preparation by the customer or by the retail food establishment.**

- Raw animal foods that are cooked (i.e., rotisserie chicken) or frozen (i.e., sushi)
- Raw fruits and vegetables that are washed
- Fruits and vegetables that are cooked for hot-holding
- All potentially hazardous foods that are cooked and then cooled
- Bakery items, such as bread, cakes, pies, fillings, or icing, for which further cooking is not required for food safety
- Substances derived from plants, such as spices, seasonings, and sugar
- Plant foods for which further washing, cooking, or other processing is not required for food safety and from which rinds, peels, husks, or shells, if naturally present, are removed
- Dry, fermented sausages (i.e., dry salami or pepperoni), salt-cured meat and poultry products (i.e., prosciutto ham, country cured ham, and Parma ham), and dried meat and poultry products (i.e., jerky or beef sticks) produced in accordance with USDA guidelines and treated to destroy pathogens
- Thermally processed low-acid foods (i.e., smoked fish or meat) packaged in hermetically sealed containers.

Foodborne Illness Caused by Bacteria

Biological hazards are important for the retail food establishment manager to control because they lead to the majority of foodborne illnesses. Bacteria are one of the most common agents that lead to foodborne illness. Bacteria are classified as sporeforming and non-sporeforming organisms.

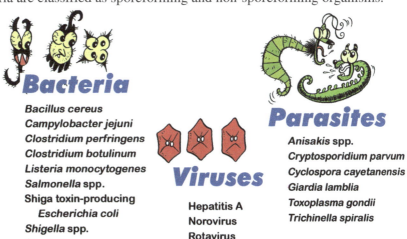

Bacteria
Bacillus cereus
Campylobacter jejuni
Clostridium perfringens
Clostridium botulinum
Listeria monocytogenes
Salmonella spp.
Shiga toxin-producing *Escherichia coli*
Shigella spp.
Staphylococcus aureus
Vibrio spp.

Viruses
Hepatitis A
Norovirus
Rotavirus

Parasites
Anisakis spp.
Cryptosporidium parvum
Cyclospora cayetanensis
Giardia lamblia
Toxoplasma gondii
Trichinella spiralis

Common biological hazards in food establishments

Foodborne Illness Caused by Sporeforming Bacteria

A spore structure enables a cell to survive environmental stress, such as cooking, freezing, high-salt conditions, drying, and high-acid conditions.

Spores are not harmful if ingested except in a baby's digestive system, where *Clostridium botulinum* spores can cause a disease called infant botulism. It is often recommended parents avoid serving honey to babies due to the possible presence of *Clostridium botulinum* spores. If conditions in the food are suitable for bacterial growth and the spore turns into a vegetative cell, the vegetative cell can grow in the food and cause illness if eaten.

Sporeforming bacteria are generally found in foods grown in soil, like vegetables and spices. They may also be found in animal products. They can be particularly troublesome in retail food establishments when foods are not cooled properly.

For example, a 10-gallon pot of chili was prepared for the next day's salad bar display. All the ingredients (beans, meat, spices, tomato base) were mixed together and cooked to a rapid boil. Vegetative forms of the cells should die, but spores may survive.

The chili was then stored in the 10gallon pot and allowed to cool overnight in a walk-in refrigerator. It can take the core temperature of the chili two to three days to cool from 135°F (57°C) to 41°F (5°C)! If given enough time at the right temperature during the cooling process, sporeforming bacteria that survived the cooking process may change into vegetative cells and begin to grow. Spores are most likely to turn into the dangerous vegetative state when:

Even proper cooking or reheating may not destroy spores.

- They are "heat-shocked" during cooking, which can allow the spores to become vegetative cells.
- Optimum conditions exist for growth (high protein or carbohydrates, high moisture, pH greater than 4.6).
- Temperatures are in the food temperature danger zone or between 41°F (5°C) to 135°F (57°C) for four or more hours.

It is critical hot food temperatures be maintained at 135°F (57°C) or above and cold foods should be held at 41°F (5°C) or below.

Always cook and cool foods as rapidly as possible (within 4 hours) to limit bacterial growth.

In the following sections, each type of biological hazard is described, the common foods and route of transmission are identified, and preventive strategies are discussed.

Sporeforming Bacteria

Bacillus cereus	
Causative Agent	• *Bacillus cereus*
Type of Illness	• Bacterial intoxication or toxin-mediated infection
Symptoms	• Diarrhea type: abdominal cramps • Vomiting type: vomiting, diarrhea, abdominal cramps
Onset	• Diarrhea type: 8 to 16 hours; usually lasts 12 to 14 hours • Vomiting type: 30 minutes to 6 hours
Common Foods	• Diarrhea type: meats, milk, vegetables, fish • Vomiting type: rice, starchy foods, grains, cereals
Prevention	• Properly cook and hold at 135°F (57°C), cool rapidly to below 41°F (5°C), and reheat foods.

Bacillus cereus is a sporeforming bacterium that can survive with or without oxygen. It has been associated with two very different types of illnesses: one vomiting, the other diarrhea. Illness due to *Bacillus cereus* is most often attributed to foods improperly stored (cooled, hot-held), permitting the conversion of spores to vegetative cells. Vegetative cells then grow in the food and produce toxin in the food that leads to illness.

Properly cook and hold at 135°F (57°C), cool rapidly to below 41°F (5°C), and reheat foods.

Clostridium perfringens

Causative Agent	• *Clostridium perfringens*
Type of Illness	• Bacterial toxin-mediated infection
Symptoms	• Intense abdominal pains and severe diarrhea
Onset	• 8 to 22 hours
Common Foods	• Spices, gravy, improperly cooled foods (especially meats and gravy dishes)
Prevention	• Properly cook, cool, and reheat foods.

Clostridium perfringens is a nearly anaerobic (can only tolerate a little oxygen), sporeforming bacterium that causes foodborne illness. PHF (TCS) that have been temperature abused [not kept hot—above 135°F (57°C); or cold—below 41°F (5°C)] are frequently associated with this problem. *Clostridium perfringens* causes illness due to a toxin-mediated infection in which the ingested cells colonize and then produce a toxin in the human intestinal tract. Illness due to *Clostridium perfringens* is most often attributed to foods that are temperature abused, especially those that have been improperly cooled and reheated. Cooked foods must be cooled from 135°F (57°C) to 70°F (21°C) within 2 hours and from 135°F (57°C) to 41°F (5°C) in 6 hours. Foods must also be reheated to 165°F (74°C) within 2 hours and held at 135°F (57°C) until served.

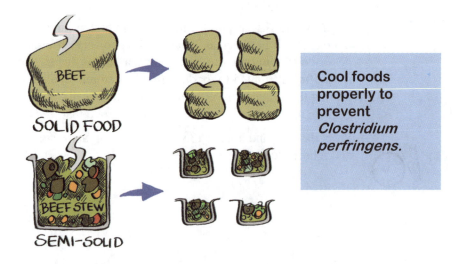

Cool foods properly to prevent *Clostridium perfringens*.

Clostridium botulinum

Causative Agent	• *Clostridium botulinum*
Type of Illness	• Bacterial intoxication
Symptoms	• Dizziness, double vision, difficulty in breathing and swallowing, headache
Onset	• 12 to 36 hours; usually lasts several days to a year
Common Foods	• Low-acid foods (pH above 4.6) that are inadequately heat-processed and then packaged anaerobically (metal can or vacuum pouch) and held in the food temperature danger zone; examples: home-canned green beans, meats, fish, and garlic or onions stored in oil or butter respectively
Prevention	• Properly heat-process and cool vacuum-packaged and other reduced-oxygen packaged foods; DO NOT use home-canned foods.

Clostridium botulinum is an anaerobic (must not have oxygen), sporeforming bacterium that causes foodborne intoxication due to improperly heat-processed foods, especially home canning. Do not can foods in a retail food establishment. The organism produces a neurotoxin that is one of the most deadly biological toxins known to man. This toxin is not heat stable and can be destroyed if the food is boiled for about 20 minutes. Illness due to *Clostridium botulinum* is almost always attributed to ingestion of foods that were not heat-processed correctly and packaged anaerobically.

Purchase only manufactured and inspected vacuum-packaged foods.

Foodborne Illness Caused by Non-Sporeforming Bacteria

Compared to bacterial spores, vegetative cells are easily destroyed by proper cooking. There are numerous examples of non-sporeforming foodborne bacteria that are important in the food industry.

Non-Sporeforming Bacteria

Campylobacter jejuni	
Causative Agent	• *Campylobacter jejuni*
Type of Illness	• Bacterial infection
Symptoms	• Watery, bloody diarrhea
Onset	• 2 to 5 days; usually lasts 2 to 7 days
Common Foods	• Raw poultry, raw milk, raw meat
Prevention	• Properly handle and cook raw meats and poultry, properly clean and sanitize food-contact surfaces, and properly wash hands.

Campylobacter jejuni has been reported as the No.1 cause of bacterial foodborne infection in the United States. This organism tolerates only 3% to 6% oxygen to grow. *Campylobacter jejuni* is often transferred from raw meats to other foods by cross contamination, typically from a food-contact surface (such as a cutting board or knife) or a food employee's hands.

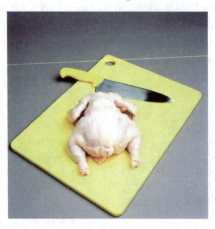

Campylobacter jejuni is commonly found in raw chicken.

Shiga toxin-producing *Escherichia coli*

Causative Agent	• Shiga toxin-producing *Escherichia coli*
Type of Illness	• Bacterial infection or toxin-mediated infection; at special risk are children up to 16 years old and elderly people
Symptoms	• Bloody diarrhea followed by kidney failure and hemolytic uremic syndrome (HUS) in severe cases
Onset	• 2 to 72 hours; usually lasts from 1 to 3 days
Common Foods	• Raw and undercooked beef and other red meats, raw finfish, improperly pasteurized milk, unpasteurized apple cider, lettuce
Prevention	• Practice good food sanitation, hand washing; properly handle and cook ground meats to an internal temperature of at least 155°F (68°C) for 15 seconds; prevent cross contamination and keep hot foods above 135°F (57°C) and cold foods below 41°F (5°C); wash lettuce in sinks used only for food preparation; use only pasteurized apple cider or fruit juice and milk products.

The *Escherichia coli* (or *E. coli*) group of bacteria includes four foodborne pathogens: enterotoxigenic *E. coli*, enteropathogenic *E. coli*, enterohemorrhagic *E. coli*, and enteroinvasive *E. coli*. Of particular importance is a type of enterohemorrhagic *E. coli* called Shiga toxin-producing *E. coli*. This facultative anaerobic bacteria lives in the intestines of humans and warm-blooded animals, especially cows. Most types of *E. coli* are harmless. However, Shiga toxin-producing *E. coli* can cause an infection or a toxin-mediated infection. Only a small amount of bacteria is required to produce illness. A PHF (TCS) is not needed for bacterial survival. That's why apple cider, which has a pH lower than 4.6, has been implicated in cases of foodborne illness. Shiga toxin-producing *E. coli* is usually transferred to foods, such as beef, through contact with the intestines of slaughtered animals. Apples used for juice from orchards where cattle grazed are also suspected. Transmission can occur if employees who are carriers do not wash their soiled hands properly after going to the toilet. Cross contamination by soiled equipment and utensils may also spread Shiga toxin-producing *E. coli*.

Listeria monocytogenes

Causative Agent	• *Listeria monocytogenes*
Type of Illness	• Bacterial infection
Symptoms	• Healthy adult: flu-like symptoms • At-risk population: septicemia, meningitis, encephalitis, birth defects • Stillbirth
Onset	• 1 day to 3 weeks; indefinite duration depending on when treatment is administered
Common Foods	• Raw meats, raw poultry, dairy products, processed luncheon meats and hot dogs, raw vegetables, and seafood
Prevention	• Properly store and cook foods, avoid cross contamination, rotate processed refrigerated foods using first-in-first-out (FIFO) to ensure timely use.

Listeria monocytogenes is a facultative anaerobic (can grow with or without oxygen) bacterium that causes foodborne infection. This microbe is important to retail food establishment operations because it has the ability to survive under many environmentally stressful conditions such as in high-salt foods and, unlike most other foodborne pathogens, can grow at refrigerated temperatures below 41°F (5°C). Transmission to foods can occur by cross contamination by people or equipment or if foods are not cooked properly.

Listeria monocytogenes **can grow at refrigerated temperatures.**

Salmonella spp.

Causative Agent	• *Salmonella* spp.
Type of Illness	• Bacterial infection
Symptoms	• Nausea, fever, vomiting, abdominal cramps, diarrhea
Onset	• 6 to 48 hours; usually lasts 2 to 3 days
Common Foods	• Raw meats, raw poultry, eggs, milk, dairy products, pork
Prevention	• Properly cook foods; example: *Salmonella* bacteria will be destroyed when poultry is cooked to an internal temperature of 165°F (74°C) for 15 seconds and when eggs are cooked to 145°F (63°C) for 15 seconds. Clean and sanitize raw food-contact surfaces after use; make sure food employees wash their hands adequately before working with food; avoid cross contamination.

Salmonella are facultative anaerobic (grow with or without oxygen) bacteria frequently implicated as a foodborne infection. *Salmonella* are found in the intestinal tract of humans and warm-blooded animals. They frequently get into foods as a result of fecal contamination or cross contamination. Transmission to foods is commonly through cross contamination in which fecal material is transferred to food through contact with raw foods (especially poultry), contaminated food-contact surfaces (i.e., cutting boards), or infected food employees.

Sprouts and melons are common sources for *Salmonella* spp.

Shigella spp.

Causative Agent	• *Shigella* spp
Type of Illness	• Bacterial infection
Symptoms	• Bacillary dysentery, diarrhea, fever, abdominal cramps, dehydration
Onset	• 1 to 7 days; duration depends on when treatment is administered
Common Foods	• Foods prepared with human contact: ready-to-eat salads (i.e., potato, chicken), raw vegetables, milk, dairy products, raw poultry, non-potable water, ready-to-eat meat
Prevention	• Wash hands and practice good personal hygiene, properly cook foods, avoid cross contamination, wash produce and other foods with potable water (water that is safe to drink). Do not allow individuals who have been diagnosed with shigellosis to handle food.

Shigellae are facultative anaerobic bacteria that account for about 10% of foodborne illnesses in the United States. These organisms can be found in the intestines and feces of humans. They cause shigellosis, a foodborne infection. The bacterium produces a toxin that causes watery diarrhea. Water contaminated by fecal material and food and utensils handled by employees who are carriers of the bacteria can cause this problem. Illnesses from *Shigellae* are most often attributed to contaminated ready-to-eat foods handled by an infected food handler.

Shigella spp. are most often attributed to foods prepared with human contact.

Staphylococcus aureus	
Causative Agent	• *Staphylococcus aureus*
Type of Illness	• Bacterial intoxication
Symptoms	• Nausea, vomiting, abdominal cramps, headaches
Onset	• 1 to 6 hours, usually 2 to 4 hours; usually lasts 1 to 2 days
Common Foods	• Foods prepared with human contact; processed ready-to-eat foods (such as luncheon meats), ready-to-eat meat, deli salads (such as taco, potato, egg, and tuna salads), meat, poultry, custards, high-salt foods (such as ham), milk and dairy products, processed foods
Prevention	• Wash hands and practice good personal hygiene; avoid coughing and sneezing near food; do not reuse tasting spoons and ladles; properly clean and bandage cuts, burns, or wounds on hands; and wear plastic gloves. Cooking WILL NOT inactivate the toxin.

Staphylococcus aureus is a facultative anaerobic bacterium that produces a heat-stable toxin as it grows on foods. This bacterium can also grow on cooked, and otherwise safe, foods recontaminated by food employees who mishandle the food. *Staphylococcus aureus* bacteria do not compete well when other types of microorganisms are present. However, they grow well when alone and without competition from other microbes. These bacteria are commonly found on human skin, hands, hair, and in the nose and throat. They may also be found in burns, infected cuts and wounds, pimples, and boils. These organisms can be transferred to foods easily, and they can grow in foods that contain high salt or high sugar and have a lower water activity. They grow well in a high-salt concentration environment, such as on hams and luncheon meats. Foods requiring considerable food preparation and handling are especially susceptible. The bacteria are also spread by droplets of saliva from talking, coughing, and sneezing near food. Food employees who improperly use tasting spoons and ladles can transfer bacteria from their mouth to food. Contaminated human hands combined with temperature abuse usually cause most problems associated with *Staphylococcus aureus*.

Vibrio spp.	
Causative Agent	• *Vibrio* spp.
Type of Illness	• Bacterial infection
Symptoms	• Headache, fever, chills, diarrhea, vomiting, severe electrolyte loss, gastroenteritis
Onset	• 2 to 48 hours
Common Foods	• Raw or improperly cooked fish and shellfish
Prevention	• Practice good sanitation, properly cool foods, implement procedures to separate raw and ready-to-eat seafood display cases, buy seafood from approved sources only.

There are three organisms within the *Vibrio* group of bacteria connected with foodborne infections. They include *Vibrio cholera*, *Vibrio parahaemolyticus*, and *Vibrio vulnificus*. All are important since they are very resistant to salt and are common in seafood.

Since the organism is inherent in many types of raw seafood, transmission to other foods by cross contamination is a concern. Most illnesses are caused by the consumption of raw or undercooked seafood.

Foodborne Illness Caused by Viruses

Viruses are now reported as the No. 1 cause of foodborne and waterborne diseases in the United States. The viruses that cause foodborne disease differ from foodborne bacteria in several ways. Viruses are much smaller than bacteria, and they require a living host (human, animal) to replicate.

Viruses do not multiply in foods. However, a susceptible person needs to consume only a few viral particles in order to experience an infection.

Viruses are usually transferred from one food to another, from a food employee to a food, or from a contaminated water supply to a food. A PHF (TCS) is not needed to support survival of viruses. The viruses of primary importance to retail food establishments are Norwalk-like virus and Hepatitis A virus. Proper hand washing, no bare hand contact with ready-to-eat foods, and separation of raw and ready-to-eat foods are important keys to controlling the spread of foodborne viruses.

Norovirus (Norwalk-like virus)	
Causative Agent	• Norwalk virus
Type of Illness	• Viral infection
Symptoms	• Vomiting, diarrhea, abdominal pain, headache, low-grade fever
Onset	• 24 to 48 hours; usually lasts 1 to 3 days
Common Foods	• Sewage-contaminated water; contaminated salad ingredients; raw clams, oysters; foods contaminated by infected food employees
Prevention	• Use potable water; cook all shellfish; handle food properly; meet time, temperature guidelines for PHF; practice good personal hygiene and wash hands and fingernails thoroughly; keep raw and ready-to-eat seafood products separate.

KEY CONCEPT

Norovirus is a common foodborne virus associated with many foodborne infections. The CDC estimates that at least one-half of all foodborne outbreaks of gastroenteritis can be attributed to noroviruses. Outbreaks of norovirus gastroenteritis occur when people consume water and/or food that is contaminated with the virus. Food and beverages are easily contaminated with norovirus because the virus is so small. Outbreaks are frequent because it usually takes only 10 to 100 norovirus particles to make a person sick.

Hepatitis A

Causative Agent	• Hepatitis A virus
Type of Illness	• Viral infection
Symptoms	• Fever, nausea, vomiting, abdominal pain, fatigue, swelling of the liver, jaundice
Onset	• 10 to 50 days; a mild case usually lasts several weeks, more severe cases can last several months
Common Foods	• Raw and lightly cooked oysters and clams harvested from polluted waters; raw vegetables that have been irrigated or washed with polluted water; foods prepared with contact by infected employee including salads, sliced luncheon meats, salad bar items, sandwiches, bakery products; contaminated water
Prevention	• Buy clams, oysters, and molluscan shellfish from approved sources; keep raw and ready-to-eat foods separate during storage and display; handle foods properly and cook them to recommended temperatures; wash hands and practice good personal hygiene.

Hepatitis A is a foodborne virus associated with many foodborne infections. Hepatitis A causes a liver disease called infectious hepatitis. The Hepatitis A virus is a particularly important hazard to retail food establishments because employees can harbor the virus for up to six weeks and not show symptoms of illness. Food employees are contagious for one week before onset of symptoms and two weeks after the symptoms of the disease appear. During that time, infected employees can contaminate foods and other employees by spreading fecal material from unwashed hands and nails. Hepatitis A virus is very hardy and can live for several hours in a suitable environment. The virus is transmitted by ingestion of food and water that contain the Hepatitis A virus. Raw seafood and foods handled by infected human hands are the largest threat of transmission and disease from Hepatitis A. Additional information about controls and prevention of Hepatitis A is available in the *Hepatitis A Information Guide* published by the FMI.

Foodborne Illness Caused by Parasites

Foodborne parasites are another important foodborne biological hazard. Parasites are small or microscopic creatures that need to live on or inside a living host to survive. Many parasites can enter the food system and cause foodborne illness. In this chapter, we list a few of the most troublesome ones that may appear in retail food establishments. Parasitic infection is far less common than bacterial or viral foodborne illnesses.

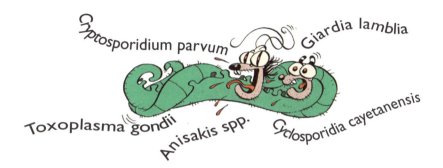

Worldwide food trade and consumption of raw and undercooked foods increase exposure to parasitic illness.

Anisakis spp.	
Causative Agent	• *Anisakis* spp.
Type of Illness	• Parasitic infection
Symptoms	• Coughing if worms attach in throat, vomiting and abdominal pain if worms attach in stomach, sharp pain and fever if worms attach in large intestine
Onset	• 1 hour to 2 weeks
Common Foods	• Raw or undercooked seafood; especially bottom-feeding fish
Prevention	• Cook fish to the proper temperature throughout, freeze to meet FDA *Food Code* specifications, inspect seafood and handle carefully, purchase seafood from approved supplier.

Anisakis spp. are nematodes (roundworms) associated with foodborne infection from fish. The worms are about 1 to 1-1/2 inches long and the diameter of a human hair. They are beige, ivory, white, gray, brown, or pink. Other names for this parasite are "cod worm" (not to be confused with common roundworms found in cod) and "herring worm." The natural hosts of the parasite are walruses and perhaps sea lions and otters. The worms are transferred to fish, their intermediate host, in the water in which the walruses live. Humans become the accidental host upon eating fish infested with the parasites. Humans do not make good hosts for the parasites. The worms will not complete their life cycles in humans and eventually die.

Bottom-feeding fish, such as salmon, are a common source of *Anisakis* spp.

Cyclospora cayetanensis

Causative Agent	• *Cyclospora cayetanensis*
Type of Illness	• Parasitic infection
Symptoms	• Watery and explosive diarrhea, loss of appetite, bloating
Onset	• Usually within 1 week; symptoms persist for weeks or months if untreated
Common Foods	• Contaminated water, strawberries, raspberries, and fresh produce
Prevention	• Use good sanitation and personal hygiene, purchase foods from reputable supplier.

Cyclospora cayetanensis is a parasite that has been reported much more frequently beginning in the 1990s. *Cyclospora* frequently finds its way into water and then can be transferred to foods. It can also be transferred to foods during handling. The most recent outbreaks of cyclosporiasis have been associated with fresh fruits and vegetables that were contaminated at the farm. *Cyclospora* is passed from person to person by fecal-oral transmission. Foods usually become contaminated after coming in contact with fecal material from polluted water or a contaminated food employee. The *Cyclospora* parasite may take days or weeks after a person eats a contaminated food to become infectious.

Wash berries to remove contaminants.

Trichinellae spiralis

Causative Agent	• *Trichinellae spiralis*
Type of Illness	• Parasitic infection from a nematode worm
Symptoms	• Early symptoms: nausea, vomiting, diarrhea, sweating, abdominal pain; in later stages: fever, swelling of tissues around eyes, muscle stiffness
Onset	• 2 to 28 days; death may occur in severe cases
Common Foods	• Primarily undercooked pork products and wild game meats (bear, walrus)
Prevention	• Cook foods to the proper temperature throughout (i.e., no pink color in cooked pork products).

Trichinella spiralis is a foodborne roundworm that causes a parasitic infection. It must be eaten with the infected fleshy muscle of certain meat-eating animals to be transmitted to a new host. Meat-eating, scavenger animals frequently carry this parasite. These animals are exposed to the parasite when they eat infected tissues from other animals and garbage that contains contaminated raw-meat scraps.

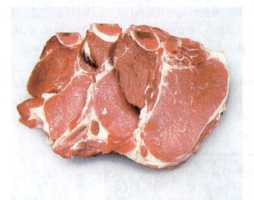

Cook raw pork to the proper temperature.

Cryptosporidium parvum

Causative Agent	• *Cryptosporidium parvum*
Type of Illness	• Parasitic infection
Symptoms	• Severe watery diarrhea
Onset	• Within 1 week of ingestion
Common Foods	• Contaminated water, food contaminated by infected food employees
Prevention	• Use potable water supply, practice good personal hygiene and hand washing.

Cryptosporidium parvum is a parasite found in water that has been contaminated with cow feces. The parasite causes foodborne infection and is considered an important source of nonbacterial diarrhea in the United States. It is primarily transmitted by a water supply contaminated with feces and by fecal contamination of food and food-contact surfaces. Parasite prevention starts with providing a potable water supply in the retail food establishment and handling foods carefully to prevent contamination and cross contamination. Food employees must practice good personal hygiene and wash hands thoroughly before working with food and after going to the toilet.

Problems Caused by Fungi

Yeast and molds make up the group called fungi. Yeasts and molds mainly contribute to food spoilage. When yeast grows in a food, it leads to undesirable characteristics of a food including production of gases and alcohol. The food may taste or smell "spoiled," and the package may swell. Yeasts do not lead to foodborne illness. Yeasts are often used to produce fermented foods, such as beer, wine, and cheeses. Molds usually grow in foods low in moisture (bread or cheese), acidic (fruit juices), or high in sugar (jams and jellies). They often appear very colorful, "cotton-like," or "powdery" in appearance. Like yeasts, molds themselves do not cause foodborne illness. However, if they grow long enough on foods, they can produce a substance called a "mycotoxin." Mycotoxins can cause foodborne illness and some forms of cancers. Mycotoxins are usually considered chemical hazards.

Foodborne Illness Caused by Chemicals

Chemical hazards are usually classified as either naturally occurring or man-made chemicals. Naturally occurring chemicals include food allergens and toxins produced by a biological organism. Man-made chemicals include substances added, intentionally or accidentally, to a food during processing. A summary of some of the more common naturally occurring and man-made chemicals is provided below.

Types of Chemical Hazards in a Retail Food Establishment	
Naturally Occurring:	**Man-made Chemicals:**
• Allergens • Ciguatoxin • Mycotoxins • Scombrotoxin • Shellfish toxin.	• Cleaning solutions • Food additives • Pesticides • Heavy metals.

Source: FDA *Food Code*

Naturally Occurring Chemicals

Food Allergens

According to the current *Food Code*, over 12 million Americans suffer from one or more food allergies. It is estimated that approximately 4% of the U.S. population are allergic to certain chemicals in foods and food ingredients. These chemicals are commonly referred to as **food allergens**. A food allergen causes a person's immune system to overreact. Some common symptoms of food allergies are hives or other itchy rashes, nausea, abdominal pain, vomiting and/or diarrhea, wheezing, shortness of breath, and swelling of various parts of the body. These symptoms can occur in as little as five minutes. In severe situations, a life-threatening allergic reaction called anaphylaxis can occur. Anaphylaxis is a condition that occurs when many parts of the body become involved in the allergic reaction. Symptoms of anaphylaxis include itching and hives, swelling of the throat and difficulty breathing, lowered blood pressure, and unconsciousness.

The FDA has identified eight different foods or food groups as "Major Food Allergens." About 90% of all food allergies are caused by one of these foods or a food ingredient that contains protein derived from one of these foods. The only way for a person who is allergic to one of these foods to avoid an allergic reaction is to avoid the food containing the allergen. In many cases, it does not take much of the food to produce a severe reaction. As little as half a peanut can cause a severe reaction in highly sensitive people.

Major Food Allergens

- Milk
- Eggs
- Wheat
- Peanuts
- Soybeans
- Tree nuts (i.e., almonds and pecans)
- Fish
- Crustacean shellfish (i.e., lobster and shrimp)

Allergies can be very serious. You need to know which foods in your establishment contain these ingredients. The FDA now requires ingredients to be listed on the label of packaged foods. Always read label information to determine if food allergens may be present. FMI has created a poster to provide an overview of the requirements of the FDA Food Allergen Labeling and Consumer Protection Act as they apply to retailers. Copies of the food allergen awareness poster in English and Spanish may be obtained from the FMI Web site at www.fmi.org/foodsafety/

The responsibility of retailers in the case of prepackaged foods is to assure that appropriate label warnings are given to potential purchasers. Retailers have special responsibilities in regard to foods sold from open containers (i.e., on delicatessen counters). When such foods contain a major food allergen, the warning should be clearly displayed by the foods in question. Moreover, staff must be trained to take great care to avoid cross contamination, such as might occur when using the same ladle or other handling equipment for a food containing a major food allergen and one that does not contain it.

The Food Allergy and Anaphylaxis Network (FAAN) urges retailers to take customer food allergy requests and questions seriously. FAAN advises retailers to always let customers make their own informed decision about what foods to buy and eat. FAAN recommends when a customer informs a food employee that someone has a food allergy, they follow the following four Rs:

- *Refer* the food allergy concern to the manager or person in charge.
- *Review* the food allergy with the customer and check ingredient labels.
- *Remember* to check the preparation procedure for potential cross-contact.
- *Respond* to the customer and inform him or her of your findings.

If a customer has an allergic reaction, call 911 and assist emergency medical personnel dispatched to attend to the allergic person.

Foods containing "major food allergens" must be properly labeled.

Natural Toxins

Ciguatoxin	
Causative Agent	• Ciguatoxin
Type of Illness	• Fish toxin originating from toxic algae of tropical waters
Symptoms	• Vertigo, nausea, hot or cold flashes, diarrhea, vomiting, shortness of breath
Onset	• 30 minutes to 6 hours; usually lasts a few days but death can occur from concentrated dose of toxin
Common Foods	• Marine finfish including grouper, barracuda, snapper, jack, mackerel, triggerfish, reef fish
Prevention	• Purchase fish from a reputable supplier. Cooking WILL NOT inactivate the toxin.

Ciguatoxin poisoning is an example of an intoxication caused by eating contaminated tropical reef fish. The toxin is found in tiny, free-swimming sea creatures called algae that live among certain coral reefs. When small reef fish eat the toxic algae, it is stored in the flesh, skin, and organs. When bigger fish, such as barracuda, eat the small reef fish, such as mackerel, mahi-mahi, bonito, jackfish, and snapper, the toxin accumulates in the flesh and skin of the consuming fish. The toxin does not affect the contaminated fish. The toxin is heat stable and not destroyed by cooking. At the present time, there is no commercially known method to determine if ciguatoxin is present in a particular fish. The toxin is transferred to finfish when they eat toxin-containing algae or other fish that contain the toxin.

Ciguatoxin can be found in marine finfish, such as red snapper.

Scombrotoxin

Causative Agent	• Scombrotoxin
Type of Illness	• Seafood toxin originating from histamine- producing bacteria
Symptoms	• Dizziness; burning feeling in the mouth; facial rash or hives; shortness of breath; peppery taste in mouth; headache; itching, teary eyes; runny nose
Onset	• Few minutes to 30 minutes; recovery usually occurs in 8 to 12 hours
Common Foods	• Tuna, mahi-mahi, bluefish, sardines, mackerel, anchovies, amberjack, abalone, Swiss cheese
Prevention	• Purchase fish from a reputable supplier; store fish between 32°F (0°C) and 39°F (4°C) to prevent growth of histamine-producing bacteria; toxin IS NOT inactivated by cooking.

Eating foods high in a chemical compound called histamine causes scombrotoxin, also called histamine poisoning. Histamine is usually produced by certain bacteria when they decompose foods containing the protein histidine. Dark meat of fish has more histidine than other fish meat. Histamine is not inactivated by cooking. Over time, bacteria inherent to a particular food can break down histidine and cause the production of histamine. Leaving fish out at room temperature usually results in histamine production.

Scombrotoxin can be found in fish, such as tuna.

Shellfish Toxins-PSP, DSP, DAP, NSP

Causative Agent	• Shellfish toxins produced by certain algae called dinoflagellates
Type of Illness	• Intoxication
Symptoms	• Numbness of lips, tongue, arms, legs, neck; lack of muscle coordination
Onset	• 10 to 60 minutes
Common Foods	• Contaminated mussels, clams, oysters, scallops
Prevention	• Purchase shellfish only from a reputable supplier, avoid buying shellfish harvested by sport fishermen or poached from polluted waters.

Shellfish toxins are known to cause a variety of illnesses including Paralytic Shellfish Poisoning (PSP), Diarrhetic Shellfish Poisoning (DSP), Domoic Acid Poisoning (DAP), and Neurotoxic Shellfish Poisoning (NSP). The toxins are produced by certain algae called dinoflagellates. When filter-feeding shellfish, such as mussels, clams, oysters, and scallops, feed on the toxic algae, they accumulate the toxins in their internal organs and become toxic to humans. The amount of toxin in the shellfish depends on the amount of toxic algae in the water and the amount of water filtered by the shellfish. Most cases of seafood toxin are caused by contaminated shellfish that have been harvested by sport fishermen or poached from polluted waters. Commercially harvested shellfish are rarely involved in foodborne disease outbreaks because regulatory agencies monitor the level of toxin in the water and shellfish during high-risk periods (May to October).

Purchase shellfish only from a reputable supplier.

Mycotoxins	
Causative Agent	• Toxic chemicals produced by some types of mold
Type of Illness	• Intoxication
Symptoms	• Acute symptoms: hemorrhage, acute liver damage and fluid buildup • Chronic onset: cancer from small doses over a long period of time
Onset	• Acute symptoms can occur within a month, while chronic forms of the disease occur after years of exposure to low levels of the toxin
Common Foods	• Moldy grains, corn, corn products, peanuts, pecans, walnuts, milk produced by cows that have ingested mold with their feed
Prevention	• Purchase food from a reputable supplier, keep grains and nuts dry, and protect products from humidity.

Molds, yeasts, and mushrooms are common examples of fungi. Molds and yeasts are able to withstand more extreme conditions, such as those associated with higher acid, low-moisture foods. Most molds and yeasts are spoilage organisms, which cause foods to deteriorate. However, some types of fungi produce toxic chemicals called mycotoxins that are capable of causing illness. Many mycotoxins have been shown to cause cancer. Aflatoxin is an important foodborne mycotoxin produced by *Aspergillus* spp. molds. Many mycotoxins are not destroyed by cooking. Foodborne illness from mycotoxins can be prevented by purchasing food from reputable suppliers and keeping grains and nuts dry and protected from humidity.

Man-made Chemicals

There is an extensive list of chemicals added to foods that may pose a potential health risk. Intentionally added chemicals may include food additives, food preservatives, and pesticides. Pesticides leave residues on fruits and vegetables and can usually be removed by a vigorous washing procedure. Non-intentionally added chemicals may include contamination by chemicals, such as cleaning and sanitary supplies. Also, chemicals from containers or food-contact surfaces of inferior metal that are misused may lead to heavy-metal or inferior-metal poisoning (cadmium, copper, lead, galvanized metals, etc.).

Employee medications can be another potential source of chemical contamination. According to the *Food Code*, only those medications necessary for the employee's health are allowed in a

Store employee medications away from food.

retail food establishment. This does not apply to medicines stored or displayed for retail sale. Employee medication must be clearly labeled and stored in an area away from food, equipment, utensils, linens, and single-use items like straws, eating utensils, and napkins. Medications stored in a refrigerator where food is stored must be kept in a clearly labeled and covered container located on the lowest shelf of the unit. Medications cannot be stored in display or storage cases, or walk-in units.

Foodborne Illness Caused by Physical Hazards

Physical hazards are foreign objects in food that can cause illness and injury. They include items such as fragments of glass, metal shavings from dull can openers, unfrilled toothpicks that may contaminate sandwiches, human hair, jewelry, or bandages that may accidentally be lost by a food handler and enter food. Stones, rocks, or wood particles may contaminate raw fruits and vegetables, rice, beans, and other grain products.

Common physical hazards in a food establishment

Physical hazards commonly result from accidental contamination and poor food-handling practices that can occur at various points in the food chain from harvest to consumer.

To prevent physical hazards:

- Wash raw fruits and vegetables thoroughly
- Visually inspect foods that cannot be washed (such as ground beef).

Food employees must be taught to handle food safely to prevent contamination by unwanted foreign objects, such as glass fragments and metal shavings. Finally, food employees should not wear jewelry when involved in the production of food, except for a plain wedding band.

Summary

Back to the Story . . . The 2006 outbreak described in the vignette at the beginning of this chapter was the first time fresh spinach had been the source of E. coli O157:H7 bacteria to cause a foodborne illness. However, lettuce and other leafy green vegetables have been implicated on several previous occasions. The foodborne disease outbreaks and food product recalls linked to contaminated fresh produce have caused retailers to become concerned about the safety of the fresh fruit and vegetable products they sell and consumers to be concerned about these types of products they consume.

The number of cases of foodborne illness associated with fresh-cut produce is on the rise due to three factors. First, people are eating more fruits and vegetables because of their nutritional value. Second, the United States imports much of its produce from foreign countries which provides opportunities for contamination as the products flow from farm to market. Finally, most fresh-cut produce is considered ready-to-eat and is consumed without being cooked or processed in some way to reduce pathogens on the produce to safe levels.

Several things are being done to prevent future outbreaks of this type. First, the FDA has published a Guide to Minimize Microbial Food Safety Hazards of Fresh-Cut Fruits and Vegetables (http://www.cfsan.gov/~dms/prodgui4.html) which recommends measures that growers and companies that import fresh-cut produce can take to prevent microbial contamination during the processing of fresh-cut produce. Retailers can reduce the risk of foodborne illness asso-

ciated in produce by purchasing these products from suppliers that follow the FDA guidelines. Once retailers wash unpackaged produce, it then is considered a ready-to-eat product. Packaged and unpackaged ready-to-eat produce must be held at proper cold temperatures to prevent the growth of disease-causing organisms during storage and display. Finally, retailers should educate their customers they can reduce the risk of foodborne illness by thoroughly washing produce before it is eaten.

- ✔ Biological hazards, such as bacteria, viruses, and parasites, continue to cause problems. An increase in foodborne illness associated with fresh produce was described at the beginning of this chapter. This change is due to several factors. An increase in the number of people in the immunocompromised population exposes more individuals to foodborne illness. The number and types of hazards also seem to be increasing. Retail food establishment managers need to be aware of the change in eating habits, marketing patterns, and emerging pathogens in our food supply.

- ✔ With fruit and vegetable products, we learned PHF (TCS) are not the only problems. Apple cider, for example, has a pH well below 4.6, not a potentially hazardous food. However, certain microbes like Shiga toxin-producing *Escherichia coli* in apple cider can survive and still cause illness.

- ✔ There are many foodborne hazards a retail food establishment may encounter. They are classified as biological, chemical, or physical hazards. These hazards differ depending on the type of food and method of preparation involved. Retail food establishments are typically toward the end of the food production chain. This is where foods are prepared or sold for consumer preparation. Therefore, it is very important to control and prevent foodborne hazards as much as possible to reduce the risk of foodborne illness associated with your establishment. Control and prevention of foodborne hazards in a retail food establishment start with understanding the different types of foodborne hazards. The next step is to understand how to control foodborne hazards with time/ temperature control, good personal hygiene, cleaning and sanitation, and prevention of cross contamination. Prevention, using these four approaches, is the focus of Chapter 3.

Discussion Questions (Short Answer)

1. Briefly explain the difference among an infection, an intoxication, and a toxin-mediated infection. Give an example of each.
2. What groups of people have a greater risk of acquiring foodborne illness?
3. Identify the three categories of hazards that can cause foodborne illness and give examples of each.
4. What types of biological hazards should be of greatest concern to retail food establishment managers? Why?
5. What does FATTOM represent?
6. At what pH and water activity (A_w) levels do disease-causing bacteria grow best?
7. What is the food temperature danger zone?
8. What is a bacterial spore? Why is it important for the retail food establishment manager to understand these forms of bacterial cells?
9. What are PHF (TCS)? What characteristics do they share?
10. What are viruses? What are parasites?

Quiz 2 (Multiple Choice)

Choose the **best** answer for each question.

1. Bacteria grow best within a narrow temperature range called the temperature danger zone. The temperature danger zone is between:
    a. 0°F (-18°C) and 220°F (104°C)
    b. 0°F (-18°C) and 140°F (60°C).
    c. 41°F (5°C) and 135°F (57°C).
    d. 41°F (5°C) and 220°F (104°C).
2. The pH of a food refers to:
    a. available water.
    b. acidity or alkalinity.
    c. amount of oxygen.
    d. amount of protein.

3. The most effective way to control the growth of bacteria in a retail food establishment is by controlling:

   a. time and temperature.
   b. pH and oxygen conditions.
   c. temperature and water activity.
   d. time and food availability.

4. Bacteria are a common cause of foodborne disease in a retail food establishment because:

   a. under ideal conditions, they can grow very rapidly.
   b. bacteria are found naturally in many foods.
   c. bacteria can be easily transferred from one source to another.
   d. All of the above.

5. Which of the following bacteria produce a toxin that is **most** likely to cause death if consumed?

   a. *Campylobacter jejuni.*
   b. *Clostridium botulinum.*
   c. Shiga toxin-producing *Escherichia coli.*
   d. *Listeria monocytogenes.*

6. Some bacteria form spores to help them:

   a. reproduce and grow in numbers.
   b. move more easily from one location to another.
   c. survive adverse environmental conditions.
   d. grow in high acid foods.

7. Which of the following is a histamine poisoning?

   a. Ciguatoxin.
   b. Scombrotoxin.
   c. Mycotoxin.
   d. Paralytic Shellfish Poisoning (PSP).

8. Which of the following is **not** considered a PHF (TCS)?

   a. Red meats.
   b. Fish and shellfish.
   c. Poultry and eggs.
   d. Dried grains and spices.

9. Bacteria that cause foodborne illness will only grow on foods that have a pH at _____ or above and a water activity (A_w) above _____.

   a. 3.2; .85.
   b. 4.6; .85.
   c. 6.5; .80.
   d. 8.0; .70.

10. Which of the following organisms are **most** likely to cause a foodborne disease outbreak?

    a. Mycotoxins and Ciguatoxin.
    b. *Cryptosporidium parvum* and *Giardia lamblia*.
    c. *Salmonellae* spp. and Norwalk virus.
    d. *Anisakis* spp. and *Trichinella spiralis*.

11. When an employee brings prescribed medication to work that must be refrigerated, it should be:

    a. put in a closed and labeled container in the employee lounge refrigerator.
    b. placed in the back corner of a refrigerated display case.
    c. wrapped in plastic and put in the ice machine.
    d. sent home with the employee because it is not allowed in the area.

Answers to the multiple-choice questions are provided in Appendix A.

References/Suggested Readings

Adams, M. R.; and M. O. Moss. 2000. *Food Microbiology*. Royal Society of Chemistry. London, England.

Banwart, G. J. 1995. *Basic Food Microbiology 2nd ed.* Wiley. New York, NY.

Heymann, David (Ed.). 2004. *Control of Communicable Diseases in Man, 18th ed.* American Public Health Association. Washington, D.C.

Doyle, Michael P.; Larry R. Beuchat; and Thomas J. Montville. 1997. *Food Microbiology: Fundamentals and Frontiers.* American Society for Microbiology. Washington, D.C.

Food and Drug Administration. 2009. *FDA 2009 Food Code.* U.S. Public Health Service. Washington, D.C.

FMI Hepatitis A Information Guide. 2002.

Food Protection Report. June 2002. Vol. 18(6). Pike & Fishers, Silver Springs, MD.

Institute of Food Technologists. 2001. *Evaluation and Definition of Potentially Hazardous Foods.* www.cfscan.fda.gov/~comm/ift4-toc.html.

Jay, James J.; Martin J. Loessner; and David A. Golden. 2005. *Modern Food Microbiology, 7th ed.* Springer Publishers. New York, NY.

Longrèe, K.; and G. Armbruster. 1996. *Quantity Food Sanitation.* Macmillan. New York, NY.

McSwane, D.; N. Rue; and R. Linton. 2005. *Essentials of Food Safety and Sanitation, 4th ed.* Prentice Hall. Upper Saddle River, NJ.

Suggested Web Sites

Gateway to Government Food Safety Information
www.foodsafety.gov

Centers for Disease Control and Prevention (CDC)
www.cdc.gov

The Bad Bug Book
vm.cfscan.fda.gov/~mow/intro.html

USDA/FDA Food and Nutrition Information Center
www.nal.usda.gov/fnic/

The Food Allergy Network
www.foodallergy.org

The Food Marketing Institute
www.fmi.org

U.S. Department of Agriculture (USDA)
www.usda.gov

Food and Drug Administration (FDA)
www.fda.gov

Environmental Protection Agency (EPA)
www.epa.gov

Partnership for Food Safety Education
www.fightbac.org

Suggested Web Sites

IFT Report, Evaluation and Definition of Potentially Hazardous Foods
http://www.cfsan.fda.gov/~comm/ift4-toc.html.

FMI "Quick Sheet" and allergens posters
www.fmi.org/foodsafety/

FMI Hepatitis A Information Guide
http://www.fmi.org/foodsafety/HepatitisAGuide.pdf

FDA Guide to Minimize Microbial Food Safety Hazards of Fresh-Cut Fruits and Vegetables
http://www.cfsan.gov/~dms/prodgui4.html

Learn How To:

- Identify potential problems related to temperature abuse of foods.

- Describe how to properly measure and maintain food temperatures to assure food temperatures have been controlled.

- Identify potential problems related to a food worker's poor personal hygiene.

- Explain how to improve personal hygiene habits to reduce the risk of foodborne illness.

- Identify potential problems related to cross contamination of food.

- Discuss procedures and methods to prevent cross contamination.

CHAPTER 3

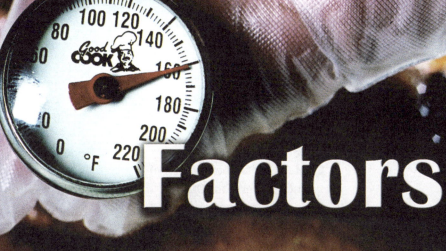

Factors that Affect Foodborne Illness

Employee Recognition Luncheon Goes Bad

The staff of the Aegean Rehabilitation Center was rewarded with an employee recognition luncheon. A party sized sub sandwich, prepared in the deli department of a local supermarket, was served. In the next 36 hours, those who ate the sandwich began to suffer nausea, vomiting, diarrhea, abdominal pain, and headache. Affected employees began to call in sick. Two days later, some of the residents from the Rehabilitation Center became ill with the same symptoms. The local health department became involved to try to identify the cause of the illness and implement measures to stop the outbreak.

Interviews of staff members who work at the rehabilitation center showed those individuals who had become ill had eaten the sub sandwich from the supermarket deli. The deli employee was wearing gloves when he prepared the sub, according to the supermarket manager.

The illness lasted about three days for many of those affected. The health department was suspicious this outbreak was caused by a highly contagious microbe. What do you think the problem might be and what measures were outlined to stop the progression of this disease?

Essential Terms

Calibrate	Food temperature–measuring device
Centers for Disease Control and Prevention (CDC)	Personal hygiene
Cross contamination	Temperature abuse
Dial-faced bi-metal thermometer	Thermocouple
Digital thermometer	T-Stick type melt devices

Factors That Contribute to Foodborne Illness

The **Centers for Disease Control and Prevention (CDC)** is an agency of the federal government. One of the CDC's primary responsibilities is to collect statistics about diseases that affect people in the United States, including foodborne illness. CDC statistics show most outbreaks of foodborne disease occur because *food is mishandled*. Some of the major contributors to foodborne illness are presented on the next page.

All five of these factors are important types of food-handling errors that could lead to foodborne illness. A foodborne outbreak may be due to one or more of these contributing factors. Poor personal hygiene and improper holding temperatures are the most common causes of foodborne illness for retail food establishments. The use of good personal hygiene practices (i.e. hand washing) helps prevent the spread of viruses and bacteria. Control of

Important contributing factors leading to foodborne illness
(Source: CDC-MMWR)

food holding temperatures (i.e., cooling and hot/cold holding) helps prevent the growth of bacteria in food. The CDC provides an estimate for the number of foodborne illnesses in the United States each year. A list of the seven most commonly found microorganisms and the estimated numbers of foodborne illness/per year are provided in the table below. For each of these organisms, common contributing factors leading to foodborne illness are provided. Note the most common microorganism associated with foodborne illness is the Norwalk-like virus, most often associated with poor personal hygiene practices.

Microorganism	Cases/Year
Norwalk-like virus	23,000,000
Campylobacter spp.	2,500,000
Salmonella spp.	1,400,000
Clostridium perfringens	250,000
Staphylococcus aureus	185,000
Escherichia coli	75,000
Listeria monocytogenes	2,500

Microorganisms leading to foodborne illness
in the United States
(Source: CDC-MMWR)

What Is Time and Temperature Abuse?

Controlling time and temperature is a very important way to assure food safety. Most cases of foodborne illness can, in some way, be linked to tem-

What Is Time and Temperature Abuse?

Controlling time and temperature is a very important way to assure food safety. Most cases of foodborne illness can, in some way, be linked to temperature abuse. As we learned in Chapter 2, **temperature abuse** is used to describe situations in which foods are:

- Exposed to temperatures in the temperature danger zone for enough time to allow growth of harmful microorganisms
- Not cooked or reheated sufficiently to destroy harmful microorganisms.

In Chapter 2, "Hazards to Food Safety," you learned harmful microbes can grow in PHF (TCS) when temperatures are between 41°F (5°C) and 135°F (57°C), the temperature danger zone. Keep the internal temperatures, inside the core of a food item, out of the temperature danger zone [41°F (5°C) to 135°F (57°C)] to prevent harmful microbes from growing. Higher temperatures destroy microbes; however, toxins produced by microbes may not be destroyed by normal cooking temperatures.

The Temperature Danger Zone

Keep cold food temperatures below 41°F (5°C) and out of the temperature danger zone to prevent most microbes from growing. Bacteria that can grow at lower temperatures do so very slowly. Proper date marking of refrigerated ready-to-eat PHF (TCS) is necessary to prevent time abuse. There are unavoidable situations during food production when foods must pass through the temperature danger zone, such as:

- Cooking
- Cooling
- Reheating
- Food handling (slicing, mixing, and sandwich assembling).

During these activities, you must minimize the amount of time foods are in the temperature danger zone to control microbial growth. When it is necessary for a food to pass through the temperature danger zone, do it as quickly as possible. In addition, foods should pass through the danger zone as few times as possible.

Heating foods improves texture and flavor and also destroys harmful microorganisms. As you learned in Chapter 2, many raw foods naturally contain harmful microbes or can become contaminated during handling. When you cook and reheat foods properly, microbes are reduced to safe levels or are destroyed. *Cooking and reheating are two very important processes for safe food management.*

How to Measure Food Temperatures

Maintaining safe food temperatures is an essential and effective part of food safety management. You must know how to measure food temperatures correctly with a **food temperature–measuring device** to prevent temperature abuse. Thermometers, thermocouples, and other devices are used to measure the temperature of stored, cooked, cooling, hot-held, cold-held, and reheated foods. The following chart shows different types of thermometers and their features.

A food temperature–measuring device with a small diameter probe must be available to measure the temperature of thin foods, such as meat patties and fish filets.

> An important rule to remember for avoiding temperature abuse is:
>
> **Keep Hot Foods Hot, Keep Cold Foods Cold, or Don't Keep the Food at All.**

Thermometer	Features/Uses
Dial face, metal stem type (bi-metallic)  Courtesy of Cooper Instrument Corp.	• Most common type of thermometer used • Used to measure internal food temperature at every stage in the flow of food • Measures temperatures ranging from 0°F (-18°C) to 220°F (104°C) with 2°F increments • Stem of bi-metallic thermometer must be inserted at least 2 inches into the food item being measured.
Digital  Courtesy of Cooper Instrument Corp.	• Displays the temperature numerically • Measures a wider range of temperatures than a dial face thermometer.
Thermocouple  Courtesy of Cooper Instrument Corp.	• Provides a digital readout of the temperature • Has a wide variety of interchangeable probes • Sensing portion is often at the tip of the probe.

(Continued)

What Is Time and Temperature Abuse?

Thermometer	Features/Uses (Continued)
Infrared Courtesy of Raytek Corporation	• Measures the surface temperature of food without actually touching the food (reduces the chance of cross contamination) • Requires about 20 minutes to adjust after use for hot and cold temperatures ("thermal shock") before use • Accuracy must be checked frequently.
T-Sticks (melt devices) Courtesy of T-Stick	• Measure only one temperature • Change color when indicated temperature is reached • Used to monitor food temperatures and to check sanitizing temperature in dishwashing machines.
Built-in	• Used to monitor air temperature in refrigerated and frozen cases.
Maximum Registering (holding) Courtesy of DeltaTRAK, Inc.	• Used to measure the temperature of hot water used to sanitize items in mechanical dishwashing machines

(Continued)

Thermometer	Features/Uses (Continued)
Thermometer Guidelines:	• Temperature-measuring devices typically measure food temperatures in degrees Fahrenheit (denoted as °F), degrees Celsius (denoted as °C), or both. • Food temperature-measuring devices scaled only in Celsius or dually scaled in Celsius and Fahrenheit must be accurate to ±1.8°F (±1°C). Food temperature-measuring devices scaled in Fahrenheit only must be accurate to ±2°F. • Mercury-filled and glass thermometers should not be used in food establishments. • Clean and sanitize thermometers properly to avoid contaminating food that is being tested. This is very important when testing raw and then ready-to-eat food items. To clean and sanitize a food thermometer, wipe off any food particles, place the stem or probe in sanitizing solution for at least 5 seconds, then air-dry. • When monitoring only raw foods, or only cooked foods being held at 135°F (57°C), wipe the stem of the thermometer with an alcohol swab between measurements.

When and How to Calibrate a Thermometer

Before you use a thermometer, you need to **calibrate** it or make sure it is working correctly. Calibrate means to compare and adjust with a known standard. Dial-faced, metal stem type (bi-metal) thermometers should be calibrated:

- Before first use
- At regular intervals
- If dropped or otherwise damaged
- If used to measure extreme temperatures
- Whenever accuracy is in question

Calibrate dial-faced thermometers by the boiling point or ice point method. See specific directions for calibration as described in the following section. Use pliers or an open-ended wrench on the hex nut to adjust the indicator needle.

Boiling Point Method

Immerse at least the first 2 inches of the stem from the tip (the sensing part of the probe) into boiling water and adjust the needle to 212°F (100°C). At higher altitudes, the temperature of the boiling point will vary. Consult your local health department if you have any questions about the boiling point temperature in your area.

Ice Point Method

Insert the probe into a cup of crushed ice. Add enough cold water to remove any air pockets that might remain. Wait until the temperature stabilizes and adjust the needle to 32°F (0°C).

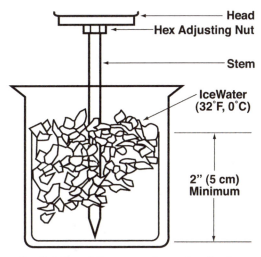

Calibration of a dial-faced thermometer using the ice point method

Source: Food Safety Inspection Service, U. S. Department of Agriculture, (www.fsis.usda.gov/Fact_sheets/kitchen_thermometers/index.asp) Nov.1, 2009

Measuring Food Temperature

The sensing portion of a food thermometer is at the end of the stem or probe. On the bi-metal thermometer, the sensing portion extends from the tip to the "dimple" mark that is typically 1 inch up the stem. An average of the temperature is measured over this distance. The sensing portion for digital and thermocouple thermometers is closer to the tip of the probe.

Accurate readings are only possible when the sensing portion of the temperature-measuring device is inserted deeply into the food. For bi-metal thermometers, immerse the needle tip at least 2 inches into the food to be measured. For digital and thermocouple thermometers, the tip must be inserted 1 inch or more. Always insert the sensing element of the thermometer into the center or thickest part of the food. When possible, stir the food before measuring the temperature.

Insert the probe at least 2 inches into the product.

Measure the temperature of packaged salads with an infrared thermometer.

Wait for the temperature to stabilize before removing probe.

The approximate temperature of packaged foods can be measured accurately without opening the package. Place the stem or probe of the thermometer between two packages of food or fold the package around the stem or probe to make good contact with the packaging.

Place thermometer between packages of prepared foods to measure temperature.

How to Accurately and Safely Measure Food Temperatures:

- Use an approved temperature-measuring device that measures temperatures from 0°F (-18°C) to 220°F (104°C).
- Locate the sensing portion of the measuring device.
- Calibrate the measuring device using the ice or boiling point method.
- Clean and sanitize the probe of the temperature–measuring device according to procedure.
- Measure the internal temperature of the food by inserting the probe into the center or thickest part of the item, at least 2 inches for a dial thermometer and 1 inch for digital thermometers.
- Always wait for the temperature reading to stabilize.

Preventing Temperature Abuse

Controlling temperatures of PHF (TCS) is important in almost all stages of food handling. Measuring temperatures of PHF (TCS) is an important responsibility for all food handlers. The following chart lists safe temperature guidelines for working with food throughout the flow of food. Each of these guidelines will be discussed throughout the remainder of this book.

Time and Temperature

Receiving and Storing:

Frozen and refrigerated receiving/storage practices prevent or slow the growth of harmful microorganisms

Food Product	Internal Temperature
Frozen Foods	Solidly frozen
Refrigerated Foods	41°F (5°C) or lower
Raw Shell Eggs	45°F (7°C) ambient temperature or below

Thawing:

Take food from frozen to nonfrozen to minimize the product's time in the temperature danger zone. Keep PHF (TCS) below 41°F (5°C) at all times.

Method	Internal Temperature	Times
In refrigerator	41°F (5°C) or lower	typically takes 2-3 days
Submerged under cool running water 70°F (21°C)	Ready-to-eat product not to exceed 41°F (5°C); Water temperature not to exceed 70°F (21°C)	Thawed portions of raw animal foods requiring cooking should not be allowed to rise above 41°F (5°C) for more than 4 hours, including the time the food is being thawed and prepared for cooking.

Cooking:

Safely heating a food product from raw to ready-to-eat with minimum holding times before serving

Food Product	Minimum Internal Temperature	Times
*Meat Roast (rare)	130°F (54°C)	112 minutes
	140°F (60°C)	12 minutes
Meat and Pork (other than roast), Fish	145°F (63°C)	15 seconds
Ground Meat, Mechanically Tenderized Meat, Ground Pork, Ground Game Animals	155°F (68°C)	15 seconds
Meat Roast (medium), Pork Roast, Ham	145°F (63°C)	4 minutes
Poultry, Ground Poultry, Stuffed Meats, and Stuffed Food Products	165°F (74°C)	15 seconds

* See additional cooking times and temperatures in FDA Food Code - paragraph 3-401.11(B)(2)

2009 FDA Food Code

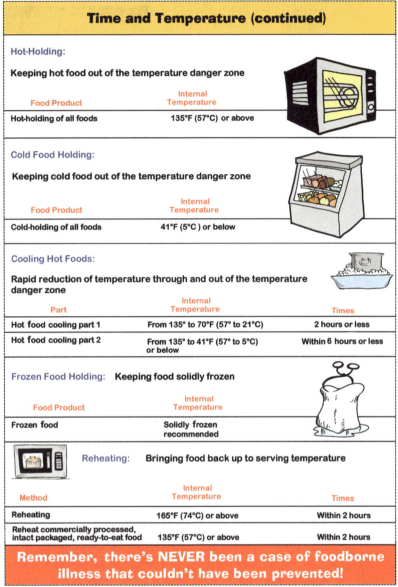

2009 FDA *Food Code*

Keep Cold Foods Cold and Hot Foods Hot!

Frozen foods should be kept solidly frozen until they are ready to be used. Freezing helps retain product quality. Proper frozen food temperatures do not permit disease-causing and spoilage microorganisms to grow. Cold temperatures also help preserve the color and flavor characteristics of food. Frozen foods can be stored for long periods of time without losing their wholesomeness and quality.

Refrigerated foods are held cold, but not frozen. Cold foods should be maintained at 41°F (5°C) or below. Do not forget that some disease-causing bacteria and many spoilage bacteria can grow at temperatures below 41°F (5°C), although their growth is very slow. By keeping cold foods at 41°F (5°C) or below, you can reduce the growth of most harmful microorganisms and extend the shelf life of the product. For maximum quality and freshness, hold cold foods for the shortest amount of time possible.

Deli salads are maintained at 41°F (5°C) or below.

> **Keep cold foods at 41°F (5°C) or below.**

Applying heat is another method used to preserve food. Heat food to proper temperatures to destroy harmful bacteria. Established safe cooking temperatures are based on the type of food and the

> **Improper holding temperature is an important factor that leads to foodborne illness.**

method used to heat the product. Cooked foods, as well as those foods that have been cooled and then reheated, must be maintained at 135°F (57°C) or above until used. You must keep foods hot to stop the growth of disease-causing bacteria.

There are times during food production when foods must be in the temperature danger zone. Recognize the time spent in the temperature danger zone should be minimized for PHF (TCS) items.

Improper holding temperature is the No. 1 contributing factor that leads to foodborne illness. Spores of certain bacteria like *Clostridium botulinum*, *Clostridium perfringens*, and *Bacillus cereus* can survive cooking temperatures. Remember, if spores survive and are exposed to ideal conditions, they can again become vegetative cells and begin to grow in foods.

The *Food Code* contains cooling guidelines that permit foods to be in the temperature danger zone for a total of 6 hours. The FDA *Food Code* specifically states foods must be cooled from 135°F (57°C) to 70°F (21°C) in 2 hours, and from 135°F (57°C) to 41°F (5°C) or less within 6 hours.

Keep Cold Foods Cold and Hot Foods Hot!

To destroy many of the bacteria that may have grown during the cooling process, reheat foods to 165°F (74°C) within 2 hours to prevent the number of organisms from reaching levels that can cause foodborne illness.

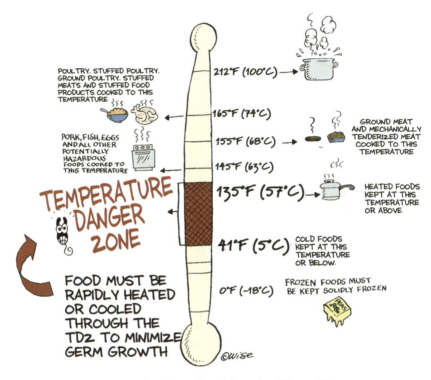

Keep it hot, keep it cold, or don't keep it!

KEY CONCEPT

The preferred method for thawing foods is in the refrigerator at 41°F (5°C) or below. This prevents the food from entering the food temperature danger zone.

Other acceptable methods for thawing include using a microwave oven, as a part of the cooking process, or submerging under cool running water [70°F (21°C)] for a controlled amount of time. Proper thawing reduces the chances for bacterial growth, especially on the outer surfaces of food.

More detailed strategies for minimizing the amount of time a food is in the temperature danger zone during cooling, thawing, and food preparation are presented in the next chapter.

The Importance of Handwashing and Good Personal Hygiene

KEY CONCEPT

The cleanliness and personal hygiene of food employees are extremely important. If a food employee is not clean, the food can become contaminated. Good personal hygiene is essential for those who handle foods. Desirable behaviors include:

- Knowing when and how to properly wash hands
- Wearing clean clothing
- Maintaining good personal habits (bathing, washing and restraining hair, keeping fingernails short and clean, washing hands after using toilet, etc.)
- Maintaining good health and reporting when sick to avoid spreading possible infections.

Just think of all the things a food handler's hands touch during a typical work day. They may take out the trash, cover a sneeze, scratch an itch, or mop up a spill. When you touch your face or skin, run your fingers through your hair or beard, use the toilet, or blow your nose, you transfer potentially harmful germs to your hands. *Staphylococcus aureus*, Hepatitis A, Norovirus, and *Shigella* spp. are examples of pathogens that are commonly transferred to foods by bare hand contact. Proper handwashing helps remove visible hand dirt and the microorganisms it contains.

KEY CONCEPT

The CDC says handwashing is the single most important means of preventing the spread of infection. Personnel involved in food preparation and service must know how and when to wash their hands. Using approved cleaning compounds (soap or detergent), food employees must vigorously rub surfaces of fingers and fingertips, front and back of hands, wrists, and forearms for at least 10-15 seconds. Remember, soap, warm water, and friction are needed to remove bacteria and viruses from skin. A significant number of germs are removed by friction alone. A brush can be helpful when cleaning hands and under fingernails. However, the brush must be made of nonabsorbent materials and be kept clean and sanitary.

> **The entire handwashing process should take approximately 20 seconds.**

When washing hands, thoroughly rinse under clean, warm running water and around fingernails and between fingers. Dry hands using a single-service paper towel, an electric hand dryer, or clean section of continuous rolled cloth towel (if allowed in your jurisdiction). Do not dry hands on your apron or a dish towel.

In addition to proper handwashing, fingernails should be trimmed, filed, and maintained so hand washing will effectively remove soil from under and around them. Unless wearing intact gloves in good repair, a food employee must not wear fingernail polish or artificial fingernails when working with exposed food.

According to the *Food Code*, hands shall be washed in a separate sink specified as a handwashing sink. An automatic handwashing facility may be used by food employees to clean their hands. However, the system must be capable of removing the types of soils encountered in the food operation. Food employees may not clean their hands in a sink used for food preparation or warewashing, or in a service sink used for the disposal of mop water and liquid waste. Hand antiseptic may be used by food employees in addition to handwashing. However, **hand antiseptic lotions must never be used as a replacement for handwashing.**

Always Wash Hands:

- Before food preparation
- After touching bare human body parts, except clean hands and clean exposed arms
- After using the toilet
- After coughing, sneezing, using a handkerchief or disposable tissue, using tobacco, eating, or drinking
- During food preparation when switching between working with raw foods and ready-to-eat products
- After engaging in any activities that may contaminate hands (taking out the garbage, wiping counters or tables, handling cleaning chemicals, picking up dropped items, etc.)
- After caring for or touching service animals or aquatic animals.

It is critical hand antiseptics be formulated with safe and approved ingredients because it is likely a food employee's hands will touch food, food-contact surfaces, or equipment and utensils after using the product.

Except when washing fruits and vegetables, food employees should not contact exposed ready-to-eat foods with their hands. Instead, they should use single-use gloves or suitable utensils, such as deli tissue, spatulas, and tongs.

Proper handwashing technique

Complying with the "no bare hands" policy is especially important when handling food for sale to immunocompromised populations.

Food employees not serving immunocompromised populations may contact exposed, ready-to-eat foods with their bare hands if certain, specific conditions are met. Examples are:

- The permit holder obtains prior approval from the regulatory authority.
- Written procedures are maintained in the food establishment and made available to the regulatory authority upon request.
- A written policy details how the food establishment complies with employee health requirements and documentation that food employees acknowledge they have received training in risks of contacting ready-to-eat foods with bare hands, proper handwashing, when and where to wash hands, and proper fingernail maintenance.

Food employees shall also minimize bare hand and arm contact with exposed food that is not in ready-to-eat form.

See 3-301.11 (D) of the *Food Code* for complete requirements and information.

Handwashing sink

Using Disposable Gloves

Retail food establishments sometimes allow their food employees to use disposable gloves as an extra barrier to help prevent contamination of foods. Gloves can protect food from direct contact by human hands. Gloves must be impermeable, meaning they do not allow anything to penetrate the porous texture of the glove. Use of gloves is often a good idea for foods handled extensively by hands, such as deli sandwiches or tacos, or when conducting food demonstrations. You must treat disposable gloves as a second skin. Whatever can contaminate a human hand can also contaminate a disposable glove. Therefore, hands should always be washed prior to putting on a new pair of single-use gloves. For example, if food handlers are wearing disposable gloves and handling raw food, they must discard those gloves, wash their hands, and put on a fresh pair of gloves before they handle ready-to-eat foods. This procedure is very important in the seafood department and other areas where raw and ready-to-eat foods are handled and displayed.

Food handlers must not handle money with gloved hands unless they immediately remove and discard the gloves. Because money is handled and exchanged by human hands, it is often contaminated with bacteria. Employees must also wash their hands and put on a clean pair of gloves after they complete cleaning, mopping, and similar activities within their department.

If an employee removes gloves by rolling them inside out, the inner surface of the glove is very contaminated from his or her skin. Again, if you take disposable gloves off, throw them away. Never reuse or wash disposable gloves—always throw them away after each use.

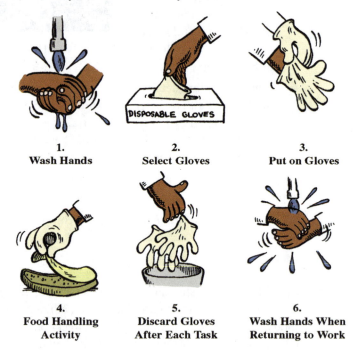

Proper use of disposable gloves

Personal Habits

Personal hygiene is related to health habits including bathing, washing hair, wearing clean clothing, and frequent hand washing. A food employee's fingers may be contaminated with saliva during eating and smoking. Saliva, sweat, and other body fluids can be harmful sources of contamination if they get into food.

Supervisors should enforce rules against eating, chewing gum, and smoking in food preparation, service, and warewashing areas. The *Food Code* permits food employees to drink beverages to prevent dehydration. The beverage must be in a covered container. The container must be handled in a way that prevents contamination of the employee's hands, the container, exposed food, equipment, and single-use articles.

Jewelry can harbor germs that cause foodborne illness, and it can fall into food causing a potential physical hazard. Therefore, food employees may not wear jewelry, including medical information jewelry, on their arms and hands while preparing food. The only exception to this policy is a plain ring such as a wedding band. Food employees should check with their supervisor to determine if their employer has additional restrictions on wearing jewelry during food production.

Outer Clothing and Apparel

Work clothes and other apparel should always be clean. The appearance of a clean uniform is more appealing to your customers.

Things You Can Do to Prevent Food Contamination:

- Wear clean clothing.
- If your clothing is contaminated, change into a new set of work clothes.
- Change your apron between working with raw foods and ready-to-eat foods. Aprons should be left in the department when going on break or to the restroom.
- Don't dry or wipe your hands on your apron.
- Wear a hat, hair coverings or nets, and beard restraints to discourage you from touching your hair or beard. These restraints also prevent hair from falling into food or onto food-contact surfaces.
- Keep in mind, however, protective apparel is similar to a disposable glove. They no longer protect food when contaminated.

Personal Health

In order to reduce the risk caused by ill food workers, the *Food Code* requires food employees and conditional food employees to report to the person in charge information about their health and activities related to the following disease-causing agents:

- Norovirus
- Hepatitis A Virus
- *Shigella* spp.
- Enterohemorrhagic or Shiga toxin-producing *Escherichia coli*
- *Salmonella* Typhi.

If a food employee or conditional food employee is directly or indirectly exposed to one of the disease agents listed above, it must be reported to the person in charge. All these diseases can potentially be transmitted by food and are considered severe health hazards.

Food employees and conditional food employees are also required to report to the person in charge when they are experiencing symptoms of gastrointestinal illness, such as vomiting, diarrhea, and jaundice, or a sore throat with fever. These employees must also report a lesion containing pus, such as a boil or infected wound that is open or draining and is located on the hands or wrists, exposed portion of the arms, or on other parts of the body unless the lesion is effectively covered and protected by an impermeable cover or tight-fitting bandage.

Food employees who have been exposed to any of these pathogens or organisms of concern must be excluded from work or be assigned to restricted activities having no food contact. In addition, food employees diagnosed with one of these diseases must not handle exposed food or have contact with clean equipment, utensils, linens, or unwrapped single-service utensils.

Sick employees cannot work with food.

The person in charge shall notify the regulatory authority when a food employee is jaundiced or diagnosed with an illness due to one of the pathogens listed previously. In addition, the person in charge must assure a conditional employee who exhibits or reports a symptom or who reports being diagnosed with one of the pathogens listed previously is prohibited from becoming a food employee until the conditional employee meets the criteria for removal of exclusions and restrictions.

A detailed summary of reportable diseases; conditions that require exclusions and restrictions; and criteria for removal, adjustment, or retention of exclusions and restrictions for food employees and conditional food employees is provided in Appendix D of this book.

To date, there has not been a medically documented case of acquired immune deficiency syndrome (AIDS) transmitted by food. Therefore, AIDS is not considered a foodborne illness.

The Americans with Disabilities Act (ADA) prohibits discrimination against people with disabilities in jobs and public accommodations. Employers may not fire or transfer individuals who have AIDS or test positive for the HIV virus away from food-handling activities. Employers must also maintain the confidentiality of employees who have AIDS or any other illness.

Cross Contamination

Contaminated food contains germs or harmful substances that can cause foodborne illness. The transfer of hazardous substances from one food item to another is called **cross contamination**. This commonly happens when germs from raw food are transferred to a cooked or ready-to-eat food via contaminated hands, equipment, or utensils. For example, bacteria from fish can be transferred to ready-to-eat seafood (such as cooked shrimp and imitation crab) in a display case where the products are not properly separated or by an employee's gloves. Cutting boards are also common vehicles for cross contamination. The leftover juices from raw chicken can lead to contamination of ready-to-eat salad items.

Cross contamination also happens when raw foods are stored above ready-to-eat foods. Juices from the raw product can drip or splash onto a ready-to-eat food. This poses a serious health risk because ready-to-eat items will not be cooked to destroy microorganisms prior to being eaten.

In a retail food establishment, germs can be transferred by a food employee, equipment and utensils, or another food. The following preventive measures can be used to eliminate the possibility of cross contamination between products:

- Always store cooked and ready-to-eat foods above raw products.
- Keep raw and ready-to-eat foods separate during storage.

Don't mix raw and ready-to-eat foods!

- Use good personal hygiene and handwashing.
- Keep all food-contact surfaces clean and sanitary.
- Avoid bare hand contact with ready-to-eat food.
- Keep different types of meat and poultry separate.
- Use separate equipment, such as cutting boards, for raw foods and
- ready-to-eat foods (color coding may be helpful for this task).
- Use clean, sanitized equipment and utensils for food production.
- Prepare ready-to-eat foods first—then raw foods.
- Prepare raw and ready-to-eat foods in separate areas of the establishment.

Use color-coded cutting boards for different types of foods.

Always keep raw foods separate from ready-to-eat foods. In the refrigerator, ready-to-eat foods must be stored above raw foods. Display cases, such as those used to display seafood items, should be designed to keep raw and cooked food items separate. In addition, separate buckets for in-place sanitizing solutions and wiping cloths should be used for cleaning food-contact surfaces in raw and ready-to-eat food production areas.

Other Sources of Contamination

Raw fruits and vegetables should be treated as ready-to-eat foods. Always wash these foods before use. Washing removes soil and other contaminants. Chemicals may be used to wash raw whole fruits and vegetables. These chemicals must be nontoxic and meet the requirements set forth in the *Code of Federal Regulations* (CFR) under Title 21 CFR 173.315.

Utensils used to dispense and serve foods can also be a source of food contamination. Utensils should be properly labeled to identify the type of food they are used to dispense. During hot- or cold-holding of foods, the utensil should be stored in the food. This helps to prevent contamination from employees or customers in self-service areas. It also keeps the utensil that contains food out of the temperature danger zone. The dispensing utensils (scoops) for ice and dry bulk foods should be clean and kept in an area protected from contamination. Scoops or tongs used in customer service areas also need to be labeled and kept clean.

Attach utensils to self-service display cases.

Customer self-service areas for bakery items and candy are becoming more popular. Contamination by food allergens, such as peanuts, has occurred in these areas. Be sure the scoop used for peanut butter cups is not used for hard candies. To assure dispensing utensils are used for the intended foods, many retail food establishments will attach the dispensing utensil to the display case with a cable or chain.

Wash hands or change gloves after touching live animals, such

Animals are not allowed in retail food establishments unless they are being used for support or special service (i.e., guide dogs for the blind). It is very important food handlers do not touch animals during food preparation and service. If employees should touch an animal for any reason, they must wash their hands before returning to work. For example, if you should remove a live lobster from a tank for sale, you should change your gloves and/or wash your hands properly.

Germs from an employee's mouth can be transferred to food when the employee uses improper tasting techniques. A food employee may not use a utensil more than once to taste food that is to be sold or served.

Animals, rodents, and pests are common sources for food contamination. Rodents and pests usually enter retail food establishments during delivery when doors are left open or when garbage facilities are not properly maintained. A good integrated pest management (IPM) program should be established and maintained in every retail food establishment. You will learn about IPM programs in Chapter 7, "Environmental Sanitation and Maintenance."

Avoid contamination from other sources.

Make Sure the Work Area Is Clean and Sanitary

Anything that comes in contact with food must be clean and sanitary. This includes human hands, equipment, utensils, storage and holding areas, and self-service areas for customers. To protect food from contamination, effective cleaning and sanitizing procedures must be implemented and monitored. The goal of cleaning is to remove visible soil. The goal of sanitizing is to reduce the number of harmful microbes that may be present on a clean surface. Chapter 6 of this book is dedicated to describing different elements of cleaning and sanitizing programs. While cleaning and sanitizing are important in all areas of a retail food establishment, they are especially critical in areas where ready-to-eat foods are handled and displayed.

Summary

***Back to the Story . . .** The source of the infection was traced back to the sub sandwich prepared at the supermarket deli. The employee who prepared the sandwich had come to work just hours after his own bout of nausea, vomiting, and diarrhea had subsided. He was observed using poor glove technique (did not change gloves after going to the restroom). Norovirus was identified as the microbe that caused the outbreak. Highly contagious, this virus is passed on through stool and vomit. Poor personal hygiene and improper handwashing spreads the virus.*

The supervisor conducted a training session to demonstrate how to use gloves properly, good handwashing technique, and when to return to work after a gastrointestinal illness. The problem of Norovirus in a healthcare facility is serious because patients with lowered immune systems are at risk for a severe illness, even death. People infected with the Norovirus are contagious from the moment they begin feeling ill until at least three days after recovery. Therefore, it is very important for people to use good handwashing and other hygienic practices all the time to prevent Norovirus and other microbes from being transmitted to others. Food workers that are diagnosed with disease from Norovirus are not permitted to work until they are medically cleared.

- ✔ Temperature abuse can occur during receiving, storing, cooking, cooling, reheating, hot-holding, and cold-holding of foods. Depending on the food type, there are specific temperature requirements to assure food safety. These requirements are discussed in the next chapter. A good rule to follow in any retail food establishment is, "Keep It Clean! Keep It Hot! Keep It Cold! Or Don't Keep It!"
- ✔ Food employees should always use good health and hygiene practices. Clean clothing, hair restraints, and proper handwashing practices are fundamental in safe food management. Effective supervision and enforcement of proper procedures form the foundation of a successful food operation.
- ✔ Control cross contamination with proper cleaning and sanitizing. Avoid cross contamination from one food to another. Keep foods separate and store raw foods below cooked and ready-to-eat foods. Always use proper food-handling techniques.

✔ Keep foods at proper temperature, use good personal hygiene, and control contamination and cross contamination. These are the essentials of safe food management.

Almost All Foodborne Illnesses Are Linked To:

- Improper holding temperature
- Poor personal hygiene
- Contaminated equipment
- Inadequate cooking
- Food from an unsafe source.

Discussion Questions (Short Answer)

1. How frequently should thermometers be calibrated? Describe the two methods for calibrating food thermometers.
2. Under what conditions are foods "time and temperature abused"?
3. What is meant by poor personal hygiene, and how can this lead to foodborne illness?
4. What does the term *cross contamination* mean?
5. Why are cleaning and sanitizing important?

Quiz 3 (Multiple Choice)

Choose the **best** answer for each question.

1. Packages of luncheon meat kept at temperatures above 50°F (10°C) for more than 6 hours are:

   a. safe to eat.

   b. cross contaminated.

   c. time and temperature abused.

   d. adulterated.

2. Good personal hygiene includes:

   a. using hand antiseptics instead of handwashing.

   b. keeping hands and clothes clean and sanitary.

   c. wearing attractive uniforms.

   d. cleaning and sanitizing food-contact surfaces.

Quiz 3 (Multiple Choice)

3. Before changing to ready-to-eat foods, a cutting board used to cut up raw chicken must be:

    a. cleaned and sanitized.

    b. turned over to use the other side.

    c. dried thoroughly with a paper towel.

    d. rinsed in cool running water.

4. After proper cooking, all foods that are to be held hot must be held at:

    a. 165°F (74°C) or above.

    b. 135°F (57°C) or above.

    c. room temperature until served.

    d. 120°F (49°C) or above.

5. After proper cooking, all foods that are to be held cold must be:

    a. cooled quickly and held at 41°F (5°C) or below.

    b. cooled quickly and held at 70°F (21°C) or above.

    c. stored at room temperature until served.

    d. cooled slowly and held at 50°F (10°C) or below.

6. The No. 1 contributing factor leading to foodborne illness in retail food establishments is:

    a. improper holding temperature of foods.

    b. cross contamination.

    c. poor personal hygiene.

    d. inadequate cleaning and sanitizing programs.

7. Foodborne illness can be caused by:

    a. poor personal hygiene.

    b. cross contamination.

    c. temperature abuse.

    d. All of the above.

8. Regarding food thermometers, which statement is **false**?

    a. They should be calibrated.

    b. They should measure temperature between 41°F and 135°F (5°C and 57°C).

    c. They should measure temperature between 0°F and 220°F (-18°C and 104°C).

    d. They should be approved for use in foods.

9. Food employees should wash their hands after which of the following?

    a. Taking out the trash.
    b. Touching their face.
    c. Handling raw food.
    d. All of the above.

10. Cross contamination is a term used to describe the transfer of a foodborne hazard from one food to another:

    a. by a food employee's hands.
    b. from a cutting board.
    c. from a knife blade.
    d. All of the above.

11. A good way to prevent cross contamination of foods is to:

    a. keep raw and cooked foods separate.
    b. properly clean and sanitize food-contact surfaces.
    c. properly wash hands.
    d. All of the above.

12. Which of the following is an accepted personal hygiene practice?

    a. Wearing jewelry and false fingernails.
    b. Smoking and eating in food production areas.
    c. Wearing caps and hats.
    d. Wiping hands on a soiled apron.

Answers to these multiple-choice questions are available in Appendix A.

References/Suggested Readings

Centers for Disease Control and Prevention. 2006. *Surveillance for Foodborne Disease Outbreaks—United States, 1998–2002.* November 10, 2006. U.S. Department of Health and Human Services. Atlanta, GA.

Code of Federal Regulations. 2001. 21 CFR 173.315. *Secondary Direct Food Additives Permitted in Food for Human Consumption—Chemicals Used in Washing or to Assist in the Peeling of Fruits and Vegetables.* U.S. Government Printing Office. Washington, DC.

Council for Agricultural Sciences and Technology. 1995. "Prevention of Food-borne Illness. Dairy." *Food and Environmental Sanitation.* Vol. 15(6), 341–367.

Food and Drug Administration. 2009. *2009 Food Code.* U.S. Public Health Service. Washington, DC.

Food and Drug Administration. 2004. *FDA Report on the Occurrence of Foodborne Illness Risk Factors in Selected Institutional Foodservice, Restaurant, and Retail Food Store Facility Types.* U.S. Public Health Service. Washington, DC. www.cfsan.fda.gov/~dms/retrsk2.html.

Suggested Web Sites

Gateway to Government Food Safety Information
www.foodsafety.gov

United States Department of Agriculture (USDA)
www.usda.gov

Centers for Disease Control and Prevention (CDC)
www.cdc.gov

Morbidity and Mortality Weekly Report (MMWR)
www.cdc.gov/mmwr/

Food and Drug Administration (FDA)
www.fda.gov

USDA/FDA Food and Nutrition Information Center
www.nal.usda.gov/fnic

Partnership for Food Safety Education
www.fightbac.org

Food Safety Day
www.foodsci.purdue.edu/publications/foodsafetyday

Handwashing for Life Institute
www.handwashingforlife.com

Clean Hands Coalition
www.cleanhandscoalition.org

Cooper-Atkins Temperature-Measuring Devices
www.cooperinstruments.com

Raytek Corporation
www.raytek.com

Brevis Corporation
www.brevis.com

Taylor Foodservice Products
www.taylorusa.com/foodsvc/food.html

DeltaTRAK, Inc.
www.deltatrak.com

Learn How To:

- Identify codes and symbols used to tag food products inspected by governmental agencies.
- Apply purchasing and receiving procedures that protect food products.
- Inspect equipment used to transport food products to retail food establishments for cleanliness and evidence of pest infestation.
- Use approved devices to measure temperatures in food products safely and accurately.
- Check for and reject defective products.
- Check for required product temperatures at receiving and storage.
- Discuss safe methods to thaw frozen foods.
- Identify internal temperature requirements for cooking foods.
- Explain the proper methods used to cool foods.
- Discuss the importance of employee health and hygiene related to food product flow.
- Employ measures to prevent contamination and cross contamination of foods.

CHAPTER 4

Following the Food Product Flow

Improperly held bakery items

An employee in the bakery department did not follow proper food-labeling procedures for pastry products. He was supposed to label each tray of pastries using the first-in, first-out method. As a result of his error, a group of egg custard-filled éclairs was left on the finishing rack for over 6 hours at room temperature before another employee at a shift change noticed it. She quickly recognized the need for refrigeration and immediately set the unlabeled éclairs in the cold case. However, she did not know how long the items had been kept in the rack at room temperature. What is the problem here, and what would have been the best solution?

Essential Terms

Aseptic processing and packaging	Inspection for wholesomeness
Cold-holding	Irradiation
Cooking	Modified atmosphere packaging (MAP)
Cooling	Pasteurization
First-in, first-out (FIFO)	Reduced oxygen packaging (ROP)
Grade standards	Reheating
Hermetic packaging	Sensory evaluation
Hot-holding	Sous vide
	Wholesome

Buying from Approved Sources

Food quality and safety begin with foods and ingredients from approved sources—processors and suppliers that comply with federal, state, and local food safety laws and regulations. These sources are routinely inspected to make sure they follow good manufacturing practices. Regulatory agencies work closely with the food industry to assure food produced and sold for human consumption is safe, **wholesome**, and accurately labeled. A food that is wholesome means it is favorable to or promotes health. Foods prepared in a private home are not from an approved source and must not be used or sold in retail food establishments. Use of "home-canned" food is prohibited because of the high risk of foodborne illness, especially botulism.

Inspecting Delivery Vehicles

Suppliers must deliver food products to your retail food establishment in vehicles that are clean and in good repair. Delivery vehicles must also:

- Maintain perishable and PHF (TCS) at safe temperatures during transport
- Be loaded in a manner that separates food items from non-food items (detergents, household cleaners, and pesticides) to prevent contamination and cross contamination
- Protect food packages from becoming damaged and torn during transit.

When delivery vehicles arrive at your establishment, receiving personnel should inspect them. Specific items to look for during these inspections are:

- Cleanliness of the cargo area
- Temperature of refrigerated and frozen storage areas (if applicable)
- Proper separation of food and non-food items
- Proper separation of raw, PHF (TCS) and ready-to-eat foods
- Signs of insect, rodent, or bird infestations
- Damaged packages that might result in contamination of food items.

Be prepared to reject or return products that do not meet your prescribed standards or that do not comply with applicable food laws.

Determining Food Quality

Sensory evaluation, or the use of smell, touch, sight, and sometimes taste, is frequently used to evaluate the quality of food received. As a first step, foods should be observed for color, texture, and visual evidence of spoilage. Quite often, spoilage is easily seen as slime formation, mold growth, and discoloration.

Inspect foods when they are received

Spoiled foods frequently give off foul odors indicative of compounds, such as ammonia and hydrogen sulfide (the smell of rotten eggs). These odors, caused by the breakdown of proteins through bacterial action, are usually very easy to smell.

Spoilage due to yeasts produces bubbles and an alcoholic flavor or smell. Milk develops an acidic taste and is often bitter or rancid when it spoils.

The quality and safety of a food are affected by many factors. A food that shows no signs of spoilage may not always be safe. Spoilage cannot be used as the only indicator of food safety.

Measuring Temperatures at Receiving and Storage

Temperature-measuring devices are used in retail food establishments to measure temperatures of food, water, and the air of food storage areas (refrigerators, ovens, etc.).

Maintaining safe product temperature is a critical part of your food safety system.

Cold-holding or hot-holding equipment used for storing PHF (TCS) should be equipped with an indicating or recording thermometer to measure the temperature of the storage environment. Equipment thermometers are either built into a piece of equipment or are fastened onto shelving or other apparatuses. Set them where they can be easily read. Place the sensor portion of the thermometer in the warmest part of a refrigeration unit or in the coolest part of a hot food storage unit. Some older equipment may need modification if they were designed with the sensor located in the discharge air.

Following the Flow of Food

The flow of food at a retail food establishment begins with receiving and storage. As foods are delivered, they are inspected by receiving personnel and then placed quickly into storage.

From storage, foods and ingredients flow into the preparation and handling stages of production or directly into a display case. Some common preparation steps in retail food establishments include grinding, cutting, trimming, dispensing, and packaging. A simple diagram showing the overall flow of food in a retail food establishment is presented at the top of the following page.

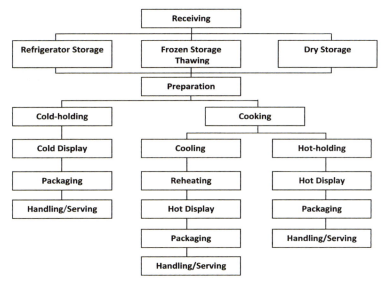

Food flow diagram

Receiving

Inspect all incoming food supplies to make sure they are at the proper temperature, in sound condition, and free from filth or spoilage. Always check product containers for tears, punctures, dents, or other signs of damage. Poor receiving procedures increase the chance of:

- Theft
- Acceptance of underweight merchandise
- Contamination
- Waste
- Acceptance of products that do not meet specifications.

Schedule deliveries for off-peak times and have enough staff and space on hand to receive products quickly and correctly. Move incoming shipments to storage as soon as they arrive. Merchandise that is damaged, spoiled, or otherwise unfit for sale or use must be properly disposed of, held by the store for credit, or returned to the distributor. Distressed merchandise must be put aside to prevent contamination of other foods, equipment, utensils, linens, or single-service or single-use articles.

Whatever the size of the establishment, receiving requires:

- Prompt handling
- Quality control procedures

> Merchandise that is damaged, spoiled, or otherwise unfit for sale should be rejected by receiving clerks. Store rejected foods away from good food.

- Trained staff who know:
  - ▲ Product specifications
  - ▲ Coding
  - ▲ Accurate checks on product temperatures
  - ▲ Proper handling of rejected merchandise.

Packaged Foods

The foods in a retail food establishment come in many different types of packages. Examples of food packaging include cans, bottles, jars, pouches, tubs, trays, bags, and boxes. The common purpose of the package is to:

- Protect the contents from contamination
- Provide a source of information about its nutritional contents
- Provide advertising material
- Make the product more convenient for customers to transport, prepare, and serve.

Dry foods, such as flour, sugar, rice, and beans, are commonly packaged in bags. These are not PHF (TCS) and can be safely stored at room temperature. At receiving, packages of dry food must be inspected for tears, signs of damage and contamination by chemicals and other substances, and infestations that could cause foodborne illness or product loss.

Reduced Oxygen Packaging (ROP)

For many foods, oxygen in the air can increase chemical breakdown and microbial spoilage. Many food processors use **reduced oxygen packaging** to help overcome the effects of oxygen and preserved foods. Some examples of reduced oxygen packaging include vacuum packaging, modified atmosphere packaging, and sous vide foods.

Vacuum packaging removes air from a package and hermetically seals the package so a near-perfect vacuum remains inside. The term **hermetic packaging** refers to a container that has been sealed to prevent the entry of gases and microorganisms. The most commonly used hermetic packages are metal cans and glass jars. These containers will also stop the entry of bacteria, yeasts, molds, and other types of contamination as long as they remain undamaged.

Upon receiving, metal cans must be checked for defects.

Defective Cans

Leaking or Bulging

- Do not accept cans if they leak or bulge at either end.
- Swollen ends on a can indicate gas is being produced inside.
- Gas may be caused by a chemical reaction between the food and the metal in the container or by the bacteria and other microbes inside the can.

Dented

- Dents in cans do not harm the contents unless they have actually penetrated the can or the seam.
- Dents found in the side seams or end seams of a can are the most important.
- Do not accept cans if damage to these areas can affect the physical integrity of the can and may allow microorganisms to enter through tiny pinhole leaks.
- Shipments with many dented cans or torn labels indicate poor handling and storage procedures by the supplier.

Rusty

- Rust does not harm contents unless it has penetrated the can or seam.
- Rusty cans indicate exposure to excess moisture.

Modified atmosphere packaging (MAP) helps preserve foods by replacing some or all of the oxygen inside the package with other gases, such as carbon dioxide or nitrogen. MAP is used with a wide range of products including meat, fish, pre-cut lettuce, baked products, cheese, coffee, nuts, and dried fruit. The MAP process has been successful in extending the shelf life of many products, and it reduces the amount of additives and preservatives required to prevent deterioration of the food. However, since low oxygen environments can create conditions conducive to the growth of anaerobic bacteria like *Clostridium botulinum* (see Chapter 2 on page 45), proper handling of MAP foods is essential. MAP technology requires adequate refrigeration be maintained during the entire shelf life of PHF (TCS). During the receiving process, employees must inspect PHF (TCS) in modified atmosphere packages to make sure the package is in sound condition and the food is at 41°F (5°C) or below when it arrives at the establishment.

Example of MAP food

Sous vide is a French term for "without air." It is a specialized packaging process where fresh raw foods are sealed in plastic pouches, and the air is removed by vacuum. The pouches are then cooked at a low temperature and rapidly cooled to 38°F (3°C) or below or frozen. The low cooking temperature of the sous vide process kills spoilage microorganisms. However, it does not destroy *C. botulinum* bacteria and their spores. Therefore, PHF (TCS) foods processed using sous vide technology must be kept out of the food temperature danger zone during transport, storage, and display. Receiving personnel must inspect sous vide products to make sure the package is in sound condition and the food is at 41°F (5°C) or below as it arrives at the establishment. Some sous vide foods may require even colder temperatures during receipt and cold storage. Check with the manufacturer about cold-holding temperatures for any sous vide foods you purchase. If extended shelf life is desired, a temperature of 38°F (3°C) or lower must be maintained at all times. After receiving, the products should be moved quickly into refrigerated storage until ready for use.

Common ROP Packaging Choices

- **Cook-chill**—A process that uses a plastic bag filled with hot cooked food from which air has been forced out and which is closed with a plastic or metal crimp.
- **Controlled Atmosphere Packaging (CAP)**—A system that maintains the desired atmosphere within a package throughout the shelf life of a product by the use of agents to bind or scavenge oxygen or a small packet containing compounds to emit a gas.
- **Modified Atmosphere Packaging (MAP)**—A process that employs a gas flushing and sealing process or reduction of oxygen through respiration of vegetables or microbial action.
- **Sous Vide**—A process in which fresh raw foods are sealed in a plastic pouch, and the air is removed by vacuum. The pouch is cooked at a low temperature and rapidly cooled to 38°F (3°C) or below or frozen.
- **Vacuum Packaging**—Reduces the amount of air from a package and hermetically seals the package so a near-perfect vacuum remains inside.

Benefits of ROP Packaging

- It creates a largely oxygen-free environment that prevents the growth of aerobic bacteria, yeast, and molds largely responsible for the off odors, slime, texture changes, and other forms of spoilage.
- It prevents chemical reactions that can produce off odors and color changes in foods.
- It reduces product shrinkage by preventing water loss.

Some products cannot be packed by ROP unless the retail food establishment is approved for the activity and inspected by the appropriate regulatory authority. These products include raw and smoked fish, soft cheeses (ricotta, cottage cheese, and cheese spreads), and combinations of cheese and other ingredients, such as vegetables, meat, or fish. Contact your local regulatory authority to obtain a complete set of guidelines for ROP foods and to seek a variance for all food manufacturing/processing operations based on the prior approval of a HACCP plan.

The *Food Code* Requirements for Retail Food Establishments That Use ROP Technology

- **Have a HACCP plan**—The retail food establishment must have a HACCP plan in place for the ROP operation that details how the seven principles (see Chapter 8) are incorporated into the operation's food safety management system.
- **Use two microbial growth barriers**—Because *Clostridium botulinum* and *Listeria monocytogenes* are significant health hazards, the establishment is required to have two microbial growth barriers. Time/temperature are commonly used as one barrier, but they need to be coupled with the use of pH, A_w, or product formulation to assure that *Clostridium botulinum* and *Listeria monocytogenes* will not grow inside the package.
- **Maintain foods at proper temperature**—All PHF (TCS) in ROP that rely on refrigeration as a barrier to microbial growth must be maintained at 41°F (5°C) or below.
- **Set shelf life**—The refrigerated shelf life is to be no more than 14 days from packaging to consumption or the original manufacturer's "sell-by" or "use-by" date, whichever comes first.
- **Proper label warnings**—Packages must be prominently and conspicuously labeled on the principal display panel with the instructions to maintain the food at 41°F (5°C) or below and to discard refrigerated food if within 14 days of its packaging it is not served for on-premises consumption or consumed if served or sold for off-premises consumption.
- **Use-by or sell-by dates**—Each container must bear a use-by or sell-by date. This date cannot exceed 14 days from packaging or repackaging to consumption, or the original manufacturer's sell-by or use-by date, whichever occurs first.

(continued)

> ### The *Food Code* Requirements for Retail Food Establishments That Use ROP Technology (continued)
>
> - **Employee training**—Employees responsible for the ROP process must receive training that will enable them to understand the key components of the process, the equipment used, and the specific procedures that must be followed to ensure critical limits identified in the HACCP plan have been met. The training program must also outline the employees' responsibilities for monitoring and documenting the process and describing what corrective actions they must take when critical limits are not met.

Food **irradiation** is a preservation technique used by some food processing industries. This process involves exposing food to controlled amounts of radiation in order to destroy disease-causing microorganisms and delay spoilage.

The acceptance of irradiated foods by shoppers has been slow due to their concerns about the safety of foods preserved in this manner. Contrary to many myths, irradiated food is not radioactive and does not pose a risk to the health and safety of people who eat it. Foods processed with irradiation are just as nutritious and flavorful as other foods that have been cooked, canned, or frozen.

Federal law requires irradiated food to be labeled with the international symbol for irradiation called a "radura." This symbol must be accompanied by the words *Treated with Irradiation or Treated with Radiation.*

Irradiation of food can effectively reduce or eliminate pathogens and spoilage microbes while maintaining the quality of most foods. This is a technology that has been proven safe and should be welcomed by customers as an effective food preservation technique.

Radura Symbol

The FDA has approved food irradiation for a variety of foods including fruits, vegetables, grains, spices, poultry, pork, lamb, and, more recently, ground meat.

Red Meat Products

Most red meat and meat products sold in the United States come from cattle (beef), calves (veal), hogs (ham, pork, and bacon), sheep (mutton), and young sheep (lamb). These products undergo **inspection for wholesomeness** by officials of the U.S. Department of Agriculture (USDA) or state agencies.

Raw red meat

Animals must be inspected for wholesomeness to make certain they are free of disease and unacceptable defects. The USDA also offers voluntary meat grading services. **Grade standards** for meat represent the culinary quality or palatability of the meat and are not measures of product safety. The figure below contains examples of inspections and grading stamps applied to products approved for use.

Inspection   **Grade**

USDA inspection and grade stamps for beef, veal, and lamb

Meat and meat products sold in retail food establishments are available in several forms, such as fresh, frozen, cured, smoked, dried, and canned. Since raw meats are PHF (TCS), never accept them if there is any sign of contamination, temperature abuse, or spoilage.

- Reject fresh meat if the product temperature exceeds 41°F (5°C) at delivery. Fresh meat should be firm and elastic to the touch and have characteristic aromas. Off odors are frequently indicators of spoilage.
  Sliminess is another characteristic of spoilage and is caused by bacterial growth on the surface of meat. Control of factors that cause

> **Reject fresh meat if the product temperature exceeds 41°F (5°C) at delivery.**

spoilage and sliminess also extends the shelf life of meat products and reduces shrink loss.

- Frozen meats should be solidly frozen when they arrive at your store. Look for signs of freezing and thawing and refreezing, such as frozen blood juices in the bottom of the container or the presence of large ice crystals on the surface of the product. Frozen meats should be packaged to prevent freezer burn.

Move fresh meat into refrigerated storage as quickly as possible. Frozen products should be moved from the delivery truck to the freezer while they are still solidly frozen.

Poultry

USDA or state inspectors must inspect all poultry products to make certain they are wholesome and not adulterated. Adulterated food contains filth or is otherwise decomposed and unfit for human consumption. Inspected poultry products carry a USDA seal on the individual package or on bulk cartons.

Inspection   **Grade**

USDA inspection and grade stamps for poultry

Usually poultry is graded also for quality. Grade A poultry must have good overall shape and appearance, be meaty, be practically free from defects, and have a well-developed layer of fat in the skin.

Poultry products support the growth of disease-causing and spoilage microorganisms. The intestinal tract and skin of poultry may contain a variety of foodborne disease bacteria, including *Salmonella* spp. and *Campylobacter jejuni*. The near neutral pH, high moisture, and high-protein content of poultry make it an ideal material for bacteria to grow in and on.

Poultry products are also vulnerable to spoilage caused by enzymes and spoilage bacteria.

Spoilage is indicated by meat tissue that:

- Is soft
- Is slimy
- Has an objectionable odor
- Has stickiness under the wings
- Has discolored or darkened wing tips.

Poultry when received should be held at or below 41°F (5°C).

Spoiled poultry

Game Animals

Game animals are not permitted for sale in retail food establishments unless they meet federal code regulations. This ban does not apply to commercially raised game animals approved by regulatory agencies, field-dressed game allowed by state codes, or exotic species of animals that must meet the same standards as those of other game animals.

Game animals commercially raised for food must be raised, slaughtered, and processed according to standards used for meat and poultry. Common examples of animals raised away from the wild and used for food are farm-raised buffalo, ostrich, and alligator. The USDA inspects the slaughter and processing of this meat in the usual manner.

Some states permit game animals, such as deer, bear, and elk that have been killed and dressed in the field, to be sold in retail food establishments. Game meat must be dressed soon after the kill to prevent rapid growth of bacteria already present in the meat. Next, the meat must be chilled rapidly, transported in a sanitary manner, and processed in an approved facility. Veterinarians are frequently appointed to inspect meat for contamination that would harm humans.

Eggs

Most retail food establishments sell and use eggs in one form or another. Eggs are usually purchased by federal grades, the most common being AA, A, and B. Grades for eggs are based on exterior and interior conditions of the egg.

Salmonella enteritidis enters the yolk of the egg as it is formed inside the hen. The eggshell surface may contain *Salmonella* spp. bacteria, especially if the shell is soiled with chicken droppings. Even if the shell is not cracked, bacteria can enter through the pores in the egg's shell.

Raw shell eggs should be clean, fresh, free of cracks or checks, and refrigerated at an ambient air temperature of 45°F (7°C) or below when delivered. Shell eggs that have not been treated to destroy all viable *Salmonella* shall be stored and displayed in refrigerated equipment that maintains an ambient temperature of 45°F (7°C) or less. These eggs must be labeled to include

Fresh eggs

USDA inspection and grade stamps for eggs

safe handling instructions. The egg, when opened, should have no noticeable odor and a firm yolk, and the white should cling to the yolk. Reject eggs that are dirty or cracked, and remember washing eggs only increases the possibility of contamination.

Ambient Air (Room Temperature)—Temperature of surrounding environment

An egg product is defined as an egg without its shell. As a safeguard against *Salmonella* spp., the FDA requires all egg products, such as liquid, frozen, and dry eggs, be pasteurized to render them *Salmonella*-free. Pasteurized egg products should be in a sealed container and kept at 41°F (5°C). Egg containers should carry labels that verify the contents have been pasteurized. These products are well-suited for facilities that offer food to immunocompromised people in highly susceptible populations.

Fluid and Dry Milk and Milk Products

This food group includes fluid and dry milk, cheese, butter, ice cream, and other types of milk products. When receiving milk and milk products, make certain they have been pasteurized. **Pasteurization** destroys all disease-causing microorganisms in the milk and reduces the total number of bacteria, thus, increasing shelf life. All market milk must be Grade A quality. Pasteurization also destroys natural milk enzymes that might shorten the shelf life of the products.

Milk that is marked "UHT" pasteurized has been heated to ultra-high temperatures using **aseptic processing and packaging.** UHT products can be stored safely for several weeks if kept under refrigeration. These products can be stored without refrigeration for short periods of time (Longrèe and Armbruster). Individual creamers are sometimes processed in this manner.

Fluid Milk

Under the Pasteurized Milk Ordinance, fluid milk should be received at 45°F (7°C) or less. It should be refrigerated immediately upon delivery and cooled within 4 hours to 41°F (5°C) or below. Individual containers of milk should be clearly marked with an expiration date and the name of the dairy plant that produced it. Check the expiration date of all dairy products before using them.

Cheese

Cheese should be received at 41°F (5°C) and checked for the proper color, flavor, and characteristics. Reject the product if it contains mold that is not a normal part of the cheese or if the rind or package is damaged. Some hard cheeses that are low in moisture may not require temperature control. Consult the cheese manufacturer's label to determine if refrigeration is required.

Butter

Butter is made from pasteurized cream. Since disease-causing and spoilage bacteria and mold may grow in butter, handle the product as a perishable item. The most common type of deterioration in butter is the development of a strong rancid odor and flavor. Ensure butter has a firm texture, even color, and is free of mold. Packaged butter should be received at 41°F (5°C), intact, and provide protection for the contents.

Fish

Fish includes finfish harvested from saltwater and freshwater, and seafood that comes mainly from saltwater. Seafood consists of molluscan shellfish and crustaceans. Molluscan shellfish includes oysters, clams, mussels, and scallops. Crustaceans include shrimp, lobster, and crab. Oysters, shrimp, catfish, salmon, and a few other types of finfish and seafood are being raised on fish farms using a technique called aquaculture.

Fish should be received at 41°F (5°C) or below and shellfish may be received at 45°F (7°C) or below. For better quality and shelf life, the optimum fish and shellfish receiving temperature often ranges from 30°F (-1°C) to 34°F (1°C). These products are generally more perishable than red meats, even when stored in a refrigerator or freezer. They are commonly packed in self-draining ice to prevent drying and to maximize the shelf life of the food. The slime covering the outside of fish contains a variety of bacteria that makes them highly susceptible to contamination and microbial spoilage. Fish are also rich in unsaturated fatty acids that are susceptible to oxidation and the development of off flavors and rancidity.

The quality of fish and seafood is measured by smell and appearance. Fresh finfish should have a mild, pleasant odor and bright, shiny skin with the scales tightly attached. Fish with the head intact should have clear, bulging eyes and bright red, moist gills. The flesh of fresh fish should be firm and elastic to the touch.

Fish must be commercially and legally caught or harvested—except when caught recreationally—and approved for sale by the regulatory authority. All fish suppliers and warehouse operations must comply with the seafood HACCP program as required in 21 CFR 123. Ready-to-eat raw, raw-marinated, partially cooked, or marinated-partially cooked fish must be frozen to time and temperature guidelines that meet *Food Code* specifications in order to kill parasites. This requirement does not apply to molluscan shellfish, tuna species specified in the *Food Code*, and aquacultured fish such as salmon. Records must be retained that show how the product was handled.

Shellfish must be purchased from sources approved by the FDA and the state shellfish authorities located along the coastline where the shellfish is harvested. Shellfish transported from one state to another must come from sources listed in the Interstate Certified Shellfish Shippers List. The reason for requiring tight control over molluscan shellfish is to reduce the risk of infectious hepatitis and other foodborne illnesses that may result from eating raw or insufficiently cooked forms of this product. Molluscan shellfish caught recreationally may not be used or sold in retail food establishments.

Purchase molluscan shellfish from approved sources.

When received at a retail food establishment, molluscan shellfish should be reasonably free of mud, dead shellfish, and shellfish with broken shells. Damaged shellfish must be discarded.

Molluscan shellfish must be purchased in containers that bear legible source-identification tags or labels fastened to the container by the harvester and each dealer that shucks, ships, or reships the shellstock. Molluscan shellfish tags must contain the following information:

- The harvester's state-issued identification number
- The date of harvesting
- The most precise harvest location or aquaculture site including an abbreviation of the state or country in which the shellfish are harvested
- The shellfish type and quantity

- A statement in bold, capitalized type that says, "THIS TAG IS REQUIRED TO BE ATTACHED UNTIL CONTAINER IS EMPTY OR IS RETAGGED AND THEREAFTER KEPT ON FILE FOR 90 DAYS FROM THE DATE THE SHELLSTOCK CONTAINER IS EMPTIED."

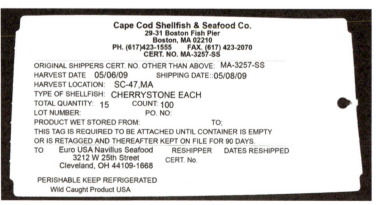
Example of shellfish tag

If seafood is suspected of being the source of foodborne illness, the investigating team can use the tags to determine where and when the product was harvested and processed.

For display purposes, shellstock may be removed from the tagged or labeled container in which it is received. The shellstock must be placed on drained ice or held in a display container. Care must be taken to protect shellstock from contamination during display.

Shellstock containers must be kept until every piece of product from that batch is gone.

The identity of the source of shellstock that has been removed from a tagged or labeled container for display must be preserved. This can be accomplished by using an approved record keeping system that keeps shellstock tags or labels in sequence based upon the date recorded on the tag or label. Shellstock from one tagged or labeled container must not be commingled with shellstock from another container before being ordered by the customer. Commingling is combining shellfish harvested on different days or from different growing areas as identified on the tag or label, or combining shellfish from containers with different container codes or different shucking dates.

Fruits and Vegetables

Most fruits and vegetables have a short shelf life. They continue to ripen even after they are picked. Therefore, they may become too ripe if not properly handled. Microorganisms found in water and soil can also cause fruits and vegetables to spoil. Fruits and vegetables hold their top quality for only a few days.

Purchase raw fruits and vegetables from approved sources and wash them thoroughly to remove soil and other contaminants before they are cut, combined with other ingredients, cooked, served, or offered for human consumption in a ready-to-eat form.

Whole raw fruits and vegetables that will be washed by customers before they are eaten do not need to be washed at the establishment before they are sold.

Most fresh fruits and vegetables are usually not considered PHF (TCS). Often the acidity and/or outer skin will prevent the entry and growth of harmful bacteria. However, sprouts, cut melons, cut tomatoes, and cut leafy greens are now considered PHF (TCS) and should be handled in the same manner as other PHF (TCS). Even so, the number of cases of foodborne illnesses linked to these kinds of products has increased in recent years. This is largely due to increased consumption of fresh fruits and vegetables and the emergence of microbes that can cause disease with a low number of organisms. Shiga toxin-producing *Escherichia coli*, *Shigella* spp., Hepatitis A, and *Cyclospora* spp. can be infective with only a few cells. Therefore, they do not require a PHF (TCS) to multiply. Though not required, whole raw fruits and vegetables may be washed using cleaners. In some cases, an additional antimicrobial rinse (water or bath) is used to reduce the number of microorganisms present on the surface. When these types of chemicals are used, they must meet the requirements in the *Code of Federal Regulations* (21 CFR 173.315). The fruits and vegetables should also be rinsed to remove as much of the residues of these chemicals as possible.

Some products, like wild mushrooms, may only be used if they have been inspected and approved by a mushroom identification expert who is approved by the regulatory authority. Beware of fresh mushrooms packaged in Styrofoam trays and covered with plastic shrink-wrap. Mushrooms use up the oxygen inside the package quickly. Unless holes are poked in the plastic wrap that covers the package to permit oxygen inside, oxygen-free conditions may occur that are favorable for the growth of *C. botulinum* bacteria.

Juice

Juice includes the liquid extracted from one or more fruits or vegetables, purees of the edible portions of one or more fruits or vegetables, or any concentrates of such liquid or puree. According to the *Food Code*, this group of foods includes juice as a whole beverage, an ingredient of a beverage, and a puree as an ingredient of a beverage.

Most of the juices sold in retail food establishments are obtained from processors in an prepackaged form. These juices must be obtained from a processor that has a HACCP system in place. In most instances, the processor will pasteurize or otherwise treat the juice to attain 99.999% reduction of the most resistant disease-causing microorganisms of public health significance.

Juice packaged in a retail food establishment must:

- Be treated under a HACCP plan as specified in 8-201.13 and 8-201.14 of the 2009 *Food Code* to attain a 99.999% reduction of the most resistant microorganisms of public health significance or, if the juice is not treated to destroy pathogens
- Bear a warning label that informs customers "This has not been pasteurized and, therefore, may contain harmful bacteria that can cause serious illness in children, the elderly, and persons with weakened immune systems."

> WARNING: This product has not been pasteurized and, therefore, may contain harmful bacteria that can cause serious illness in children, the elderly and persons with weakened immune systems.

Juice warning label

Purees of fruits or vegetables that are not used as beverages or ingredients in beverages are not required to comply with the HACCP requirements.

Frozen Foods

Frozen products must be solidly frozen when delivered. Check the temperature of frozen foods by placing the sensing portion of a thermometer between two packages. Receiving personnel should also look for signs the product has been thawed and refrozen.

Common signs of thawing and refreezing are:

- Large ice crystals or frost on the surface of the food
- Frozen liquid or juice at the bottom of the package
- Mushy soft products.

Reject frozen foods that are not solidly frozen or show signs of temperature abuse.

Storage of Food

Employees must check incoming shipments carefully and quickly move received items to proper storage. Stock rotation is a very important part of effective food storage. A **first-in, first-out (FIFO)** method of stock rotation helps assure older foods are used first. Product containers should be marked with a date or other readily identifiable code to help employees know which product has been in storage longest. When expecting food shipments, always make certain the older stock is moved to the front of the storage area to make room for the newly arriving products.

Proper stock rotation

Types of Storage

The three most common types of food storage areas in retail food establishments are:

- Refrigerator.
- Freezer.
- Dry storage.

Refrigerated Storage

Refrigerated storage is used to maintain the safety of PHF (TCS) and to maintain the quality of other perishable foods. It slows down microbial growth and controls quality by holding foods at 41°F (5°C) or below. Some common types of refrigerated storage equipment found in retail food establishments are:

- Walk-in
- Reach-in
- Coffin (a long, low unit that may or may not be equipped with a cover)
- Upright
- Under-the-counter refrigerators
- Cold display units, among others.

In order to maintain the temperature of PHF (TCS) at 41°F (5°C) or below, equipment should maintain the air temperature in the storage compartment at about 38°F (3°C). Fish and shellfish are especially vulnerable to spoilage and should be stored at colder temperatures ranging from 30°F-(-1°C) to 34°F (1°C). Some fruits and vegetables, such as bananas and potatoes, undergo undesirable chemical changes when they are refrigerated. Therefore, although fruits and vegetables are perishable products, not all types should be refrigerated. For perishability, fresh fruits and vegetables requiring refrigeration should be stored at temperatures between 33°F (1°C) and

Important Procedures for Cold Storage

- Keep refrigerated foods at 41°F (5°C) or below and frozen foods solidly frozen during storage.
- Rotate refrigerated and frozen foods on an FIFO basis and store foods in covered containers that are properly labeled and dated.
- Store foods in refrigerated and freezer storage areas at least 6 inches off the floor and space products to allow the cold air to circulate around them.
- Store raw products under cooked or ready-to-eat foods to prevent cross contamination.
- Keep different species of raw animal foods separate during storage. If limited storage space makes it necessary to store different species in the same area of the refrigerator, store poultry on the bottom shelf; ground meat and pork on the middle shelf; and fish, eggs, and other cuts of red meat on the top shelf.

41°F (5°C). Unpasteurized juices and potentially hazardous fruits and vegetables, like cut melons, cut tomatoes, cut leafy greens, and sprouts must be refrigerated at 41°F (5°C) or below.

Cut melons are a potentially hazardous food.

In order to hold PHF (TCS) at 41°F (5°C) or below, the unit should maintain air temperature of 38°F (3°C). Check temperatures daily in the warmest part of the unit to assure accuracy using an indicating or recording thermometer. Keep the unit door closed as much as possible to maintain temperature.

Freezer Storage

Freezer storage is designed to keep foods solidly frozen. Freezer equipment must also be equipped with indicating or recording thermometers to monitor the temperature of the ambient air inside the unit. If your freezer is not frost free, defrost it regularly to assure proper operation. Wrap frozen foods and transfer them to the refrigerated storage area until the defrosting process is complete.

Although bacteria are generally not destroyed by freezing, parasites can be killed if foods are frozen at the proper temperature for the proper length of time. Guidelines have been established for destroying parasites in raw-marinated and marinated, partially cooked fish.

The *Food Code* allows yellow fin, big-eye, bluefin northern, blue fin southern, and certain other species of tuna to be served or sold in a raw, raw-marinated, or partially cooked ready-to-eat form without freezing.

Food should be frozen throughout to -4°F (-20°C) and held for 7 days in a freezer,

or

Food should be frozen throughout to -31°F (-35°C) -using a blast chiller, and held at that temperature for 15 hours,

or

Food should be frozen throughout to -31°F (-35°C) and stored at -4°F (-20°C) for at least 24 hours.

Guidelines for parasitic destruction

Dry Storage

Products in dry storage areas are usually packed in labeled cans, bottles, jars, and bags. The area should have a room temperature of 50°F (10°C) to 70°F (21°C) with a relative humidity of 50% to 60% to maximize shelf life of stored products. Windows should be blocked or shaded.

- Use slatted shelves that allow circulation of air, are at least 6 inches off the floor, and are away from the wall. This allows for cleaning under the shelving and discourages pest harborage.
- When bulk items are moved into bulk food-grade containers with tight-fitting lids, include the product's common name, codes, labels, and dates.
- Scoops and other utensils should be food grade and have long handles that keep hands from touching food.
- Do not use toilet rooms, locker areas, mechanical rooms, and similar spaces for storage of food, single-service items, paper goods, or equipment and utensils. Do not expose foods to overhead water and sewer lines unless the lines are shielded to collect and remove potential drips.

Dry storage area

Store dry foods on slatted shelving.

Contamination of ready-to-eat food

Chemical Storage

Toxic chemicals, such as cleaners, sanitizers, and pesticides, are commonly used and sold in retail food establishments. Most of these products can be poisonous if consumed accidentally.

Many chemicals used in retail food establishments are poisonous if consumed. Others can cause irritation to skin and the respiratory system.

- All products must be labeled and kept separate from food products. If an adequate storage area is not available, use a locked cabinet to store the chemicals.
- Identify the chemical and include directions on proper use.
- Train employees on how to use these products safely.
- It is a good practice to post lists of instructions so users can easily see when and how to use the products.

> A good label identifies the chemical, provides directions on how to use it safely, and instructs people on what first-aid measures to use in case of accidents.

Do not store chemicals near food

Storage Conditions for Foods

Product	Storage Conditions
Meat and meat products	• Store for up to 3 weeks at temperatures between 28°F (-2°C) and 32°F (0°C) and a relative humidity between 85% and 90%. • Cold temperatures extend the shelf life of red meats by slowing down the growth of bacteria that cause spoilage and reduce shrink loss. • Store for several months when held at 0°F (-18°C) or below. • Frozen meats must be wrapped in moisture-proof paper to prevent them from drying out. • Use by manufacturer's shelf-life criteria. • Packaging for frozen foods should also be strong and flexible and protect against light. (continued)

Product	Storage Conditions (continued)
Poultry	• Store at temperatures between 28°F (-2°C) and 32°F (0°C) for short periods of time. • A relative humidity of 75% to 85% is recommended, as excessive humidity causes sliminess due to excessive bacterial growth. • Poultry should be wrapped carefully to prevent dehydration, contamination, and loss of quality. • Frozen poultry and poultry products can be stored for 4 to 6 months when held at 0°F (-18°C) or below. • Use by manufacturer's shelf-life criteria.
Whole shell eggs	• Keep fresh for up to 2 weeks when stored at 41°F (5°C) or below. • It is recommended to store eggs at 34°F (1°C) to 38°F (3°C) to maintain optimum quality. • Keep eggs covered and store them away from onions and other foods that have a strong odor. • Discard eggs that are dirty or cracked. • Always make sure to wash your hands after handling whole shell eggs. • Use by manufacturer's shelf-life criteria.
Egg products (such as whole eggs, egg whites, and yolks)	• Egg products are pasteurized to destroy Salmonella spp. bacteria. • Store at 41°F (5°C) or below. • Store frozen eggs at 0°F (-18°C) or below and keep them frozen until time for defrosting. • Once dried eggs have been reconstituted, they are considered potentially hazardous and must be stored at 41°F (5°C) or below. • Use by manufacturer's shelf-life criteria.

(continued)

Product	Storage Conditions (continued)
Milk	• Pasteurized milk may be held at 41°F (5°C) or less for up to 10 days or longer. • The optimal storage temperature for fluid milk is 34°F (1°C) to 38°F (3°C), and the shelf life of milk is shortened significantly at higher storage temperatures. • Milk also picks up odors from other foods. Store milk in an area away from onions and other foods that give off odors. • Use by manufacturer's shelf-life criteria.
Fish and shellfish	• Products are more perishable than red meats even when refrigerated or frozen. • Fish and shellfish should be stored at temperatures ranging from 30°F(-1°C) to 34°F (1°C). • Fish should be kept on crushed ice drained away from the product or solidly frozen. Use fresh fish within 24 hours or less. • Shellfish shells should close when tapped. Dead shellfish must be discarded. Lobsters and clams should be kept alive until cooked or frozen. Keep shellfish tags for 90 days after the container is emptied. If a foodborne outbreak occurs, the tags help identify the source.
Fresh fruits and vegetables	• Products require temperatures between 41°F (5°C) and 45°F (7°C) in a relative humidity of 85% to 90%, if not cut. • If fruits and vegetables arrive packed in airtight film, notify your supplier to correct this issue to allow the product to respire. • Produce should not be washed before storage—wash before using. • Proper circulation is necessary to maintain freshness and firmness. Discard fruits that begin to spoil. • Whole citrus fruits and bananas should not be refrigerated.

(continued)

Product	Storage Conditions (continued)
Modified atmosphere packaging (MAP) and sous vide products	• MAP products are perishable foods and must be kept at temperatures recommended by the processor. • Most will need refrigeration at 41°F (5°C) or below; if frozen, keep solidly frozen until thawed and used. • Check expiration dates before using; discard out-of-date products. • Do not use packages that have signs of microbial growth (slime, bubbles, molds, etc.).

Food Preparation, Handling, and Service

Preparation, handling, and service of food in retail food establishments involve one or more steps. In convenience stores, ready-to-eat products, such as sandwiches and salads, are sold to customers with minimal preparation. In larger retail food establishments, foods are prepared in consumer-sized portions using commercially available equipment for cutting, grinding, slicing, cooking, and cooling. These foods are commonly referred to as "meal solutions" or "home meal replacements."

During preparation, an important technique that can be used to promote food safety is "small batch" preparation. Food preparation is usually done at room temperature. This is several degrees into the temperature danger zone. Therefore, you must limit the amount of time the food is in the danger zone by working with small and manageable amounts of potentially hazardous ingredients. In addition, it is recommended ingredients be pre-chilled prior to preparation (i.e., ingredients used in the preparation of chicken salad).

Ingredient Substitution

For meal solutions and home meal replacements, there is normally a recipe for the products prepared in the retail food establishment. The recipe usually includes a list of ingredients and instructions for how to prepare, store, and label the food item.

- When one or more of the original ingredients are not available for a recipe, other ingredients may be substituted so the food item can still be prepared and sold.
- All ingredient substitutions should be identified in the recipe before preparation.

- Ingredient substitutions must never compromise the safety of the food and should not be allowed unless they are identified and allowed in the recipe.

Avoiding Temperature Abuse

Temperature and time abuse is when food is kept in the temperature danger zone, 41°F (5°C) to 135°F (57°C), long enough for harmful organisms to grow.

- Monitoring and controlling food temperatures are extremely effective ways to minimize the risks of foodborne illnesses.
- Thermometers are used for stored, cooked, cooling, hot-held, cold-held, and reheated foods. Before using a thermometer, make sure it is clean, sanitary, and properly calibrated. Always insert the "sensor" portion or probe stem of the thermometer into the thickest part of the food. In most instances, this will be at the center of the food product or container.

Thawing

The most common and acceptable methods for thawing foods include: in a refrigerator, under cool running water [less than 70°F (21°C)]; in a microwave oven followed by immediately cooking; and as part of the cooking process.

Thawing food in a refrigerator is the preferred method, since the temperature of foods thawed in this manner won't reach the temperature danger zone. The method requires good planning and adequate refrigeration space. It can take two or three days and sometimes longer to thaw large food masses such as turkeys, roasts, and hams. When using this method to thaw foods, you must plan ahead.

PHF (TCS) like shrimp or scallops, can be thawed by submerging them under cool [less than 70°F (21°C)] running water. When using this process, water must flow at sufficient velocity to agitate and float off loose particles in an overflow. In addition, it is desirable to thaw foods under cool running water as quickly as possible. The *Food Code* requires thawing foods for a period of time that does not allow thawed portions of ready-to-eat foods to rise above 41°F (5°C). In addition, thawed portions of raw animal foods requiring cooking should not be allowed to rise above 41°F (5°C) for more than four hours including the time the food is being thawed and the time needed to prepare it for cooking or the time it takes under refrigeration to lower the food temperature to 41°F (5°C) or below for storage.

Foods thawed in a microwave must be cooked immediately after thawing. Cooking can be done in the microwave oven or with conventional cooking equipment. Do not thaw foods in a microwave oven and then store them in a refrigerator before they are cooked.

Retail food establishments will sometimes use a slacking (defrosting) process to moderate the temperature of foods prior to cooking or reheating. During the slacking process, foods can be defrosted under refrigeration that maintains the food at 41°F (5°C) or less or at any temperature if the food remains frozen. The slacking process is typically used with previously block-frozen food, such as spinach.

Under no circumstances should foods be thawed or slacked at room temperature. Room temperature thawing puts foods in the temperature danger zone—the very thing you do not want to have happen. When foods are thawed at room temperature, the outer surface of the food thaws first and will soon reach room temperature. Microbial growth occurs very quickly at room temperature.

Guidelines for Thawing Food

Refrigeration

- Under refrigeration that maintains the food temperature at 41°F (5°C) or below.

Submerged under Running Water

- Completely submerged under running water:
- At a water temperature of 70°F (21°C) or below
- With enough water force to remove contaminants from the surface of the food
- For a period of time that does not allow thawed portions of ready-to-eat foods to rise above 41°F (5°C)
- For a period of time that does not allow thawed portions of a raw animal food requiring cooking to be in the temperature danger zone for more than a total time of 4 hours.

As Part of the Cooking Process

Thawing for Immediate Service

- Use any procedure (i.e., microwave oven) that thaws a portion of frozen ready-to-eat food prepared for immediate service in response to an individual customer's order.

Cold-holding

Most harmful microorganisms start to grow at temperatures above 41°F (5°C). Some bacteria, such as *Listeria monocytogenes*, can grow slowly at temperatures below 41°F (5°C). Proper **cold-holding** is required to control the growth of pathogenic microorganisms and extend the shelf life of perishable products.

Cold display of raw, potentially hazardous, foods

Cold-holding at a Glance: Refrigerators, Display Case, and Cold Service Bars

Cold raw PHF (TCS) (like meat)
Temperature: Below 41°F (5°C)

- Physical barriers should be in place to separate different species (meat, poultry, seafood) and to separate raw from ready-to-eat

Meat cutting operation
Temperature: Below 41°F (5°C)

- Slows bacterial growth.

Fish and seafood foods.
Temperature: Below 41°F (5°C)

- Use ice made from potable water.
- Transport ice in "approved food-contact" containers.
- Liquid must be drained from ice to prevent contamination.
- After ice has been in contact with fish and shellfish, it cannot be reused.
- Cooked and raw product should be kept separate.

Cold, ready-to-eat PHF (TCS)
Temperature: Below 41°F (5°C) up to 7 days

- If held for more than 24 hours, the *Food Code* recommends prepared and held products be marked to indicate the date or day by which the food shall be consumed on the premises, sold or discarded.

(continued)

> **Cold-holding at a Glance: Refrigerators, Display Case, and Cold Service Bars** (continued)
>
> **Cold, ready-to-eat PHF (TCS)**
> **Temperature: Below 41°F (5°C) up to 7 days**
> - The day of preparation or the day the original container is opened in the retail food store shall be counted as Day 1.
> - The day or date marked by the retail food store may not exceed a manufacturer's use-by date if the manufacturer determined the use-by date based on food safety.
>
> **Ready-to-eat salads**
> **Temperature: As cold as possible and above 32°F (0°C) and below 41°F (5°C)**
>
> - Pre-chill ingredients before using.
> - Prepare small batches to assure food is not in the temperature danger zone too long.
>
> A special note regarding cold-holding of PHF(TCS): If your target food product temperature is 41°F (5°C) or lower, you will most likely need to maintain the air temperature in the refrigeration unit at a lower temperature, such as 38°F (3°C).

Frozen, Ready-to-eat Foods

When large amounts of food are removed from the freezer, they should be marked to indicate the date by which the food must be sold. Ready-to-eat, PHF(TCS) must be used within 7 calendar days or less after the food is removed from the freezer, minus the time out of temperature control before freezing. Subtract any time if the food is maintained at 41°F (5°C) or less before freezing.

When displaying ready-to-eat PHF(TCS), like prepared salads and luncheon meats, be sure the refrigerator unit can maintain a safe, cold-holding temperature. This may be more difficult in open-top and open-front refrigerated display cases that do not have doors. Refrigerated display cases have a "safe load line." This line indicates the level below which foods must be stored to assure the food is held at the proper temperature. It is also important to store foods so the discharge or return air vents are not blocked.

Prepackaged Foods

A refrigerated, ready-to-eat, PHF(TCS) prepared and held in a retail food establishment for more than 24 hours or originating from an original con-

Prepared salads

Safe load line

Cold storage of read-to-eat foods

tainer prepared and packaged by a food processing plant and opened at the retail food establishment must be discarded if it:

- Exceeds the prescribed time and temperature requirements;
- Is in a container or package that does not bear a date or day, or;
- Is marked with a date or day that exceeds the time and temperature combinations described previously.

Cooking

The purpose of **cooking** is to make food more palatable by changing its appearance, texture, and aroma. Cooking also heats the food and destroys pathogens that may be found in and on the product.

Meat, poultry, fish, seafood, eggs, and unpasteurized milk should not be prepared and served raw or rare. Establishments that choose to serve raw foods increase the risk of causing a foodborne illness. Raw animal foods need to be cooked to the proper temperatures to be safe. Many states and jurisdictions require an advisory be posted to warn consumers of the risk.

Most foods are cooked using stoves, conventional ovens, and microwave ovens. Because heat transfer can be different depending on the heating source, final temperature requirements have been set for conventional oven cooking and microwave cooking.

The destruction of pathogens results from a combination of time and temperature. Requirements for cooking a particular food item should include a final temperature as well as a prescribed length of time at that temperature.

Casseroles and other foods that contain a combination of raw ingredients, such as meat and poultry, must be cooked to a final temperature that coincides with the highest risk food. In this case, 165°F (74°C) is required to

Cooking Guidelines for Potentially Hazardous Foods

Food Type	Minimum Internal Temperature	Minimum Time Held at Internal Temperature Before Serving
Meat Roast (Rare)	• 130°F (54°C) • 140°F (60°C)	• 112 Min. • 12 Min.
Eggs, Meat and Pork (Other than roasts), Fish	• 145°F (63°C)	• 15 Sec.
Ground meat, Mechanically Tenderized Meat, Ground Pork, and Ground Game Animals	• 155°F (68°C)	• 15 Sec.
Meat Roast (medium), Pork Roast, and Ham	• 145°F (63°C)	• 4 Min.
All Poultry, Ground Poultry, Stuffed meats, and Stuffed Food Products	• 165°F (74°C)	• 15 Sec.

Note: When microwave cooking, heat raw animal foods to a temperature of 165°F (74°C) in all parts of the food.

Serving undercooked hamburgers and other ground meats is not an option for items on a children's menu.

(Source: FDA *Food Code*)

destroy pathogens that may be found in the poultry. Food mixtures, such as chili and beef stew, must be cooked to 165°F (74°C) to assure proper destruction of disease-causing agents.

When cooking foods in the microwave oven, the distribution of heat is often uneven. Stirring and rotating the food during the cooking process will enable heat to be distributed more evenly. The *Food Code* requires raw animal foods cooked in a microwave oven to be heated

> **The internal temperature of raw animal foods cooked in a microwave oven must reach 165°F (74°C) or above.**

to 165°F (74°C) in all parts of the food. As a common practice, foods cooked in a microwave oven should be allowed to stand covered for 2 minutes before serving to allow the heat inside the product to disperse more evenly.

For most foods, the internal temperature will be measured by inserting the probe of a thermometer or thermocouple into the center or thickest part of the food mass. This will give you an accurate reading of the internal temperature of the product.

Cooling

Foods are in the temperature danger zone during **cooling**, and there is no way to avoid it. After proper cooking, potentially hazardous foods (time temperature control for safety foods) need to be cooled from 135°F (57°C) to 41°F (5°C) as rapidly as possible. **The *Food Code* recommends that hot foods not used for immediate service or hot display be cooled from 135°F (57°C) to 70°F (21°C) within 2 hours and from 135°F (57°C) to 41°F (5°C) or less within 6 hours.**

> **Improper cooling is one of the leading contributors to foodborne illness in retail food establishments**

PHF (TCS) prepared from ingredients such as reconstituted foods and canned tuna, which have been held at room temperature, must be cooled to 41°F (5°C) or less within 4 hours.

Foods must pass through the temperature danger zone as quickly as possible.

Ice bath

Place food in shallow pans 2" to 3" deep.

Safe cooling methods

Common Methods for Reducing Cooling Time

- Blast chillers
- Walk-in coolers, loosely covered
- Use containers that facilitate heat transfer (stainless steel)
- Transfer food into shallow pans that will allow for a product depth of 3 inches or less
- Transfer food into smaller containers
- Place container of hot food in an ice water bath
- Stir food while cooling
- Use cooling paddles to stir the food
- Add ice as an ingredient directly to a condensed food.

Never assume any one method is working without checking the temperature and time foods take to cool. Always depend on the thermometer reading with any of the methods you use to cool food.

Always use a thermometer to verify foods are cooling properly.

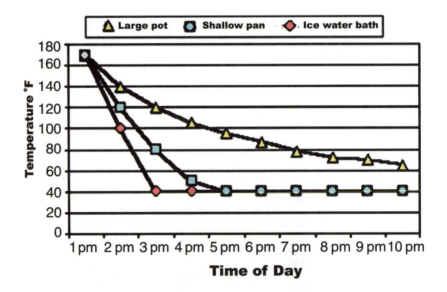

Different cooling methods for chili

Source: Laboratory Test conducted by Dr. Richard Linton at Purdue University

Hot-holding and Reheating

All PHF (TCS) that have been cooked and are intended to be held hot (not cooled, stored, and reheated) must be maintained at 135°F (57°C) or above.

- **Hot-holding** is also required when hot PHF (TCS) are delivered to sites away from the retail food establishment.
- During hot-holding, never add fresh product to existing product and always work in small batches.
- **Reheat** to at least 165°F (74°C) within 2 hours.

While temperature is usually the most important factor in controlling microbes, there are some situations in which controlling time can also be used. That is why there is an allowance of 4 hours in the temperature danger zone for ready-to-eat PHF (TCS) held for food service or immediate consumption. Sliced pizza and fried chicken are good examples. If these PHF (TCS) are hot-held at 135°F (57°C) or above, the food may dry out and the quality may deteriorate very quickly.

Ready-to-eat foods commercially prepared and packaged and from a food processing plant under regulatory inspection should be free of harmful microorganisms. Therefore, these foods may be reheated to a temperature of at least 135°F (57°C) for hot-holding [rather than a minimum of 165°F (74°C)]. Commercially prepared and cooked soups would be a good example of a food that would need to be reheated to 135°F (57°C) or above followed by hot-holding. Roasts cooked to the proper temperature and time may be held at 130°F (54°C) or above.

Hot-holding—Store hot-held foods at 135°F (57°C) or above

Avoid holding potentially hazardous foods (time/temperature control for safety foods) in the temperature danger zone. Most establishments will limit this amount of time to 20–30 minutes. In these instances, it is critical to achieve the required cooking temperature, and the amount of time foods are held in the temperature danger zone must be carefully monitored and recorded. The procedures and monitoring required when using time as a method of control vary. Consult with your local regulatory authority for requirements in your jurisdiction.

Time as a Public Health Control

The 2009 *Food Code* allows PHF (TCS) sold in ready-to-eat form to be stored without temperature control using the following guidelines:

- For up to 4 hours, after which it must be consumed or discarded; or
- For up to 6 hours for refrigerated food, if the food is 41°F(5°C) when initially removed from temperature control, and as long as the food temperature does not exceed 70°F (21°C).

This version of the *Food Code* now clarifies that ready-to-eat PHF (TCS) held for sale or service using time only as the public health control can be sold or served at any temperature upon a consumer's request. Some examples of food items affected by this provision are slices of pizza, chicken wings, and egg rolls that may be heated for taste during the holding time before being served. These foods are commonly served at short-term buffets or catered meals.

Food Handling

Employees must practice good personal hygiene when handling food. This starts with a clean uniform and an effective hair restraint.

- Food handlers in all departments should avoid touching food with their bare hands.
- They can use tongs, serving spoons, disposable gloves, or deli tissue when handling meats, cheeses, or prepared salads or when making sandwiches.
- Employees must hold serving utensils by the handle only, and they must never touch the part of the utensil that comes into contact with food.

- A single utensil should be used for each food item, and the utensil should be stored in the food between uses.
- Always store serving utensils in a way that permits the employee to grab the handle without touching the food.

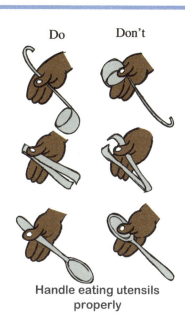

Handle eating utensils properly

Discarding or Reconditioning Food

A food that is unsafe, adulterated, or not honestly presented shall be reworked or reconditioned using a procedure approved by the regulatory authority in the jurisdiction, or it must be discarded.

Food must be discarded if it is not from an approved source or has been contaminated by food employees, consumers, or other persons via soiled hands, bodily discharges (i.e., coughs and sneezes), or other means.

Ready-to-eat foods must be discarded if they have been contaminated by an employee who has been restricted or excluded as described in Appendix D of this book.

Refilling Returnable Containers

A take-home food container returned to a retail food establishment may not be refilled with a PHF (TCS) at the establishment. A food-specific container for beverages may be refilled at a food establishment if:

- Only a beverage that is not a PHF (TCS) is dispensed into the container
- The design of the container and of the rinsing equipment and the nature of the beverage, when considered together, allow effective cleaning of the container at home or in the retail food establishment
- Facilities for rinsing before refilling returned containers with fresh, hot water that is under pressure and not recirculated are provided as part of the dispensing system

- The consumer-owned container returned to the retail food establishment for refilling is refilled for sale or service only to the same consumer
- The container is refilled by an employee of the retail food establishment or the owner of the container if the beverage system includes a contamination-free transfer process that cannot be bypassed by the container owner.

Personal take-out beverage containers, such as thermally insulated bottles, nonspill coffee cups, and promotional beverage glasses, may be refilled by employees or the consumer if the refilling process will protect the food and food-contact surface of the container from contamination.

Self-service Bar

Self-service salad and hot food buffet bars are very popular in retail food establishments. They offer convenience and a wide range of selections for customers. The most important food safety goals for this type of operation are to:

Self-service bar

- Protect foods from contamination by customers
- Keep foods out of the temperature danger zone.

Rules for Self-service Bars

- A properly installed sneeze guard protects the food from contamination by your customers.
- Never place raw animal foods, such as oysters, on a self-service bar except for ready-to-eat foods like sushi. Keep hot-held PHF (TCS) foods at 135°F (57°C) or above and cold foods at 41°F (5°C) or below.
- Use clean and sanitized utensils in a self-service bar and replace any utensils that become contaminated or soiled.
- Use only one utensil for each food item and store it in the food between uses.

If customers are allowed to visit the self-service bar more than once, they must be given a clean plate or bowl for each trip. This will reduce the risk of contaminating food on display at the bar. Beverage cups and glasses may be reused to get refills.

Checkout and Bagging

Sneeze guards help prevent the spread of foodborne illness.

The last step in the flow of food in retail food establishments takes place at the checkout counter. Food employees must practice good personal hygiene and not allow their hands to transfer bacteria from raw animal foods to cooked and ready-to-eat foods. Juices from raw meat, poultry, fish, and shellfish can contaminate produce and other ready-to-eat foods. These juices must be routinely wiped off conveyor belts, and employees must wash hands properly.

Keep checkout counters clean and sanitary.

Baggers must be careful not to put raw meat, poultry, and fish in the same bags with fresh fruits and vegetables. In addition, non-food items, such as detergents, pesticides, and lightbulbs, must not be

Checkers and baggers must work carefully to prevent contamination and cross contamination.

put in the same bag with foods to avoid contamination with chemical and physical hazards. Freezer bags should also be used to separate frozen goods.

Sometimes customers change their mind about purchasing a particular item. Whenever these are PHF (TCS), the product must be put back into the proper storage or display environment as quickly as possible.

Temporary Facilities and Mobile Food Facilities

A temporary food establishment (TFE) is defined by the *Food Code* as a food establishment that operates for a period of no more than 14 consecutive days in conjunction with a single event or celebration. TFEs may operate either indoors or outdoors and often have limited physical and sanitary facilities available.

Some food establishments are offering food by way of temporary and mobile facilities. A variety of foods can be prepared and served from temporary stands and trailers. Some examples include sandwiches, pizza, BBQ ribs, gyros, corn on the cob, confections (i.e., cotton candy, funnel cakes, or elephant ears), and beverages.

Mobile food facility

Temporary food facility

Mobile facilities are trucks and trailers used to cater events located away from the establishment. The extent of food items offered through catering operations is practically unlimited.

The same food safety practices employed in other areas of the establishment must also be applied at temporary facilities, mobile facilities, and in-store product demonstrations. In particular, food must be protected from:

- Temperature abuse
- Infected employees who practice poor personal hygiene and use improper food-handling practices
- Contamination and cross contamination.

Employees should use tongs, utensils, and deli tissue to avoid bare hand contact with food. Disposable gloves can provide an additional barrier against contamination. However, gloves must not be viewed as a substitute for proper handwashing.

> **Employees must not eat and smoke around food, and they must wash their hands whenever they are contaminated.**

Food must be protected from contamination and cross contamination. Food on display must be protected from contamination by customers and employees. Food equipment must be designed and constructed to make it smooth, easily cleanable, nontoxic, and nonabsorbent.

Use disposable utensils whenever possible. When it is necessary to use multiple-use utensils, they must be washed and sanitized using a four-step process:

1. Wash in hot, soapy water.
2. Rinse in clean water.
3. Use chemical sanitizing rinse.
4. Air-dry.

Garbage and paper wastes should be placed in containers lined with plastic bags and equipped with tight-fitting lids. Food and wastes must be kept covered to avoid attracting insects, rodents, and other pests.

Vending Machines

A vending machine is a self-service device that dispenses individual-size servings of food and beverages after a customer inserts a coin, paper currency, token, card, or key or makes a payment by another means. Some vending machines dispense food and beverages in bulk while others dispense products in individually wrapped packages. Vending machines are available that will dispense PHF (TCS), ready-to-eat foods (i.e., sandwiches, french fries, dairy products, and soup) and non-PHF (TCS) (candy, snack chips, pastries, coffee, and soft drinks).

Vending machines that store and dispense PHF (TCS) must have adequate refrigeration and/or heating units, insulation, and controls to keep cold foods cold and hot foods hot. These machines must also be equipped with an automatic control that prevents the machine from vending food if there is a power failure, mechanical failure, or other condition that prevents cold food from being maintained at 41°F (5°C) or below and hot food maintained at 135°F (57°C) or above.

The temperature cutoff requirement does not apply:

- In a cold food machine during a period not to exceed 30 minutes immediately after the machine is filled, serviced, or restocked, or;
- In a hot food machine during a period not to exceed 120 minutes immediately after the machine is filled, serviced, or restocked.

Refrigerated, ready-to-eat PHF (TCS) prepared in a food establishment and dispensed through a vending machine (with an automatic shutoff control) shall be discarded if it (a) exceeds the time and temperature combinations prescribed by the *Food Code* or (b) is not correctly date labeled.

Home Meal Replacement

Home meal replacements and *meal solutions* are the terms most often used to refer to high-quality meals prepared away from home but eaten at home. These types of products are now a multi-billion dollar business for retail food establishments throughout the country.

> Home meal replacements come in "ready-to-cook," "ready-to-heat," and "ready-to-eat" varieties.

The move toward prepared food has retail food establishments selling complete meals instead of just ingredients. Retail food establishments and restaurants are now competing head-to-head for the "heat and eat" business that has become very popular with today's customers.

> **It is a good idea to establish sell-by or best-if-used-by dates and codes for these ready-to-eat foods.**

All three varieties are designed to save time and effort for families too tired to cook at the end of the day.

Ready-to-eat foods are a common variety of home meal replacements.

Home replacement meals should be labeled so customers understand how to keep the product safe when they take it home. Warn them against keeping the food in the car while they do more shopping or keeping it at room temperature when they get home. Pamphlets and brochures stuffed into bags or stapled to the front of bags can help educate customers about safe handling of home replacement meals. Retailers must be able to show they've done everything in their power, including written documentation and following industry standards, to make the food safe.

Summary

***Back to the Story . . .** In this case, the best solution is to discard the éclairs because they are not labeled properly, and it is unknown how long they were left at room temperature. Proper labeling using the FIFO method is an important way to monitor and identify foods as they pass through the food product flow. The éclairs are PHF (TCS) because they contain eggs in the custard and if stored improperly could lead to foodborne illness. Salmonella or Staphylococcus aureus microbes thrive in this type of custard. The management at this establishment should set up training programs so employees understand the importance of labeling food products during the flow of food.*

- ✔ Not all retail food establishment managers will actually purchase food products. However, knowledge of the rules, regulations, and procedures for receiving and storing food is a must for everyone responsible for food safety.
- ✔ The flow of food must be monitored and considered when preparing safe food.
- ✔ Foods should only be allowed in the temperature danger zone for a short time during thawing, heating, and cooling activities. The three main contributors to foodborne illness in retail food establishments are:
  - Time and temperature abuse
  - Cross contamination
  - Poor personal health and hygiene practices by food handlers.

These factors must be controlled throughout the flow of food to assure food safety. Preparation and service are critical processes in your establishment because they are the last steps you take before your customer eats the food.

Discussion Questions (Short Answer)

1. Why should buyers purchase foods only from approved sources that comply with all applicable food laws?
2. Discuss the differences between grading and inspection services for meat and poultry.
3. Why should cans with swollen ends be rejected and sent back to the supplier?
4. What are typical signs to spoilage for red meats, poultry, and fish?
5. What is the meaning of FIFO?
6. Why should raw products be placed below cooked or ready-to-eat foods during storage?
7. Describe safe procedures for storing cleaning and sanitizing agents and pesticides.
8. Why should products be located at least 6 inches off the floor during storage?

Quiz 4 (Multiple Choice)

Please choose the **best** answer for each question.

1. The safest way to thaw food is:

    a. at room temperature.
    b. in the refrigerator.
    c. under ultra-violet light.
    d. none of the above.

2. What is the minimum number of days shellfish tags must be kept after the date a container of shellstock is emptied?

    a. 15.
    b. 30.
    c. 60.
    d. 90.

Quiz 4 (Multiple Choice)

3. Which of the following PHF (TCS) can be received at 45°F (5°C) or below rather than 41°F (5°C) or below?

   a. Milk.
   b. Liquid eggs.
   c. Fish.
   d. Ground lamb.

4. Foods that are held hot, like soup, should be at or above temperatures of:

   a. 165°F (74°C).
   b. 155°F (68°C).
   c. 145°F (63°C).
   d. 135°F (57°C).

5. Which of the following is **not** a rule that should be closely followed when purchasing food?

   a. Foods prepared in a private home may not be used or offered for human consumption in a retail food establishment.
   b. Buyers should only purchase food that is safe, wholesome, and from an approved source.
   c. Avoid the use of commercially raised game animals as meat and poultry items.
   d. Only buy meat and poultry that have been inspected by the USDA or state agency officials.

6. The **best** method for measuring the temperature of frozen food products is by:

   a. inserting the sensing probe into the center of a frozen food package until the recorded temperature stabilizes.
   b. inserting the sensing probe between two packages of frozen foods until the recorded temperature stabilizers.
   c. measuring the ambient temperature of the frozen food compartment of the delivery vehicle.
   d. looking for signs of freezing and thawing, such as large ice crystals and frozen juices in the bottom of the box.

7. Frozen foods should **not** be accepted at a retail food establishment if:

   a. they have large ice crystals on the surface.
   b. there are frozen juices on the bottom of the package.
   c. if the temperature is above 32°F (0°C).
   d. All of the above.

8. Which of the following foods should **not** be rejected upon delivery?

   a. Fresh fish that has dull, sunken eyes and soft flesh.
   b. Poultry with darkened wing tips and soft flesh.
   c. Canned fruit with small amounts of surface rust on the lid of the can.
   d. Fresh beef products that are delivered at 45°F (7°C).

9. Which of the following statements about fish and seafood is **false**?

   a. Fish and shellfish are less likely to spoil than red meat and poultry.
   b. Quality in fish and shellfish is measured by smell and appearance.
   c. Fish that may be eaten raw must be commercially frozen prior to consumption.
   d. Molluscan shellfish tags must be kept for 90 days from the date a container of shellstock is emptied.

10. Which of the following storage practices should prompt a manager to take corrective action?

    a. Products in the dry storage area being rotated on first-in, first-out stock basis.
    b. Foods stored in the walk-in freezer are stored on slatted shelves that are 6 inches above the floor.
    c. Raw poultry is stored above potato salad in the walk-in refrigerator.
    d. Cleaning and sanitizing agents and pesticides are stored in a locked and labeled cabinet in the dry food storage area.

11. Pork roasts should be cooked to an internal temperature of at least _____ for 4 minutes to be considered safe.

    a. 140°F (60°C).
    b. 145°F (63°C).
    c. 155°F (68°C).
    d. 165°F (74°C).

12. Hot foods should be held at _____ or above, and cold foods should be held at _____ or below.

    a. 165°F (74°C); 41°F (5°C).
    b. 165°F (74°C); 32°F (0°C).
    c. 135°F (57°C); 41°F (5°C).
    d. 135°F (57°C); 32°F (0°C).

13. Poultry and stuffed meats should be cooked to an internal temperature of _____ for 15 seconds to be considered safe.

    a. 135°F (57°C).
    b. 145°F (63°C).
    c. 155°F (68°C).
    d. 165°F (74°C).

14. Ground meats should be cooked to an internal temperature of _____ for 15 seconds to be considered safe.

    a. 135°F (57°C).
    b. 145°F (63°C).
    c. 155°F (68°C).
    d. 165°F (74°C).

15. All PHF (TCS) that have been cooked and cooled need to be reheated to an internal temperature of _____ within 2 hours to be considered safe.

    a. 135°F (57°C).
    b. 145°F (63°C).
    c. 155°F (68°C).
    d. 165°F (74°C).

16. According to the *Food Code*, foods that are cooked and then cooled must be cooled in which of the following ways?

    a. From 135°F (57°C) to 41°F (5°C) in 12 hours.
    b. From 135°F (57°C) to 41°F (5°C) in 8 hours.
    c. From 135°F (57°C) to 70°F (21°C) in 2 hours, and from 135°F (57°C) to 41°F (5°C) within 6 hours.
    d. From 135°F (57°C) to 70°F (21°C) in 4 hours, and from 70°F (21°C) to 41°F (5°C) in an additional 2 hours.

17. Temperatures in refrigerated storage should be measured daily with the thermometer placed in the _____ part of the unit.

    a. Coldest.
    b. Warmest.
    c. Highest.
    d. Lowest.

Answers to these multiple-choice questions are provided in Appendix A.

References/Suggested Readings

Food and Drug Administration. 2009. *2009 Food Code*. U.S. Public Health Service. Washington, DC.

Food and Drug Administration. 2001. *Fish and Fishery Products Hazards and Control Guide, 3rd ed.* U.S. Public Health Service. Washington, DC.

Longrèe, Karla; and G. Armbruster. 1996. *Quantity Food Sanitation.* John Wiley and Sons. New York, NY.

Thayer, David W., et al. 1996. *Radiation Pasteurization of Food.* Council for Agricultural Science and Technology Issue Paper, No. 7. April.

Suggested Web Sites

Gateway to Government Food Safety Information
www.foodsafety.gov

United States Department of Agriculture (USDA)
www.usda.gov

Centers for Disease Control and Prevention (CDC)
www.cdc.gov

Food and Drug Administration (FDA)
www.fda.gov

The American Egg Board
www.aeb.org

American Meat Institute
www.meatami.org

The National Chicken Council
www.eatchicken.com

U.S. Poultry and Egg Association
www.poultryegg.org

USDA Foods Safety and Inspection Service (FSIS)
www.fsis.usda.gov

USDA/FDA Food and Nutrition Information Center
www.nal.usda.gov/fnic

Environmental Protection Agency (EPA)
www.epa.gov

Partnerships for Food Safety Education
  www.fightbac.org

The Food Marketing Institute www.fmi.org

Food Irradiation Processing Alliance
  www.fipa.us

International Food Information Council
  www.ific.org

Produce Marketing Association
  www.pma.com

Learn How To:

- Understand the importance of properly maintaining equipment and utensils and the influence it has on food safety.
- Describe how work tasks are conducted in work centers.
- Understand how the preparation and service of food flows through retail food establishments.
- Understand the basic, design requirements that apply to floor and counter-mounted equipment used in retail food establishments.
- Recognize the different types of cooking, refrigeration, preparation, and dishwashing equipment available for use in retail food establishments.
- Describe how proper installation and maintenance affect the operation of equipment used during the course of food production, holding, display, and handling.
- Explain the role of proper lighting in food production and warewashing areas.
- Explain how proper heating, air conditioning, and ventilation affect food sanitation, employee comfort, and productivity in retail food establishments.

CHAPTER 5b

Facilities, Equipment, and Utensils

Facilities, Equipment, and Utensils

Proper Equipment Usage

The local health inspector arrived for a routine visit at the store. The inspection consisted of a walk-through of every department, checking for overall compliance. During the visit, the inspector found the refrigerated display case containing a variety of gourmet cheeses had a temperature of 51°F. The case contained over $2,000 of hard cheeses and soft cheeses. The manager called over an employee and told him to take care of the situation. What is the problem and how should the employee correct the situation?

Essential Terms

Easily movable	Non-food contact surface
Easily cleanable	Sealed
Equipment	Smooth
Kitchenware	Work centers
Tableware	
Utensils	
Single-use articles	

Design, Layout, and Facilities

The design, layout, and facilities provided in a retail food establishment must be consistent with the types of foods being sold there. The equipment used in the various departments must be properly designed and sized to meet the production needs of the area. A layout that works well in one establishment may not necessarily be suitable for another that produces and sells different food items. Most equipment and facilities will be used for several years. Therefore, managers should seek a design that meets current needs and accommodates increased sales and new items are offered for sale in the future. Some general areas commonly found in retail food establishments are:

- Delivery and receiving
- Storage
- Preparation

Design, Layout, and Facilities

- Hot- and cold-holding
- Display
- Handling and service
- Warewashing, cleaning, and sanitizing
- Waste storage and pickup
- Housekeeping
- Toilet facilities.

It is important you develop a flow diagram of your establishment's operation in order to plan the physical facilities for each function.

Display area

When planning a retail food establishment:

- Understand and visualize each function that will be conducted within the different departments
- Determine the specific tasks employees must complete when performing the function
- Arrange the tasks in a way that allows a smooth and sequential flow within that department or area.

The activities carried out by employees in the various departments are called functions.

Regulatory Considerations

When planning facilities for retail food establishments, you must know about and comply with national, state, and local standards and codes related to:

- Health
- Safety
- Building
- Fire
- Zoning
- Environmental code standards.

The **equipment** used in retail food establishments should meet the American National Standards Institute (ANSI) standards and bear the stamp of approval of recognized third-party certification organizations. Some examples of these organizations include:

- NSF International
- Underwriters Laboratories (UL), Inc.
- American Gas Association (AGA).

Buyers who purchase equipment approved by these organizations are assured quality materials are used in the construction. Also, the items are designed and constructed to meet accepted food sanitation criteria.

UL and NSF seals

Work Center Planning

The departments in a retail food establishment are commonly organized into **work centers**. These are areas where a group of closely related tasks are performed by an individual or individuals. The number of work centers required in a department depends on the number of functions to be performed and the volume of material to be handled.

An employee should be able to complete the related tasks at the work center without moving away from it. The work center should also be large enough to do the job yet small enough to reduce travel and conserve time and effort. A properly designed work center will provide adequate facilities and space for:

Plan work centers carefully.

- Efficient production
- Fast handling and service
- A pleasant environment
- Effective cleanup.

Equipment Selection

It is extremely important to select the right piece of equipment for the job. Compare different pieces of equipment for a particular job and look at such features as:

- Design
- Construction
- Durability
- Easily cleaned
- Size
- Cost
- Safety
- Overall ability to do the job.

> **Purchase equipment that will improve the quality of food, reduce labor and material costs, improve sanitation, and contribute to the bottom line of the establishment.**

Size and Design

> **Purchase equipment that fits into the space available and can handle your anticipated future needs.**

Design is an important feature of food equipment since the equipment used in a retail food establishment is subject to constant use and abuse. Equipment and utensils must be designed to function properly when used for their intended purposes.

Equipment that sits on the floor must be:

- Elevated on 6-inch (15 cm) legs, or;
- Sealed to the floor, or;
- Mounted on casters to make it **easily movable**.

Clearance space and mobility make it easier to clean the floor under and behind the equipment. Equipment **sealed** to the floor will prevent the accumulation of debris and the harborage of pests.

In retail food establishments, display shelving units, display refrigeration units, and display freezer units located in the customer shopping areas do not have to be elevated or sealed to the floor. However, the floor under these units must be maintained in a clean and sanitary manner.

Floor-mounted equipment

Counter-mounted equipment

Counter-mounted equipment (that is not easily movable) should be on 4-inch (10-cm) legs. This provides clearance between the counter top and the bottom of the equipment and makes it easier to clean under and around the equipment. The equipment may also be sealed to the counter.

Major Costs Associated with the Purchase of Equipment:

- Purchase price
- Installation cost
- Operating costs
- Maintenance costs
- Finance charges.

Construction Materials

The *Food Code* and construction standards, such as those from ANSI, require food equipment and utensils to:

- Be **smooth**
- Be seamless
- Be **easily cleanable**
- Be easy to take apart
- Be easy to reassemble
- Have rounded corners and edges.

Materials used in the construction of utensils and food-contact surfaces of equipment must be nontoxic and not impart colors, odors, or tastes to foods. Under normal use, these materials must also be safe; durable; corrosion-resistant; and resistant to chipping, pitting, and deterioration.

Metals

Metals are very popular materials in retail food establishments. Chromium over steel gives an easily cleanable, high-luster finish. It is commonly used in conjunction with small appliances. Noncorrosive metals formed by the alloys of iron, nickel, and chromium may also be used in the construction of food equipment.

Lead, brass, copper, cadmium, and galvanized metal can cause a chemical poisoning when they come into contact with high-acid foods (foods that have a low pH). Therefore, these materials must not be used as food-contact surfaces for equipment, utensils, and containers.

Stainless Steel

Stainless steel is one of the most popular materials in retail food establishments. It is commonly the material of choice for food containers, counter tops, sinks, dish tables, dishwashers, and ventilation hood systems. Stainless steel has a durable, shiny surface that easily shows soil and is easy to clean and maintain. Stainless steel also resists high temperatures, rust, and stain formation.

One factor that influences the cost of stainless steel is the extent of polishing desired, because polishing requires labor, material, and energy. Finish No. 4 (on a scale of 1–8) is most commonly preferred for food production areas whereas higher finishes are usually preferred in display and handling areas.

Plastic

You must be sure to buy food equipment that is made of only food-grade plastics. Select the one that works best for you based on intended use and durability. The harder, more durable plastics are easier to clean and sanitize. Some examples of plastics used in retail food establishments are:

- Acrylics (used to make covers for food containers)

Food-contact surfaces are the parts of equipment and utensils that normally come into contact with food or from which food may drain, drip, splash, or spill into food or onto a surface that is normally in contact with food.

Non-food contact surfaces are the remaining parts of the equipment and utensils and the surrounding area that should not make contact with food during production.

Abrasive cleaners and scouring pads can scratch the surface of the metal and cause harborage areas for disease-causing microorganisms.

- Fiberglass (used in boxes, bus trays, and trays)
- Polyethylene (used in storage containers and bowls).

Plastic and fiberglass are very popular in retail food establishments because they are durable, inexpensive, and can be molded into different combinations.

Wood

The *Food Code* permits limited use of wood materials including hard maple or an equally hard, close-grained wood for cutting boards, cutting blocks, and baker's tables. Wood is also approved for paddles used in pizza operations.

Wood versus plastic materials

Advantages of Wood:	Disadvantages of Wood:
- Light in weight - Economical.	- Porous to bacteria and moisture - Absorbs food odors and stains - Wears easily under normal use - Requires frequent maintenance and replacement.

The consensus seems to be that the disadvantages of using wood for food-contact surfaces outweigh the advantages. This is primarily because of the high degree of maintenance required and problems with keeping the equipment clean and sanitary.

Types of Equipment

The NSF and UL provide independent evaluations of equipment and materials. The NSF and UL emblems on a piece of equipment verify the equipment has been tested and meets the requirements prescribed in their standards.

Cooking Equipment

The most important criteria to use when selecting cooking equipment are the types and quantities of food prepared, ease of cleaning, durability, and energy conservation. The frame, door, exterior, and interior materials of cooking equipment should contribute to the durability and cleanability of the equipment. The type and thickness of insulation materials contribute to the energy efficiency of this equipment.

Ovens

Ovens are important pieces of equipment in the bakery and may well be used by other departments in a retail food establishment. The heat in an oven is distributed by radiation, conduction, or convection, depending on the type oven being used. A good oven's temperature should rise to 450°F (232°C) within 20 minutes, and proper heat circulation is important. Ovens should be able to cool quickly when a drop in temperature is required. All ovens should be well insulated to prevent heat loss. Ovens should be in a well-ventilated area.

Types of Ovens	
Range	**Primary Department: Bakery** **Heat Distribution: Conduction** • Commonly used in small operations • Cooking surface on top of oven.

(continued)

Types of Ovens (continued)

Rotisserie 	**Primary Department: Bakery** **Heat Distribution: Conduction** • Used to cook and hold poultry and meats • Powered by gas, electricity, or wood burning.
Deck 	**Primary Department: Bakery** **Heat Distribution: Conduction** • Multiple ovens stacked on top of one another • Each oven contains separate heating elements.
Convection 	**Primary Department: Bakery** **Heat Distribution: Conduction** • High-speed fan circulates heated air around food to reduce cooking time. • Multiple racks allow for more cooking in a smaller space.
Microwave 	**Primary Department: Bakery** **Heat Distribution: Conduction** • Used for thawing, heating, and reheating foods • Cooks small quantities of food quickly.

Other types of ovens may be used in retail food establishments. These include rotary, infrared, conveyor, and roll-in units. Each of these pieces of equipment has unique features and has been designed for special applications. You should contact your equipment supplier to determine if this type of equipment is best suited to carry out the functions required in your operation.

Refrigeration and Low-temperature Storage Equipment

Refrigeration is an important feature of the safe transport and storage of perishable foods. Cold-holding permits us to have an ample supply of meats, poultry, fish, dairy products, fruits, and vegetables throughout the country during practically all seasons of the year. Refrigeration during transportation, combined with improved cold storage facilities, has helped to stabilize the price of perishable foods.

Refrigerators and freezers are used to keep perishable foods fresh and preserve the safety and wholesomeness of PHF (TCS). Many foods deteriorate rapidly at room temperature. Retail food establishments can reduce spoilage, waste, and shrinkage by keeping foods at lower temperatures until they are used.

Proper cooling requires removing heat from food quickly enough to prevent microbial growth. Improper cooling of PHF (TCS) is consistently identified as one of the leading contributors to foodborne illness. Bacteria grow best at temperatures between 70°F (21°C) and 120°F (49°C). **The *Food Code* states cooked PHF (TCS) must be cooled from 135°F (57°C) to 70°F (21°C) within 2 hours and from 135°F (57°C) to 41°F (5°C) or below within 6 hours.**

All types of refrigerators and freezers have a maximum capacity for cooling foods. Too often, employees put large amounts of hot food in a unit and rely on it to "cool" the food. On the contrary, the addition of large amounts of hot food causes the inside temperature of the unit to rise above acceptable storage temperatures. This, in turn, causes food in the unit to be stored in the temperature danger zone. Don't forget the primary purpose of a refrigerator is to take foods already at or near the proper cold-holding temperature and keep them out of the temperature danger zone.

The efficient operation of a refrigeration unit depends on several factors including:

- Design
- Construction
- Capacity of the equipment.

> **Proper air circulation both inside and outside the refrigerator makes it more efficient.**

The storage of food in shallow containers placed on slatted shelves or tray slides to permit good circulation of the chilled air is essential for both short- and long-term storage. Do not line shelves in refrigerators and freezers with sheet pans, foil, plastic, or cardboard. This decreases airflow in the storage compartment and reduces the cooling capacity of the equipment. Store raw products under cooked and ready-to-eat foods to prevent cross contamination.

Proper construction of cold storage units includes sturdy construction of doors, hardware, and fixtures. Doors may be full-length or half-length, and shelving should be adjustable. Door gaskets should be durable and easy to clean. They must be replaced when worn.

The size of the refrigerator or freezer needed depends on the size of the work area and the type and amount of food to be stored in the unit. Refrigeration and low-temperature storage equipment must be adequately sized and properly installed to assure reliable and efficient operations. If your target food product temperature is 41°F (5°C) or lower, you will most likely need to maintain the air temperature in the refrigeration unit at a lower temperature, such as 38°F (3°C).

Maintenance of the refrigeration equipment in the various departments is an important responsibility. These units must be cleaned on a regular basis to maintain good sanitary conditions and eliminate odors. The inside walls, floor, shelves, and other accessories of a walk-in refrigeration unit must be cleaned regularly to remove spills and debris. Don't forget to clean the fan grates and condenser as part of your routine cleaning.

Refrigeration equipment

Reach-in Refrigeration

Several types of reach-in refrigeration units can be used for cold storage in retail food establishments. Some of the more popular models are upright, under-the-counter, and mobile units. Reach-in refrigerators are commonly found in the deli, bakery, and other departments of a retail food establishment. The capacity of reach-in refrigerators varies greatly.

Types of Refrigeration

Reach-in

Courtesy of Hobart Corp.

Primary Departments:
- Bakery
- Deli
- Convenience Store.

- Models range in capacity
- Can have multiple doors
- May have external thermometer attached to a sensing device inside the warmest part of the refrigeration unit.

Walk-In

Primary Departments:
- Dairy
- Meat
- Seafood
- Deli
- Produce
- C-Store.

- Stores large quantities of perishable foods between 32°F (0°C) and 41°F (5°C)
- Used to thaw products
- Can be combined with reach-in dairy/deli display cases that are loaded from inside the walk-in
- Should be located at a site that is easy to get to from the receiving and production areas
- Door openings may have 4-inch-wide plastic strips called strip curtains, which reduce cool air loss when the door is open
- May have external thermometer attached to a sensing device placed at the warmest location in the refrigeration unit.

(continued)

Types of Refrigeration (continued)

Display

Primary Departments:
- Grocery
- Meat
- Seafood
- Deli
- Dairy
- Produce
- C-Store.

- Keep cold foods out of the temperature danger zone and frozen foods solidly frozen while on display.
- Avoid stocking above the maximum load line.
- Avoid covering vents and return air openings.
- Properly control defrost cycles.
- May be open air or have closing doors.

Cook-chill and Rapid-chill Systems

Cook-chill is a system in which food is:

- Cooked using conventional cooking methods
- Rapidly chilled using a chiller
- Stored for a limited time
- Reheated before service to the customer.

The food is typically chilled to 37°F (3°C) in 90 minutes or less and is stored at temperatures between 33°F (1°C) and 38°F (3°C) for 5 days. Day 1 is considered the day of production and Day 5 is the day of service.

Rapid-chill equipment
Courtesy of Hobart

The advantages of this system include reduction of peaks and valleys in production and readily available foods. The disadvantages of this system include the high cost of the chiller and the storage space requirements.

Rapid-chill systems are designed to cool hot foods very quickly. This type of equipment can typically get a few hundred pounds of hot food through the temperature danger zone in 2 hours or less. Although this equipment is somewhat expensive, it can be a very good investment for some retail food establishments that work with large masses of food or with foods that are challenging to cool quickly.

Watch out for metal fasteners on plastic pouches. They are a physical hazard and should be discarded immediately upon removal.

Be Prepared in Case of a Power Failure:

1. Keep refrigerator doors closed.
2. Monitor product temperatures.
3. Discard products that are in the temperature danger zone for more than 4 hours.

Hot-holding Equipment

PHF (TCS) that has been cooked and is to be eaten hot must be held at 135°F (57°C) or above. An important fact to remember is hot-holding equipment will not raise the temperature of foods very much. In order for hot-holding equipment to work properly, the food must be at 135°F (57°C) or above when it is put into or onto this equipment.

Hot-holding equipment uses steam, heating elements, or light bulbs to keep foods hot. This equipment should be checked regularly to make sure it is working properly. Food temperatures must be monitored to -assure they are being maintained at 135°F (57°C) or above. Hot-holding units must be cleaned regularly, and food should be rotated using an FIFO procedure.

Hot-holding equipment

Other Types of Food Equipment

Slicers

The basic design of food slicers includes a circular knife blade and carriage that passes under the blade. Foods to be sliced are placed on the carriage and fed either automatically or by hand. Slicers can be dangerous if not used properly. The manufacturer's instructions should always be followed, and employees should receive training on safe operation and proper cleaning of this equipment.

Slicer
Courtesy of Hobart Corp.

Mixers, Grinders, Choppers, Tenderizers, and Saws

Mixers, grinders, choppers, tenderizers, and saws are examples of equipment commonly found in a retail food establishment. Some of these pieces of equipment are available as counter and floor models.

Mixers can also be used to shred and grind when different accessories and attachments are used. Floor model mixers have three standard attachments: (1) a paddle beater for general mixing, that can be used to mash, mix, or blend foods and ingredients; (2) a whip to incorporate air into products; and (3) a dough hook used to mix and knead dough.

Mechanical tenderizers are commonly used to improve the edible quality of meat. Tenderizers cut connective tissue in meats and poultry by making incisions with stainless steel blades. The depth and the spacing of the blades and the frequency with which the meat is penetrated control the amount of tenderizing.

Meat grinder
Courtesy of Hobart Corp.

Grinders and choppers work well with a variety of fresh foods and ingredients including meats and vegetables.

Band saws are commonly used in meat and fish processing areas. Heavy-duty saws are best suited for large volume retail food establishments. These saws are designed to cut meat and bone and hold up under continuous heavy use. Counter-top and light-duty saws are commonly used in small delis, meat shops, and small establishments. This equipment is excellent when cutting boneless meats, chicken, and fish.

Band saws must be durable, easily cleanable, and safe to use. Food-contact surfaces must be made of nontoxic materials that provide good sanitation qualities. Employees must be able to disassemble this equipment for easy cleaning, preferably without tools. Band saws must be properly guarded or have a "dead man" switch to protect the operator from contact with the blade.

Band saw
Courtesy of Hobart Corp.

Ice Machines

Ice is an important item in retail food establishments. It is used to chill beverages and preserve the freshness of fish and some produce items during display.

Ice must be made from potable water, and ice machines must protect the ice during production and storage.

> **Ice is food and must be handled with the same degree of care as other food items.**

The parts of an ice machine that come into contact with the ice must be smooth, durable, easily cleanable, and constructed of nontoxic materials. These food-contact surfaces must be cleaned and sanitized regularly to prevent the growth of mold and other microorganisms. The drain line from the ice machine must be equipped with an air gap to protect the ice from contamination due to backflow. You will learn more about backflow and air gaps in Chapter 7.

Scoops, shovels, carts, and other equipment used to dispense or transport ice must meet the

Ice machine

design and construction criteria for food-contact surfaces. When not in use, this equipment should be stored in a manner that will protect it from contamination.

Employees must never dispense ice by passing a glass or cup through the ice. This can cause glass from the container to break off and become a physical hazard in the ice. Food and beverage containers must not be stored in ice that will be used for drinking purposes. This prevents contamination of the ice your customers may consume. When scoops are stored inside an ice machine, they must be placed in a bracket mounted to a wall of the ice storage compartment. This will permit employees to use the handle of the scoop without their hands touching the ice or the food-contact surface of the scoop.

Do not store food and beverage containers in ice served to customers.

Ambient Temperature Display Equipment

Many foods in retail food establishments are displayed at room temperature. These include shelf-stable products, certain types of produce, bakery items that have a low water activity (bagels, cookies, doughnuts, etc.) and bulk foods, such as candy, peanuts, and cereals. These are not considered PHF (TCS), and they can be held safely at room temperature. However, they must be protected from contamination by customers and the environment.

Ambient display equipment can have both food-contact and non-food–contact surfaces. The food-contact surfaces of the equipment must be cleaned and sanitized regularly to remove contaminants. Non-food–contact surfaces must be cleaned regularly to remove spills and eliminate soil.

> Stock on display should be rotated using the FIFO method, and utensils should be provided so customers will not contaminate unpackaged food with their bare hands.

Some produce display equipment is equipped with misters that help assure the freshness of fruits and vegetables and prevent wilting, dehydration, and shrinkage. These misters must be connected to a potable water supply, and the system and heads of the system must be properly cleaned and maintained to assure maximum freshness, safety, and wholesomeness of produce exposed to the mist.

Ambient temperature display equipment

Live Seafood Display and Holding Tanks

Fish, crustacean shellfish (crabs, lobsters, and shrimp), and molluscan shellfish (oysters, clams, and mussels in the shell) are live and perishable products that must be protected to remain safe, wholesome, and attractive to customers. The quality of the product in live seafood tanks is only as good as the water in the tank. Water quality is critical, and the key to maintaining optimum water quality is filtration.

Produce case with misting heads

There are two different types of seafood display tanks, one for fish and one for molluscan shellfish.

To operate a fish or crustacean shellfish tank, the water quality and tank maintenance are important to maintain the health of the animals, but these products are not ready-to-eat and are intended to be cooked by the consumer.

To operate a live molluscan shellfish tank, additional precautions are required because the shellfish may be eaten raw. Before an operator installs and sells raw molluscan shellfish from a live tank, a variance must be acquired from the regulatory authority.

Some important handling and maintenance steps to use with live molluscan shellfish tanks are:

- Clean and replace the ultraviolet light to assure proper intensity to kill pathogens.
- Cull out and discard dead, cracked, and weak molluscan shellfish daily.
- Before adding molluscan shellfish to a tank, make sure they are cleaned thoroughly and cull out dead, cracked, and weak shellfish.
- Never mix molluscan shellfish with crustacean shellfish.
- Never allow molluscan shellfish to be submerged in the system.
- Never cook dead or dying shellfish from live displays as a way to reduce shrinkage.
- Clean the tank interior to keep it free of algae and prevent slime buildup that may harbor bacterial pathogens.

Life seafood display system

Single-service and Single-use Articles

Single-service articles include tableware, carryout utensils, and other items, such as bags, containers, stirrers, straws, and wrappers designed and constructed to be used only one time by only one person. After one use, the article is discarded.

Single-use articles include items, such as wax paper, butcher paper, deli paper, plastic wrap, and certain types of food containers that are designed to be used once and discarded.

A retail food establishment should provide single-use and single-service articles for food handlers if it does not have proper facilities for cleaning and sanitizing multi-use kitchenware and tableware (see Chapter 6). These establishments must also provide single-service articles for use by consumers.

Materials used to make single-service and single-use articles must not permit the transfer of harmful substances or pass on colors, odors, or tastes to food. These materials must be safe and clean when used in retail food establishments.

Warewashing Equipment

Warewashing is the process used to clean and sanitize the equipment, utensils, dishes, glasses, and so on, that are used during the preparation, handling, and consumption of foods. Proper warewashing is one of the most important jobs in a retail food establishment. As you learned in Chapter 3, contaminated equipment and utensils have been identified as sources of contamination and cross contamination that can cause foodborne illness.

> **Equipment and utensil warewashing should be performed in a room or area separate from food production areas.**

Warewashing areas must be well lighted and well ventilated. Noise-absorbing materials may be installed on walls and the ceiling to lower noise levels in warewashing areas.

Some of the items most frequently washed and sanitized in a retail food establishment are:

- **Utensils,** such as knives, forks, spoons, and tongs
- **Kitchenware,** such as pots, pans, cutting boards, slicers, grinders, and mixers
- **Tableware,** such as dishes, glasses, and eating utensils.

The purpose of warewashing is to clean and sanitize equipment and utensils. It consists of two phases:

1. A cleaning phase in which visible soil is removed from the surface of the item through washing and rinsing.

2. A sanitizing phase in which the number of disease-causing microorganisms on a cleaned surface is reduced to safe levels.

Cleaning and sanitizing operations can be performed either manually or mechanically. Most retail food establishments use manual warewashing operations to clean and sanitize equipment and utensils. Some larger establishments may use a mechanical dishwashing machine to perform these tasks.

Manual Warewashing

A manual warewashing area must provide adequate space to store soiled equipment and utensils. Items to be cleaned must be pre-flushed or pre-scraped and, if necessary, pre-soaked to remove food particles and soil. A hose and nozzle or other device must be provided to pre-flush and pre-scrape food soil into a garbage container or disposal. This equipment must be located at the soiled end of the warewashing operation to avoid contaminating cleaned and sanitized equipment and utensils.

Manual warewashing can also be performed using a bucket and brush, wall-mounted hose units, and spray units. These processes are explained in more detail in Chapter 6 of this book.

Three-compartment sink

The compartments of the three-compartment sink must be large enough to accommodate the largest pieces of equipment and utensils used in the retail food establishment. Supply each compartment with hot and cold potable running water. Provide drainboards or easily movable dish tables of adequate size for proper handling of soiled utensils prior to washing, and for air-drying cleaned and sanitized items.

Mechanical Warewashing

Mechanical warewashing machines may be used by retail food establishments but are far less common than a three-compartment sink. Dishwashing machines can be used to clean and sanitize equipment and utensils that do not have electrical parts and that will fit into the machine. When using a single-tank, stationary-rack dishwashing machine, the dishes are placed on racks and washed one rack at a time with jets of water within a single tank. They are operated by opening a door, inserting a rack of dishes, closing the door, and starting the machine.

The Most Common Types of Mechanical Dishwashers Used in Retail Food Establishments Are:

- Single-tank
- Stationary-rack
- Low-temperature.

A dishwashing machine must automatically dispense detergents and sanitizers. These machines must have a visual means to verify detergents and

KEY CONCEPT

sanitizers are delivered or a visual or audible alarm to signal if the detergent and sanitizers are not delivered to the respective washing and sanitizing cycles. The machine must be large enough to accommodate the size and volume of equipment and utensils to be cleaned and sanitized.

Low-temperature dishwashers are similar in design to the single-tank, stationary-rack dishwashing machine. However, they use chemicals to sanitize equipment and utensils. This allows lower water temperatures, which conserves energy.

When purchasing a dishwashing machine, you should also consider the cost of operation and maintenance. An adequate supply of very hot water is required for the final rinse in a high-temperature dishwashing machine. The high temperatures required for effective sanitization make it expensive and unsafe to maintain general purpose hot water at these temperatures. Therefore, a separate booster heater is needed to raise the temperature of the sanitizing rinse water to the proper temperature. The booster heater must be properly sized, installed, and operated to deliver water at the volume, flow pressure, and temperature required for the operation.

Single-tank dishwashing machine
Courtesy of Hobart Corp.

Installation

Proper installation is required to assure equipment functions properly. The best design and construction will be worthless if electrical, gas, water, or drain connections are inadequate or improperly installed. The dealer who sells you equipment may or may not be responsible for its installation. Arrangements for installation will usually be specified in your purchase agreement. Following installation, employees must be trained to operate equipment correctly and safely.

Maintenance and Replacement

The cost of care and upkeep on a piece of equipment may determine whether or not its purchase and use are justified. Successful maintenance of equipment requires definite plans to prolong its life and maintain its usefulness. Such plans place emphasis on a few simple procedures:

- Keep the equipment clean.
- Follow the manufacturer's printed directions for care and operation.
- Post the instruction card for a piece of equipment near it.
- Stress careful operation and maintenance schedules.
- Make needed repairs promptly.

Some valuable suggestions for the care of equipment are:

- Assign the care of a machine to a responsible person.
- Check the cleanliness of machines daily.
- Have repairs performed promptly and by a properly trained person.

Lubricants used on food equipment may directly or indirectly end up in food. Therefore, all lubricants used on food-contact surfaces, bearings and gears, and other components of equipment that are located so the lubricants may leak, drip, or be forced into food or onto food-contact surfaces must be approved as food additives or generally recognized as safe. These lubricants should be used in the smallest amount needed to get the job done.

Lighting

Proper lighting in production and dishwashing areas:

- Increases productivity
- Improves workmanship
- Reduces eye fatigue and employee irritability
- Decreases accidents and waste due to employee error
- Shows when a surface is soiled and when it has been properly cleaned.

Glass and food do not mix.
Courtesy of Shat-R-Shield, Inc.

Food production and warewashing areas should be furnished with the proper amount of lighting and soft colors that reduce glare. Locate lights to eliminate shadows on work surfaces or glare and excessive brightness in the field of vision.

The amount of light required in a department or area depends on the kind of work performed there. The following light intensity levels are recommended in the *Food Code*:

Recommended Light Intensity Levels

10 foot-candles at a distance of 30 inches above the floor

- Walk-in refrigeration units
- Dry food storage areas
- Other areas and rooms during periods of cleaning.

20 foot-candles at a distance of 30 inches above the floor

- Areas where fresh produce and packaged foods are offered for sale and consumption
- Areas used for handwashing
- Areas used for dishwashing
- Areas used for equipment and utensil storage
- Toilet rooms.

50 foot-candles at the work surface

- Where an employee is working with unpackaged, potentially hazardous food
- Where an employee is working with food, utensils, and equipment, such as knives, slicers, grinders, or saws
- Where employee safety is an overriding concern.

The food regulations in some state and local jurisdictions may require higher illumination levels in retail food establishments, especially during periods of cleaning. Consult the food regulation in your jurisdiction to determine what lighting levels are required for your store.

Light bulbs must be shielded, coated, or otherwise shatter-resistant when used in areas where there is exposed food; clean equipment, utensils, and linens;

Plastic-coated shatterproof bulbs
Courtesy of Shat-R-Shield, Inc.

or unwrapped single-service and single-use utensils. This is to prevent glass fragments from getting into food and onto food-contact surfaces. Shielded or shatter-resistant bulbs are not required in areas where packaged foods are stored and will not be affected by broken glass falling onto them, and the packages are capable of being cleaned of debris from broken bulbs before being opened.

Light bulbs over self-service buffets and salad bars must also be shielded or shatter-resistant. In addition, this lighting must not mislead customers about the quality of the food items on display.

Use shielded lighting over exposed foods.

Heating, Ventilation, and Air Conditioning (HVAC)

Air conditioning in retail food establishments means more than simply "cooling the air." It includes heating, humidity control, circulation, filtering, and cooling of the air. HVAC systems must filter, warm, humidify, and circulate the air in the winter and maintain comfortable air temperature in the summer.

The National Fire Protection Association recommends all hoods be equipped with a fire extinguishing system.

Ventilation in food production and warewashing areas is typically provided by mechanical exhaust hood systems. These systems keep rooms free of excessive heat, steam, condensation, vapors, obnoxious odors, smoke, and fumes. The standard ventilation system used in retail food establishments consists of a hood, fan, and intake and exhaust air ducts and vents. Ventilation hood systems must be designed and constructed to prevent grease or condensation from dripping onto food, equipment, utensils, linens, or single-service and single-use articles. The capacity of the ventilation system should be based on the quantity of vapor and hot air to be removed.

Hoods are usually constructed of stainless steel or a comparable material that provides a durable, smooth, and easily cleanable surface. The hood

Ventilation hood system

should be equipped with filters or other grease-extracting equipment to prevent drippage onto food.

Filters and other grease-removal equipment must be:

- Easily removed for cleaning and replacement
- Designed to be cleaned in place.

Fires at retail food establishments have been caused by the combustion of grease that accumulates in filters and ducts. Cleaning and replacement of filters must be part of your routine maintenance program. Intake and exhaust air ducts must be cleaned so they do not become a source of contamination of dust, dirt, and other materials. If vented to the outside, ventilation systems must not create a public health nuisance or unlawful discharge.

Summary

Back to the Story . . . Cheeses must be stored and displayed in refrigerated equipment that maintains an ambient temperature of 41°F (54°C) or less. While hard cheeses are less susceptible to contamination than soft cheeses, when the ambient temperature is above the required temperatures for more than 4 hours, or when the time is unknown, all product should be destroyed. The employee should dispose of all the cheese and the refrigeration unit should be repaired. Routine monitoring and maintenance of equipment is essential for smooth operation and efficiency. The establishment should establish routine checks of equipment and maintain equipment logs to verify the equipment is working properly.

✔ The basic needs of a retail food establishment will determine the type and size of equipment purchased. When purchasing equipment, look for items that:
- Will serve the current and future needs of the operation
- Can be properly cleaned and sanitized
- Do not require extraordinary maintenance and repair.

✔ The *Food Code* and construction standards from the American National Standards Institute (ANSI) require food equipment and utensils to be:
- Smooth
- Easily cleanable
- Easy to take apart
- Easy to reassemble
- Equipped with rounded corners and edges.

✔ Materials used as food-contact surfaces must be safe, durable, corrosion-resistant, nonabsorbent, and resistant to chipping, pitting, and deterioration. These materials must not allow the transfer of harmful substances, colors, odors, or tastes to food.

✔ Always install equipment in accordance with local building, plumbing, electrical, health, and fire safety codes. The best possible design and construction of equipment is worthless if electrical, gas, water, or drain connections are inadequate or the equipment is poorly installed.

Discussion Questions (Short Answer)

1. In what ways do layout, design, and facilities planning influence a retail food establishment?
2. What is a work center? What layout features are important to the efficiency of a work center?

3. What design and construction factors should a manager consider before buying a particular piece of equipment?

4. What standards organizations are commonly involved in the testing of food equipment? How can these organizations be helpful to a retail food establishment manager?

5. What kinds of materials are commonly used in the construction of equipment and utensils? What are the advantages and disadvantages of each kind of material?

6. How does a food-contact surface differ from a non-food-contact surface?

7. What are some features that make a piece of equipment easily cleanable?

8. How do proper lighting and ventilation affect sanitation in a retail food establishment?

Quiz 5 (Multiple Choice)

Choose the **best** answer for each question.

1. Floor-mounted equipment on legs must be a minimum of _____ inches above the floor.

    a. 2.
    b. 4.
    c. 6.
    d. 8.

2. The cooling efficiency of a refrigerator is greatly reduced by:

    a. spacing products evenly throughout the storage area.
    b. placing products on shelves 6 inches above the floor.
    c. loosely covering the foods to be cooled in the unit.
    d. lining the shelves of the refrigerator with paper or aluminum foil.

3. Which of the following materials is not recommended for use as a food-contact surface in retail food establishments?

    a. Soft wood.
    b. Stainless steel.
    c. Plastic.
    d. Chrome-plated steel.

4. Good sanitation requires adequate lighting in food production areas in order to:

   a. provide a comfortable work environment for employees.
   b. show when a surface is soiled and when it has been properly cleaned.
   c. decrease accidents and waste due to employee error.
   d. reduce glare that causes eye fatigue.

5. Which of the following statements about ventilation is **false**?

   a. Ventilation is typically provided by means of a mechanical exhaust hood system.
   b. Ventilation hood systems must be designed and constructed to prevent grease or condensation from dripping onto food and food-contact surfaces.
   c. The hood should be equipped with filters or other grease-catching devices to prevent drippage into food.
   d. Intake and exhaust air ducts do not need cleaning if filters or other grease-catching devices are provided to collect grease and other condensation.

6. The design, layout, and facilities in a retail food establishment should be based on the:

   a. number of employees working in the store.
   b. amount of food sold each day.
   c. type of foods prepared and sold.
   d. amount of space available in food production areas.

7. Which of the following organizations does **not** routinely evaluate the design and construction of food equipment?

   a. The Food and Drug Administration.
   b. NSF International.
   c. The American Gas Association.
   d. Underwriters Laboratories, Inc.

8. Which of the following questions is **least** important when determining a retail food establishment's need for a particular piece of equipment? Will the equipment:

   a. result in improved quality of food?
   b. produce a significant savings in labor and material?
   c. improve sanitation?
   d. make the facility more attractive to customers?

9. When buying equipment, retail food establishment managers should look for equipment that:

   a. can meet the need and demands of the operation.
   b. can be used for a long time.
   c. does not require excessive repair and upkeep.
   d. All the above.

10. Which of the following statements is **false**?

    a. The size of equipment should be such that it can easily be fitted in the space available in the layout of the facility.
    b. Construction requirements for equipment vary according to whether the surface or area is a "food-contact surface" or a "splash zone."
    c. Wood is a preferred material for food-contact surfaces of equipment because it resists moisture and bacterial growth.
    d. Floor-mounted equipment that is not easily movable must be elevated on 6-inch legs or sealed to the floor on a base that is sealed to the floor.

11. Which of the following statements about ovens is **false**?

    a. A convection oven cooks food by circulating heated air around the product.
    b. Newer microwave ovens are sized to permit quantity cooking in a retail food establishment.
    c. The range oven is commonly used in retail food establishments.
    d. Deck ovens contain separate heating elements and controls for each unit.

12. Which of the following statements about refrigeration equipment is **false?**

    a. The size of the refrigerator or freezer needed depends on whether a walk-in unit is available, what is going to be stored, and how much.
    b. Mechanical refrigeration during transportation and storage is important to preserve perishable foods.
    c. Pass-through refrigeration units open from both sides and are used for storage between production and service areas.
    d. The cleanliness and care of refrigerated equipment are not important, since it is only used to store and display foods.

13. What type of equipment is required when a retail food establishment uses a manual dishwashing operation?

    a. A three- or four-compartment sink with hot and cold potable running water and drainboards or easily movable dish tables.
    b. A two-compartment sink with hot and cold potable running water and drainboards or easily movable dish tables.
    c. A two-compartment sink with suitable facilities for pre-flushing and pre-scraping the dishes before they are washed.
    d. A single-tank dishwashing machine large enough to accommodate the largest pieces of equipment and utensils used in the operation.

Answers to these multiple-choice questions are available in Appendix A.

References/Suggested Readings

Baraban, Regina S. and Joseph F. Durocher (2010). *Successful Restaurant Design*. John Wiley and Sons. New York, NY.

Birchfield, John C., and John Birchfield, Jr. (2008). *Design and Layout of Foodservice Facilities*. John Wiley and Sons. Hoboken, NJ.

Food and Drug Administration and Conference for Food Protection (2000). *Food Establishment Plan Review Guide*. Washington, DC.

Food and Drug Administration (2009). *2009 Food Code*, Chapter 4. U.S. Public Health Service. Washington, DC.

Food and Nutrition Service (1999). *A Guide for Purchasing Food Service Equipment*. U.S. Department of Agriculture. Washington, DC.

Fullen, Sharon L. (2003). *The Food Service Professional's Guide to Restaurant Design: Designing, Constructing & Renovating a Food Service Establishment*. Atlantic Publishing Group. Ocala, FL.

Katsigris, Costas, and Chris Thomas (2006). *Design and Equipment for Restaurants and Foodservice: A Management View*. John Wiley and Sons. New York, NY.

Suggested Web Sites

AK Steel Stainless Steel
www.aksteel.com/markets/stainless_steels.asp

NSF International
www.nsf.org

Underwriters Laboratories, Inc.
www.ul.com

Hobart Corporation
www.hobartcorp.com

Hussmann Company
www.hussmann.com

Katchall Industries International
www.KatchAll.com

Shat-R-Shield, Inc.
www.shat-r-shield.com

Specialty Steel Industry of North America
www.ssina.com

The Food Marketing Institute
www.fmi.org

Gateway to Government Food Safety Information
www.foodsafety.gov

San Jamar
www.sanjamar.com

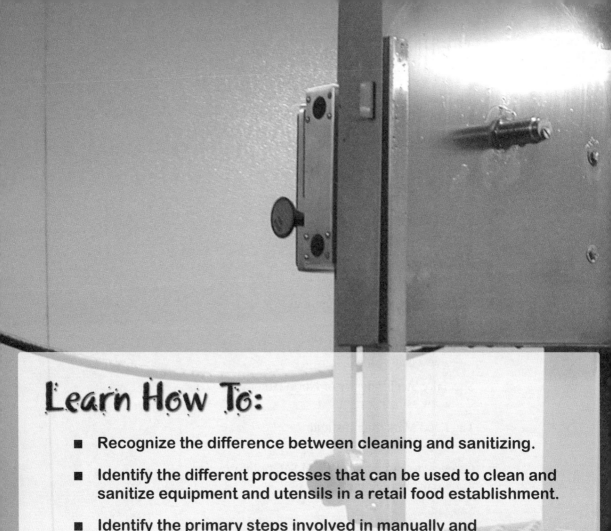

Learn How To:

- Recognize the difference between cleaning and sanitizing.

- Identify the different processes that can be used to clean and sanitize equipment and utensils in a retail food establishment.

- Identify the primary steps involved in manually and mechanically cleaning and sanitizing equipment and utensils.

- Describe the factors that affect cleaning efficiency.

- Identify the procedures used to clean environmental areas in a retail food establishment.

CHAPTER 6

Cleaning and Sanitizing Operations

Children Suffer Allergic Reaction to Peanuts in Cookies

Two children were taken to the emergency room of a local hospital when they experienced allergic reactions after eating chocolate chip cookies prepared in the bakery at a local retail food establishment. The children's symptoms included red, itchy skin; swelling in their lips; and difficulty breathing.

The children's parents knew each child was allergic to peanuts. However, peanuts were not supposed to be an ingredient in the chocolate chip cookies eaten by the children. Samples of the suspect cookies were tested and traces of peanuts were found in the product.

The emergency room physician contacted the local health department, and an investigation of the incident was conducted. Health department personnel conducted an inspection of the bakery and interviewed the employees who were on duty the day the contaminated cookies were made. The recipe for the chocolate chip cookies was reviewed, and it was verified that peanuts were not an ingredient in that product. However, interviews with bakery employees revealed peanut butter cookies had been baked before the chocolate chip cookies. Each batch was baked on clean cookie sheets, lined with parchment paper to keep them from sticking. The parchment paper was reused with several batches of cookies.

How did the peanuts get into the chocolate chip cookies? What must the bakery employees do to prevent similar episodes from occurring in the future?

Essential Terms

Cleaning	Sanitizers
Cleaning agent	Chlorine
Clean-in-place (CIP)	Iodine
Detergent	Iodophors
In-place sanitizers	Quaternary ammonium compounds (quats)
Potable water	Selectivity
Sanitizing	Soap

Principles of Cleaning and Sanitizing

Cleaning and **sanitizing** are important activities in all retail food establishments. Proper cleaning and sanitizing enhance the safety and quality of

Principles of Cleaning and Sanitizing

food, increase the life expectancy of equipment and facilities, and improve overall sanitary conditions.

Cleaning and sanitizing are two distinct processes used for very different purposes. Cleaning is the physical removal of soil from surfaces of equipment and utensils. Most of the soil is food wastes and residues. The equipment and supplies used for cleaning are different from those used for sanitizing. Single-use items do not need to be cleaned. They must be discarded after use.

Sanitizing (sometimes called sanitization) is the treatment of a clean surface to reduce the number of disease-causing microorganisms to safe levels.

Water is the primary component of cleaning materials used in retail food establishments. The water supply serving an establishment must be safe to drink (potable). **Potable water**, also called safe drinking water, is free from harmful microorganisms, chemicals, and other substances that can cause disease. While the water supply must be potable, it may contain substances that bring about hardness, taste, and odors. Therefore, cleaning agents must be compatible with the characteristics of your water supply and the nature of your operation.

"Hard" water is caused by dissolved salts of calcium, magnesium, and iron. Water hardness reduces the effectiveness of detergents and leaves "lime" scale deposits on the surface of equipment. The degree of water hardness varies considerably from place to place. In severe cases, hard water must be softened to permit effective cleaning. If the water is not softened, cleaners should contain softening agents that inactivate the iron and manganese in the water without settling them out.

If there is an extended interruption in the water supply to a retail food establishment, the facility should cease operations or sell only prepackaged or pre-prepared food using single-use utensils until water service is restored.

Effective Cleaning Consists of Four Separate Events:

1. A detergent or other type of cleaner is brought into contact with the soil.
2. The soil is loosened from the surface being cleaned.
3. The loosened soil is dispersed in the wash water.
4. The dispersed soil is rinsed away along with the detergent to prevent it from being redeposited onto the clean surface.

Removal of Food Particles

Scrape and flush food particles from the surfaces of equipment and utensils before the items are placed in a cleaning solution. Use warm water when pre-flushing and pre-scraping equipment and utensils. Avoid using very hot water or steam because they tend to "bake" food particles onto the surface of equipment and utensils and that makes cleaning more difficult.

Pre-flushing makes washing easier.

Application of Cleaning Agents

A **cleaning agent** is a chemical compound formulated to remove soil and dirt. It is important to choose the cleaning agent that is right for the particular job you have. There are many methods of applying cleaning agents to equipment surfaces.

Soaking

Small equipment, equipment parts, and utensils may be immersed in cleaning solutions in a sink. By soaking equipment or utensils for a few minutes before scrubbing, you will increase the effectiveness of manual and mechanical warewashing.

Principles of Cleaning and Sanitizing

Cleaning agents typically include an acid or alkaline detergent and may include degreasers, abrasive materials, or a sanitizer.

Spray Methods

Cleaning solutions can be sprayed on equipment surfaces by using either fixed or portable spray units that use hot water or steam. These methods are used extensively in meat departments of retail food establishments.

Soaking

Clean-in-place Systems

The **clean-in-place (CIP)** method is an automated cleaning system generally used in conjunction with permanent-welded pipeline systems, such as milk pasteurization equipment. The strength and velocity of the cleaning solution moving through the pipes are chiefly responsible for removing soil in CIP operations.

Abrasive Cleaning

Abrasive cleaners, in the form of powders and pastes, are used to remove soil firmly attached to a surface. Always rinse these cleaners completely and avoid scratching the surface of equipment and utensils. Abrasive-type cleaners are not recom-

Spray cleaning

mended for use on stainless steel surfaces. Never use metal or abrasive scouring pads on food-contact surfaces because small metal pieces from the pads may promote corrosion or may be picked up in food to become a physical hazard.

Rinsing

Immediately after cleaning, thoroughly rinse all equipment surfaces with hot, potable water to remove the cleaning solution. This very important rinse step is necessary because the product or detergent used for washing can interfere with the effectiveness of the sanitizer.

Factors Affecting Cleaning Efficiency

Factors	Impact on Cleaning	Description
Type of soil to be removed	Type of soil determines cleaning agents and process used to remove soil.	Soil consists of: • Food deposits (proteins, carbohydrates, fats, and oils) • Mineral deposits (salts) • Microorganisms (bacteria, viruses, yeasts, and molds) • Dirt and debris.
Water quality	Affects soap efficiency.	• Must be potable (safe to drink) water • Cleaning agents must be compatible with the characteristics of your water supply.
Detergent or cleaner to be used	Cleaning agent or solvent—dissolves dirt and soil.	• See cleaning chart on pages 202 and 203 for more detailed information.

(continued)

Factors Affecting Cleaning Efficiency (continued)

Factors	Impact on Cleaning	Description
Water temperature	Increased water temperature helps decrease the strength of the bonds that hold soil to the surface.	• Hot enough to remove soil but not to bake it on • Heat-stable detergents work best when the water temperature is 130°F (54°C)–160°F (71°C).
Velocity or force	Removes soil and film from food-contact surfaces.	• Scrubbing or force to move soil/film from food-contact surfaces • Less force is required when detergent is working correctly.
Amount of time detergent/cleaner remains in contact with the surface	Reduces scrubbing necessary to remove soil.	• Soaking items increases cleaning efficiency.
Concentration of cleanser	Using the recommended amount of detergent improves cleaning power.	• Using too much detergent is a waste of money and may not improve cleaning.

Detergents and Cleaners to Be Used

The origin of the word **detergent** is from the Latin *detergere*, meaning "to wipe away." Water acts as a detergent when soils are readily soluble. However, we can improve the cleansing action of water by adding **soap**, alkaline detergents, acid detergents, degreasers, abrasive cleaners, detergent sanitizers, or other cleaning agents to it. The water supply serving an establishment must be safe to drink (potable). Potable water is free from harmful microorganisms, chemicals, and other substances that can cause disease.

> If there is an extended interruption in the water supply to a retail food establishment, the facility should cease operations or sell only prepackaged or pre-prepared food using single-use utensils until water service is restored.

Advantages and Disadvantages of Different Types of Detergents and Cleaners

Cleaning Agent	Advantages	Disadvantages
Soaps	• Effective for hand-washing in soft water • Limited applications as cleaners.	• Form precipitates and films in hard water • Not compatible with some sanitizers • Lose cleaning power in hard water.
Alkaline detergents	• Good general-purpose cleaners • Dissolve proteins and other organic material • Good buffers and enhance detergency	• Strong alkalis are corrosive and can harm metals, equipment surfaces, and skin.
Acid detergents	• Frequently used to remove food, mineral deposits, and hard water deposits from the surfaces of equipment and utensils	• Strong acids are corrosive to metals and irritating to skin.

(continued)

Advantages and Disadvantages of Different Types of Detergents and Cleaners (continued)

Cleaning Agent	Advantages	Disadvantages
Degreasers	• Remove grease and oily soils from hard surfaces • May be used for pre-treatment.	• Can be irritating to skin and can leave a residue.
Abrasive	• When mixed with a detergent are useful for jobs that require scrubbing, scouring, or polishing.	• Can scratch equipment surfaces • Abrasive particles may also contaminate food.
Detergent sanitizers	• Effectively cleans and sanitizes a food-contact surface when applied to a food-contact surface two times—to clean the surface and to sanitize it • Product may be used at two-bay sink where there is no distinct water rinse between the washing and sanitizing steps.	• Can leave chemical residue if used at too high a level of concentration.

Cleaning Frequency

Under normal circumstances, food-contact surfaces and equipment used to prepare and serve PHF (TCS) must be cleaned throughout the day to prevent the growth of microorganisms on those surfaces. Some guidelines for cleaning food-contact surfaces include:

- Before each use with a different type of raw animal food, such as beef, fish, lamb, pork, or poultry, except when the surface is in contact with a series of different raw animal foods each requiring a higher cooking temperature

- Each time there is a change from working with raw foods to working with ready-to-eat foods
- Between uses with raw fruits and vegetables and with PHF (TCS)
- Before using or storing a food temperature-measuring device
- At any time during the operation when contamination may have occurred.

There are some exceptions to the 4-hour cleaning rule. One exception is when equipment and utensils are used to prepare PHF (TCS) in a refrigerated room or area. The following chart shows the *Food Code* prescribed cleaning frequency for refrigerated areas.

> The *Food Code* requires food-contact surfaces of equipment and utensils used to prepare PHF (TCS) to be cleaned at least every 4 hours when used at room temperature.

> Retail food establishments must maintain records of the cleaning frequency based on the ambient temperature of the refrigerated room or area.

Room Temperature and Cleaning Frequency	
Room Temperature	Cleaning Frequency
41°F (5°C) or less	at least once every 24 hours
41°F (5°C)–45°F (7°C)	at least once every 20 hours
45°F (7°C)–50°F (10°C)	at least once every 16 hours
50°F (10°C)–55°F (13°C)	at least once every 10 hours

Source: *Food Code*

In all cases, equipment and utensils that contact PHF (TCS) must be cleaned every 24 hours.

Iced tea dispensers, carbonated beverage dispenser nozzles, water dispensing units, ice makers, and ice bins are examples of equipment that routinely come into contact with food that is not potentially hazardous. These types of equipment must be cleaned on a routine basis to prevent the development of slime, mold, or soil residues that may contribute to an accumulation of microorganisms. The *Food Code* recommends surfaces of utensils and equipment contacting food that is not potentially hazardous be cleaned:

- At any time when contamination may have occurred.
- At least every 24 hours for iced tea dispensers and customers' self-service utensils, such as tongs, scoops, or ladles.
- Before restocking customers' self-service equipment and utensils, such as condiment dispensers and bulk food display containers.
- Whenever possible, follow the manufacturer's guidelines for regular cleaning and sanitizing of the food-contact surfaces of equipment and utensils. If the manufacturer does not provide cleaning instructions, the person in charge should develop a cleaning regimen that will effectively remove soil, mold, and other contaminants from equipment and utensils.

Guidelines for Cleaning Food-contact Surfaces That Touch PHF (TCS)

Item and Condition	When to Be Cleaned
• Storage containers for PHF(TCS) when properly maintained for hot- and cold-holding temperatures.	• When empty.
• Containers in serving situations (salad bars, delis, cafeteria lines) that are periodically combined with same food refills at required temperatures.	• At least once every 24 hours.
• Temperature-measuring device maintained in contact with food (deli food or roast).	• At least once every 24 hours.
• Refrigerated equipment used for storage of packaged or unpackaged food (reach-in refrigerator).	• Frequency necessary to preclude accumulation of soil residue
• In-use utensils stored in water (containers with water at 135°F (57°C).	• At least once every 24 hours.

Sanitizing Principles

Heat and chemicals are the two types of **sanitizers** most commonly used in retail food establishments. Sanitizing does not provide the same level of microbial destruction as sterilization, because some bacterial spores and a few highly resistant vegetative cells generally survive the sanitizing process.

In all instances, a food-contact surface must be thoroughly cleaned and rinsed to remove soil and detergent residues before it can be properly sanitized.

Sanitizers destroy disease-causing microorganisms that may be present on equipment and utensils even after cleaning.

Heat Sanitizing

Heat sanitizing in manual warewashing operations requires cleaned equipment and utensils to be submersed in hot water maintained at 171°F (77°C) or above for at least 30 seconds. A properly calibrated thermometer is needed to routinely check the temperature of the sanitizing water. Employees must use dish baskets or racks to lower equipment and utensils into the sanitizing water. Manual warewashing operations rarely employ this type of sanitizing due to concerns about employee safety and the large amount of energy required to keep the water hot.

Heat Has Several Advantages over Chemical Sanitizing Agents Because it:

- Can penetrate small cracks and crevices
- Is noncorrosive to metal surfaces
- Kills all types of microorganisms equally effectively
- Leaves no residue
- Is easily measurable.

Sanitizing with hot water is most commonly performed as part of mechanical warewashing operations. The *Food Code* requires the hot water used for these purposes to be between 180°F (82°C) and 194°F (90°C) when it leaves the final rinse spray nozzles. This assures the temperature of the water will be at 171°F (77°C) or above when it reaches the surfaces of the equipment and utensils being sanitized. The only exceptions to these temperature requirements are single-tank, stationary-rack, and single-temperature machines, where the final rinse water temperature must be at least 165°F (74°C) as it leaves the spray nozzles.

Steam is an excellent agent for treating pieces of food equipment. The equipment shown here is an example of a low-pressure, high-temperature steam/vapor cleaning system. When steam in a flow cabinet is used, it should be sufficient to achieve 171°F (77°C) for at least 15 minutes or 200°F (93°C) for at least 5 minutes.

Low-pressure, high-steam cleaning system

Steam is sometimes produced in remote steam boilers. Most boiler systems will require the periodic addition of boiler water additives to prevent the buildup of scale and corrosion in the boiler system. When there is a chance steam produced in these boilers will come into direct or indirect contact with food, the chemicals added to boiler water must be approved for use as a food additive and labeled for that use as per Title 21 CFR Part 173.310—Boiler Water Additives.

When using heat for sanitizing, the temperature at the surface of the equipment and utensils must reach at least 160°F (71°C) to assure proper destruction of disease-causing microorganisms. The temperature at the surface can be measured by using irreversible heat-sensitive labels or tapes attached to a clean dry dish and then run with a load of soiled dishes through a regular wash cycle. The labels change from white to black when the indicated temperature is reached.

Heat-sensitive label

T-Stick

Measuring the sanitizing temperature in dishwashing machines

Another commonly used device for measuring the temperature of hot water sanitizers is the "maximum registering" or "holding" thermometer. This type thermometer will continue to hold the highest temperature measured until shaken down like a medical thermometer. Be sure to use only the newer maximum registering thermometers that don't contain any mercury.

Maximum registering thermometers

Deltra TRAK, Inc.

Chemical Sanitizing

The chemical **sanitizers** most commonly used in retail food establishments are **chlorine**, **iodine**, and **quaternary ammonium compounds (quats)**.

There are two ways to sanitize surfaces using chemical compounds:

- Immerse a piece of equipment or a utensil into a sanitizing solution at the prescribed concentration
- Swab, brush, or pressure spray the sanitizing solution directly onto the surface of the equipment and utensils.

Chemical test strips

Requirements for Sanitizing Equipment and Utensils			
Concentration Range of Sanitizer Solution as Expressed in Parts per Millions (ppm) or mg/L	pH 10.0 or Less and Minimum Water Temperature	pH 8.0 or Less and Minimum Water Temperature	Contact Time
Chlorine 25-49	120°F (49°C)	120°F (49°C)	Greater than or equal to 10 seconds.

(continued)

Source: 2009 *Food Code*

Requirements for Sanitizing Equipment and Utensils (continued)

Concentration Range of Sanitizer Solution as Expressed in Parts per Millions (ppm) or mg/L	pH 10.0 or Less and Minimum Water Temperature	pH 8.0 or Less and Minimum Water Temperature	Contact Time
Chlorine 50-99	100°F (38°C)	75°F (24°C)	Greater than or equal to 7 seconds.
Chlorine 100	55°F (13°C)	55°F (13°C)	Greater than or equal to 10 seconds
Iodine Greater than or equal to 12.5 and less than or equal to 25	pH less than or equal to 5.0 or per label and water temperature at 68°F (20°C) or above.		Greater than or equal to 30 seconds
Quaternary Ammonium Per label	Slightly alkaline pH is preferred, water hardness must be 500 ppm or less or per EPA-registered label use instructions, and water temperature at 75°F (24°C) or above.		
Hot Water Sanitize Three-compartment sink with integral heating device	Water temperature must be maintaed at 171°F (77°C) or above and equipment and utensils completely immersed in rack or basket.		
Steam	Water temperature must be maintained at 200°F (93°C) or above.		For at least 5 minutes

Source: 2009 *Food Code*

A chemical test kit or test strips must be available so warewashing personnel can routinely check the strength of the sanitizing solution. The sanitizing solution should be replaced with a fresh solution whenever it becomes contaminated or if the concentration falls below the minimum level recommended by the manufacturer of the sanitizer.

Factors That Affect the Action of Chemical Sanitizers

The effectiveness of chemical sanitizers is affected by many different factors. The following are some of the most important factors to consider.

- **Contact of sanitizer**—In order for the chemical to react with and destroy microorganisms, it must achieve close contact.
- **Selectivity of sanitizer**—Some sanitizers are nonselective and destroy a wide variety of microorganisms. Others exhibit a certain degree of **selectivity**.
- **Concentration of sanitizer**—In general, increasing the concentration of a chemical sanitizer proportionately increases its rate of microbial destruction. But there are limitations as the increased activity only extends to a certain maximum concentration and then levels off. More is not always better, and high concentrations of sanitizers can be toxic and wasteful. Always follow the manufacturer's label use instructions to assure peak effectiveness of chemical sanitizers.

- **Temperature of solution**—All of the common sanitizers increase in activity as the solution temperature increases. The standard range of water temperatures for chemical sanitizing solutions is between 68°F (20°C) and 120°F (49°C). Water temperatures as low as 55°F (13°C) can be used with chlorine under special circumstances, and temperatures above 120°F (49°C) should be avoided when using chlorine and iodine. At high temperatures, the potency of these sanitizers is lost by its evaporation into the atmosphere.
- **pH or acidity of solution**—Water hardness can affect the pH of water that exerts a significant influence on most sanitizers. Most soaps and detergents are alkaline with a pH between 10 and 12. That is why soap and detergent must be rinsed off the surfaces of equipment and utensils before they are sanitized.
- **Time of exposure**—Allow sufficient time for chemical reactions to destroy the microorganisms. The amount of exposure time depends on the preceding factors as well as the size of the microbial populations and their susceptibility to the sanitizer.

Chlorine

Chlorine is a chemical component of hypochlorites. These compounds are commonly used as chemical sanitizers in retail food establishments. Hypochlorites are available as powders and liquids. The germicidal effectiveness of chlorine-based sanitizers depends, in part, on water temperature and the pH of the sanitizing solution.

Iodine

The **iodine**-containing sanitizers commonly used in retail food establishments are called **iodophors**. Iodophors are effective against a wide range of bacteria, small viruses, and fungi. They are especially effective for killing disease-causing microorganisms found on human hands. Iodophors kill more quickly than either chlorine or the quats. They function best in water that is acidic and at temperatures between 68°F (20°C) and 120°F (49°C). Iodophors must be applied at 12.5 parts per million (ppm) when immersion sanitizing and at 25 parts per million in swab and spray applications.

Quaternary Ammonium Compounds

Quaternary ammonium compounds (quats) are ammonia salts used as chemical sanitizers in retail food establishments. Quats are effective sanitizers, but they do not destroy the wide variety of disease-causing microorganisms that chlorine and iodophor sanitizers do. Quats are noncorrosive and have no taste or odor when used in the proper dilution. Quats are more heat stable and can be used in hotter water than either hypochlorites or iodophors. At concentrations above 200 ppm, quats can leave a residue on the surface of an item. This is undesirable for food-contact surfaces. *Always follow the manufacturer's directions for proper use and concentration of quats.*

The FDA Food Code recommends not using quats above 200 parts per million (ppm) for immersion sanitizing of food-contact -surfaces.

A summary of the advantages and disadvantages of the chemical sanitizers used most frequently in retail food establishments is shown below.

Advantages and Disadvantages of Selected Chemical Sanitizerss

Sanitizer	Advantages	Disadvantages
Chlorine compounds	• Economical cost • Kills many types of microbes • Good for most sanitizing applications • Deodorize and sanitize • Nontoxic to humans when used at recommended concentrations • Colorless and nonstaining • Easy to handle • Economical to use.	• Corrosive to equipment • Can irritate human skin and hands.
Iodophors	• Less corrosive to equipment • Less irritating to skin • Good for killing microbes on hands.	• Moderate cost • Can stain equipment.
Quats	• Stable at high temperature • Stable for a longer contact time • Good for in-place sanitizers • Noncorrosive • No taste or odor.	• Very expensive • Hard water can reduce effectiveness • Destroy a narrow range of microorganisms, which may limit their use in some retail food establishments.

Mechanical Warewashing

Mechanical warewashing is performed in a dishwashing machine that cleans and sanitizes multi-use equipment and utensils automatically. Dishwashing machines are designed to clean and sanitize equipment and utensils that have no electrical parts and will fit into the machine. When properly maintained and operated, mechanical warewashing is as effective at removing soil and disease-causing microorganisms as is manual warewashing.

Single-tank dishwashing machine

Mechanical Warewashing Process

Mechanical warewashing uses an eight-step process to clean and sanitize equipment and utensils.

1. Pre-scrape and pre-flush soiled equipment and pre-soak utensils to remove visible soil.

2. Rack equipment and utensils so wash and rinse waters will spray evenly on all surfaces and the equipment will freely drain.

3. Wash equipment and utensils in a detergent solution.

4. Rinse equipment and utensils in clean water at a temperature consistent with the type of dishwashing machine being used.

5. Sanitize equipment and utensils in a fresh, hot water sanitizing rinse between 180°F (82°C) and 194°F (90°C) for at least 30 seconds, except for a single-tank, stationary-rack, or single-temperature machine, where the final rinse may not be less than 165°F (74°C) for at least 30 seconds. Water temperature at the surface of equipment and utensils must be at least 160°F (71°C) to achieve proper sanitization. The recommended final rinse temperature for low-temperature chemical sanitizing dishwashing machines is 120°F (49°C) or less.

   The flow pressure of the hot water sanitizing rinse must be in the range indicated on the machine manufacturer's data plate and not less than 5 or more than 30 pounds per square inch (PSI). The reduced water pressure is required in order to assure the sanitizing water covers the entire surface of the items being sanitized.

Cleaning and Sanitizing Operations

6. Drain properly and air-dry equipment and utensils. Do not towel dry food-contact surfaces.

AIR DRY UTENSILS
DON'T WIPE DRY

7. Store clean and sanitary items in a clean, dry area where they are protected from contamination.

8. Clean and maintain the machine to keep it in proper working condition.

The temperature of the wash water (and power rinse if applicable) is extremely important in providing effective sanitizing of equipment and utensils. Water temperatures, water pressure, and conveyor speed or cycle time must be in accordance with the dish machine data plate and the manufacturer's instructions.

> **Provide sufficient counter or table space for the accumulation of soiled equipment and utensils and keep them separate from items that are clean and sanitary.**

Warewashing Mechanical & Manual		Minimum Wash Sanitizing Temperature	Minimum Sanitizing Temperature
Spray Type warewashers: Single-tank, hot water sanitize	Stationary-rack, single temperature	165°F (74°C)	165°F (74°C)
	Stationary rack, dual temperature	150°F (66°C)	180°F (82°C)
	Conveyor, dual temperature	160°F (71°C)	
Multi-tank, hot water sanitize	Conveyor, multi-temperature	150°F (66°C)	

(continued)

Sanitizing Principles

Warewashing Mechanical & Manual (continued)		Minimum Wash Sanitizing Temperature	Minimum Sanitizing Temperature
Chemical sanitize	Any warewashing machine	120°F (49°C)	Sanitization levels as state in the FDA *Food Code* or per the labeled manfacturer's instructions on the container[1]
Three-compartment sink	Cleaning agent labeling may permit lower washing temperatures	110°F (43°C)	

[1]**Chemical sanitization units installed after the adoption of the FDA's 2001 *Food Code* must be equipped with an audible or visual "low level" sanitizer indicator to add more sanitizer.**

Cleaned and sanitized equipment and utensils must be properly drained and air-dried before storage. Soiled, multi-use cloth towels can recontaminate cleaned and sanitized equipment and utensils. The *Food Code* prohibits cloth drying of equipment and utensils, with the exception that air-dried utensils can be "polished" with cloths that are clean and dry. If drying agents are used in conjunction with sanitization, they must contain components that are generally recognized as safe (GRAS) for use in food, GRAS for the intended purpose, or have been approved for use as a drying agent under the relevant provisions contained in Title 21 of the *Code of Federal Regulations*.

Cleaned and sanitized equipment and utensils must be stored in such a way as to protect them from contamination. Cabinets and carts used to store cleaned and

Operators of dishwashing machines must be careful not to contaminate cleaned and sanitized equipment and utensils by touching them with soiled hands.

Proper storage of cleaned and sanitized equipment and utensils

sanitized equipment and utensils may not be located in locker rooms and toilet rooms and under sewer lines that are not shielded to catch drips, leaking water lines, open stairwells, or under other sources of contamination.

Manual Warewashing

Manual warewashing typically uses a three-compartment sink to clean and sanitize equipment and utensils. The manual process begins with scraping and flushing food residues off the surface of equipment and utensils. When necessary, items may be pre-soaked to remove food residues and other soil.

After pre-flushing, the equipment and utensils are washed in the first compartment of the sink with warm water and a cleaning agent. Washing removes visible food particles and grease. Warewashing personnel should always use the correct amount of detergent based on the quantity of water used in the wash compartment of the sink. The temperature of the wash water must be maintained at not less than 110°F (43°C) unless the manufacturer of the cleaning agent specifies a different temperature.

> **Always make certain surfaces are properly cleaned and rinsed before they are sanitized.**

The second compartment of the sink is used to rinse equipment and utensils in clean, warm water. Rinsing removes cleaning agents, soap film, remaining food particles, and abrasives that may interfere with the sanitizer agent. For best results, the rinse water must be kept clean and the temperature should be between 110°F (43°C) and 120°F (49°C).

Manual Warewashing			
	Compartment #1	Compartment #2	Compartment #3
Contains:	Detergent solution with hot water	Fresh warm potable water	Chemicals or hot water
Process:	Pre-scraped and pre-flushed equipment and utensils are washed.	Soap and soil are rinsed off equipment and utensils.	Sanitize the previously cleaned surfaces.

The third compartment of the sink is used for sanitizing items with either hot water or chemical sanitizers.

When using hot water:
- Temperature must be maintained at 171°F (77°C) or above at all times
- Items must be immersed in the hot water for at least 30 seconds.

Chemical sanitizers:
- Preferred in retail food establishments because they do not require large amounts of hot water.
- The standard range of water temperatures for chemical sanitizing solutions is between 68°F (20°C) and 120°F (49°C).
- Under certain conditions, chlorine sanitizers may be used with a water temperature as low as 55°F (13°C).
- Quats may be used with a water temperature above 120°F (49°C). Chlorine and iodophor sanitizers should not be used in water temperatures above 120°F (49°C) because the potency of these sanitizers is quickly lost at high water temperatures.
- Follow the manufacturer's directions for proper use and concentration of quats.

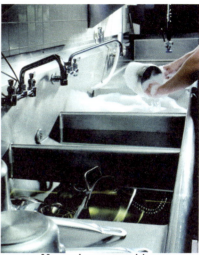
Manual warewashing

The manual warewashing sink must be equipped with sloped drain boards or dish tables of adequate size to store soiled items prior to washing and clean items after they have been sanitized.

As with mechanical warewashing, items manually cleaned and sanitized must be air-dried before they are put into storage. If drying agents are used in conjunction with sanitization they must contain components that are GRAS for the intended purpose or have been

> **Hot and cold potable water must be supplied to each compartment of the sink, and the sink should be cleaned and sanitized prior to use.**

approved for use as a drying agent under the relevant provisions contained in Title 21 of the *Code of Federal Regulations*.

The effectiveness of the manual warewashing process depends on the condition of the wash, rinse, and sanitizing solutions. Monitor wash and rinse solutions and replace them when they become soiled. When the sanitizer in the third compartment is depleted, it should be drained completely and replaced with a fresh solution at proper strength. The concentration of a chemical sanitizer solution must be tested periodically with a test kit or test strips to make sure it remains at strength. These strips provide a color comparison to indicate the strength of the sanitizer. Test kits or strips may be obtained from the manufacturer of your sanitizer.

Measuring the concentration of sanitizers using test strips

Cleaning Fixed Equipment

Fixed equipment used in retail food establishments has food-contact surfaces but cannot be cleaned using either traditional mechanical or manual warewashing processes. Common examples of fixed equipment include band saws, floor- mounted mixers, slicers, grinders, produce display cases, and live tanks used to display live lobsters and molluscan shellfish. This equipment must be disassembled to expose food-contact surfaces to cleaning and sanitizing agents. The basic steps for cleaning fixed equipment are listed in the box shown on the next page:

Cleaning fixed equipment

Large equipment, such as preparation tables and band saws, can be cleaned by using a foam or spray method. In this process, detergents and degreasers, fresh water rinse, and a chemical sanitizer are applied using foam or

Steps for Cleaning Fixed Equipment

1. Disconnect the power supply to the equipment before taking it apart for cleaning.

2. Disassemble the equipment as necessary to allow the detergent solution to reach all food-contact surfaces.

3. Use a plastic scraper to clean equipment parts and remove food debris that has accumulated under and around the equipment. Scrape all debris into the trash.

4. Carry the parts that have been removed from the equipment to the manual warewashing sink where they will be washed, rinsed, and sanitized.

5. Wash the remaining parts of the equipment using a clean cloth, brush or scouring pad, and warm, soapy water. Clean from top to bottom.

6. Rinse thoroughly with fresh water and a clean cloth.

7. Swab or spray a chemical sanitizing solution, mixed to the manufacturer's recommendations, onto all food-contact surfaces.

8. Allow all parts to drain and air-dry.

9. Reassemble the equipment.

10. Resanitize any food-contact surface that might have been contaminated due to handling when the equipment was being reassembled.

spray guns. The hoses, feed lines, and nozzles that make up the foam or spray unit should be in good condition and attached properly.

The various display cases used in meat, seafood, dairy, bakery, produce, and other departments in retail food establishments will have racks and other parts that can be removed for cleaning. Some equipment, such as produce and self-service bakery cases, may be equipped with accessory items, such as misting heads and tongs or other handling devices. These accessories must also be cleaned and sanitized regularly to assure the safety and wholesomeness of products with which they are used.

Food-contact surfaces have to be cleaned and sanitized while non-food–contact surfaces require cleaning only.

Routine cleaning and maintenance of live seafood displays and holding tanks are necessary to preserve water quality and the quality of your live seafood. Some general guidelines that should be followed when working with this equipment are:

- Clean and sanitize the ultraviolet (UV) light unit used to kill pathogens in the water.
- Clean the interior portion of the tank on a regular basis to keep it free of algae and slime buildup that may harbor pathogens.

The produce misting system in your establishment should be checked regularly to make sure it is clean and in good working order. Routine maintenance should include the following steps:

Make sure your misting system is maintained regularly.

- If there is a separate water filter for the misting system, it should be checked and replaced as needed to assure an adequate supply of clean water.
- Disassemble the nozzles and clean and sanitize the various parts to remove food debris and mineral residue.
- Flush the tubing that supplies the mister heads with clean water.
- Wipe the outside surfaces of the system (tubing, etc.) with an approved sanitizer to stop the growth of fungi, molds, and yeast.

The bucket and brush method is often used to clean equipment that could be damaged by pressure spraying or immersion in the manual warewashing sink. This system uses three separate buckets for washing, rinsing, and sanitizing.

The **clean-in-place (CIP)** method is used for equipment that is designed to be cleaned and sanitized by circulating cleaning and sanitizing solutions through the equipment. Examples of equipment that would be cleaned using this method are soft-serve ice cream or yogurt machines. The basic steps in the clean-in-place method are listed in the following box.

Clean-in-place Cleaning Method

1. Empty food product and waste from the equipment.
2. Disconnect the power to the equipment.
3. Disassemble if parts are removable and cleanable in the manual warewashing sink.
4. Clean and sanitize the removable parts using the three-compartment warewashing sink process.
5. Clean and sanitize the main unit by circulating wash, rinse, and sanitizing solutions through it. Combination detergent sanitizers can also be used on equipment that is designed for CIP cleaning.
6. Reassemble parts removed from the main unit.
7. Resanitize by circulating a manufacturer approved sanitizing solution through the equipment. Resanitize any food-contact surface that might have been contaminated due to handling when the equipment was being reassembled.

Soft-serve ice cream machine
(Courtesy of SaniServ)

Many departments will use wiping cloths to clean up spills. These cloths should be stored in a container of sanitizing solution between uses in order to prevent microbial growth on the cloth. This is often referred to as an **"in-place sanitizer."** Any standard chemical sanitizer may be used for storing wiping cloths. However, quats are preferred because they kill disease-causing microorganisms for a longer period of time.

- A clean cloth and fresh container of sanitizing solution at the proper strength must be used at the start of each day.
- The cloth should be changed whenever it becomes heavily soiled, and the sanitizer must be changed when it falls below the required concentration.
- Wiping cloths may not be used for any other purpose except removing spills.
- Cloths used to wipe spills from floors and non-food-contact surfaces must be kept separate from the cloths used to clean food–contact surfaces of equipment.

- Cloths used for wiping floors and surfaces that have come in contact with raw animal foods must be used for no other purpose.

A retail food establishment should provide single-use and single-service articles for food handlers if it does not have proper facilities for cleaning and sanitizing multi-use kitchenware and tableware. These establishments must also provide single-service articles for use by consumers.

Store and use wiping cloths properly.

Materials used to make single-service and single-use articles must not permit the transfer of harmful substances or pass on colors, odors, or tastes to food. These materials must be safe and clean when used in retail food establishments.

Single-use items must be stored and dispensed in a way that will protect them from contamination from employees, customers, and the surrounding environment.

Cleaning Environmental Areas

A regular cleaning schedule of non-food–contact surfaces should be established and followed to maintain the facility in a clean and sanitary condition. The manager or supervisor should create a master cleaning schedule that will list the following items:

- The specific equipment and facilities to be cleaned
- The processes and supplies needed to clean the equipment and facilities
- The prescribed time when the equipment and facilities should be cleaned

Cleaning environmental areas

- The name of the employee who has been assigned to do the cleaning.

Ceilings and Walls

Ceilings should be checked regularly to make certain they are not contaminating food production areas. Ceilings, lights, fans, and covers can be cleaned using either a wet- or dry-cleaning technique. When wet-cleaning ceilings and fixtures, it is best to use a bucket method to keep water away from lights, fans, and other electrical devices. Walls may be cleaned using either the bucket or spray methods. Whenever possible, disconnect power before cleaning fixtures.

> **Major cleaning should be done during periods when the least amount of food will be exposed to contamination and service will not be interrupted.**

Floors

The cleanliness of floors depends on the ability of an employee to remove soil from the surface of the floor. Floors in customer shopping areas are usually cleaned with floor cleaning machines, and floors in food production areas can be cleaned using a spray system for washing and rinsing. Floors that will be damaged by spray cleaning can be cleaned using the bucket method.

> **All floors should be sloped to drains to help remove soil and the water used to clean floors.**

If floor drains are not properly maintained, they can be a source of disease, vermin, and odors. All floor drains should be flushed, washed, rinsed, and sanitized.

The steps commonly used to clean floor drains are listed below:

1. Remove the grate or cover over the drain.
2. Clean out waste and other debris from the drain.
3. Use a sprayer or hose to flush the drain and grate or cover.
4. Pour in drain cleaner to break up grease and other waste in the drain.
5. Wash the drain using a brush or water pressure from the sprayer.
6. Rinse the drain with hot water.
7. Pour or spray sanitizer into the drain.

If not properly maintained, sewer pipes can become clogged and can cause sewage and other wastes to back up into and flood various areas of a retail food establishment. This can create both a health hazard and a nuisance. You must know what to do in the event a sewer backup occurs. Some of the steps you should follow are:

- Remove anything from the floor that might be damaged or contaminated by the wastewater.
- Remove the blockage in the pipe causing the backup. This may require the services of a professional plumber.
- Wash and sanitize all equipment, floors, walls, and any other objects that may have been contaminated by the waste that backed up into the establishment.

Equipment and Supplies Used for Cleaning

Some examples of equipment commonly used during cleaning are nylon brushes, cleaning cloths, scouring pads, squeegees, mops, buckets, spray bottles, hoses, and spray or foam guns. Commonly used cleaning supplies include hot water, cleaners, degreasers, and sanitizers.

Janitor sink

There should be a separate sink to fill and empty mop buckets, to rinse and clean mops, and to clean brushes and sponges. A janitor's sink or floor drain should be provided to dispose of wastewater produced by cleaning activities.

Containers of poisonous or toxic materials and personal care items must bear a legible manufacturer's label. Working containers used for storing poisonous or toxic materials, such as cleaners and sanitizers taken from bulk supplies, must be clearly and individually identified with the common name of the material. A container previously used to

Handwashing, food preparation, and warewashing sinks must never be used for cleaning mops and brushes.

store poisonous or toxic materials may not be used to store, transport, or dispense food.

The Occupational Safety and Health Administration (OSHA) requires employees to have the "right-to-know" about the chemicals to which they may be exposed on the job. Information about substances in the work place is provided to employees by way of material safety data sheets (MSDS). Chemical manufacturers develop these, and they must be maintained on file and accessible to employees in the retail food establishment.

Examples of information contained in an MSDS include:

- Ingredients
- Physical and chemical characteristics

MATERIAL SAFETY DATA SHEET

PRODUCT IDENTIFICATION
Product:
Product Code:
Chemical Name/Synonym: Oxypurinol Xanthine

INGREDIENTS
Oxypurinol: 1% CAS#:2465-59-0
Xanthine: 1% CAS#: 69-89-6

PHYSICAL AND CHEMICAL CHARACTERISTICS
Boiling Point: NA
Melting Point: NA
Vapor Pressure (mm Hg): NA
Vapor Density (air=1): NA
Solubility in Water: Insoluble
pH: NA
Specific Gravity: NA
Bulk Density: Not Determined
Evaporation rate: NA
Percent Volatile: NA
Appearance and Odor: Solid, slightly musty

FIRE AND HAZARD DATA
Flash Point: > 220°F
Flammable Limits: NA
Autoignition Temp: NA
Decomposition Temp: NA
NTP Teratogen or Mutagen Carcinogen: Not Determined
IARC or OSHA Potential Carcinogen: Not Determined
Fire Extinguishing Media: Carbon Dioxide, dry chemical or foam.
Special Fire Fighting Procedures: Wear self-contained breathing apparatus and protective clothing to prevent contact with skin and eyes.
Unusual Fire and Explosion Hazards: Emits toxic fumes under fire conditions.

HEALTH HAZARDS
Primary Route(s) of Entry: Skin, eye, inhalation, ingestion.
Signs of Symptoms of Exposure: May cause irritation. May cause allergic skin reaction.
Target Organs: Liver. Complete chemical, physical and toxicological properties have not been thoroughly investigated.

EMERGENCY FIRST-AID PROCEDURES
Ingestion: If swallowed, wash out mouth with water provided person is conscious. Call a physician.
Skin: Flush with copious amounts of water for at least 15 minutes. Remove contaminated clothing and shoes. Call a physician.
Eyes: Flush with copious amounts of water for at least 15 minutes. Assure adequate flushing by separating the eyelids with fingers. Call a physician.
Inhalation: Remove victim to fresh air. If breathing is difficult, call a physician.
Note to Physician: No specific antidote is available. Treatment of overexposure should be directed at the control of symptoms and the clinical conditions.

TOXICITY INFORMATION:
Oral LD_{50} (Rats): > 5,000 mg/kg
Dermal LD_{50} (Rabbits): >2,000 mg/kg (Technical)
Eye Irritation: Slight
Skin Irritation: Very slight

REACTIVITY
Stability: Stable
Conditions to Avoid: None
Incompatibility: Strong oxidizing agents
Hazardous Decomposition Products: Thermal decomposition may produce carbon monoxide, carbon dioxide, and nitrogen oxides.

SPILL, LEAK, AND DISPOSAL PROCEDURES
If material is spilled: Sweep, vacuum or shovel material into a container for reuse or disposal. Do not allow product to contaminate drains, sewers, streams, ditches or bodies of water. Prevent large quantities from contacting vegetation. Keep animals away from large spills. Dike and contain spill area, then rinse area and tools several times with soapy water. Dispose of rinse water in accordance with applicable law.
Waste Disposal: Dispose according to Federal EPA procedures as outlined in the Resource Conservation Recovery Act (RCRA) and follow state and local guidelines. Empty containers may contain some product residues and should be handled and disposed of in a similar manner to the product. All attempts should be made to utilize the product completely, in accordance with its intended use.

STORAGE AND HANDLING
Precautions: Store in a cool, dry place. Separate from other pesticides, fertilizers, seed, feed, foodstuffs and away from drains, sewers and water sources.
Other Precautions: Keep out of reach of children. Practice good care and good safety precautions when handling this product. Avoid contact with eye, skin and clothing. Avoid breathing dust. Do not swallow. Wash thoroughly after handling. This product is toxic to fish. Do not apply directly to lakes, ponds or streams. This product may be an attractant to pets and rodents. Store in a secure place.

FEDERAL REGULATORY INFORMATION:
SARA TITLE III; SEC. 311/312 Hazard Categories
Immediate (Acute) Health: NA
Delayed (Chronic) Health: NA
Fire: NA
Sudden Release of Pressure: NA
Reactivity: NA
SEC 302/SEC 304 TPQ: Not Listed
SEC 313: NA
CERCLA RQ: NA
CAA RQ: NA
EPA Reg. No.: 1001-73
HM- 181 Shipping Name: Insecticide, Agricultural, Solid, NOI

NA = Not Applicable
ND = Not Determined

Material safety data sheet

- Fire, explosion, reactivity, and health hazard data
- How to handle chemicals safely
- How to use personal protective equipment and other devices to reduce risk
- Emergency procedures to use if required.

Failure to produce the required MSDS upon demand can result in a substantial fine from OSHA.

Summary

Back to the Story . . . For sensitive individuals, the presence of allergens in food is potentially life threatening. Currently, there is no cure for a food allergy. The only successful method to manage a food allergy is avoidance of foods containing the allergen. However, as described in the case study at the beginning of this chapter, product change over provides an unintentional opportunity for a product that contains an allergen to contaminate a product that does not contain that particular allergen (i.e., peanuts). Equipment cleaning is a critical allergen control point for the production of a nonallergen containing product following product changeover. All visible and non-visible product residues must be removed from food-contact surfaces by proper cleaning and sanitizing, between products. In this case, the cookie sheets were clean, but the employee was reusing the parchment paper. The peanut oil and crumbs from the peanut butter cookies contaminated the chocolate chip cookies that were baked on the same parchment paper. A new sheet of parchment paper should be used for each pan of cookies baked. Proper cleanup and sanitation steps used by bakery personnel should be verified and proven effective.

✔ A good sanitation program starts with a neat, clean, and properly maintained building. A well-maintained facility helps protect food products from contamination, makes proper stock rotation easier, prevents entrance of pests, reduces fire hazards, and contributes to the overall safety of the work environment. Proper cleaning and sanitizing also enhance the safety and quality of food and increase the life expectancy of equipment and facilities.

✔ A retail food establishment's sanitation program consists of the standards, policies, and procedures that assure proper cleaning and sanitation. In-store sanitation standards must incorporate the requirements of government regulations and manufacturers' guidelines.

✔ The effectiveness of a retail food establishment's sanitation program is directly related to the degree of commitment and concern demonstrated by top management. Managers must motivate their employees to follow prescribed sanitation practices and reward those employees who do so successfully.

✔ Proper education and training are required to assure proper sanitation practices are followed. Employees responsible for handling food, equipment, and cleanup of the building and grounds must be trained to accept sanitation as one of their key responsibilities. A clean, well-maintained facility will become a source of pride for employees.

✔ For a sanitation program to be effective, cleaning tasks must be scheduled and individual employees assigned to complete the tasks. Employees must be given instructions that include what they are to clean, how to clean it, and what tools and supplies are required to effectively clean it. Properly trained employees must carry out cleaning activities, and they must be closely monitored by supervisors to identify and correct problems when they occur.

✔ A good sanitation program is a preventive program that anticipates and eliminates potential hazards before they become serious problems. The value of an effective program is difficult to measure in terms of dollars. Nonetheless, the value of effective sanitation can be evident in the form of diminished problems and increased goodwill with customers and the local regulatory community.

Discussion Question (Short Answer)

1. What is the difference between cleaning and sanitizing?
2. Briefly discuss some of the factors that affect cleaning efficiency.
3. What are the main functions of detergents in the cleaning process?
4. What are the basic steps in the manual warewashing process?
5. Why must cleaned and sanitized equipment and utensils be air-dried?
6. How can cleaning and sanitizing help to control food allergens in a food store operation?
7. How does water temperature affect chemical sanitizers?

8. What are some of the factors that affect the action of chemical sanitizers?

9. What is the best way to measure the strength of a chemical sanitizer?

10. What steps are commonly used to clean fixed equipment that is too large to be placed in a dishwashing machine or three-compartment sink?

11. What purposes do material safety data sheets serve in a retail food establishment?

Quiz 6 (Multiple Choice)

Choose the **best** answer for each question:

1. The process that results in the complete removal of soil and food residues from surfaces of equipment and utensils is called:

    a. cleaning.
    b. sanitizing.
    c. pre-scraping.
    d. rinsing.

2. The treatment of a clean surface to reduce the number of disease-causing microorganisms to safe levels is called:

    a. cleaning.
    b. sanitizing.
    c. pre-scraping.
    d. rinsing.

3. The Occupational Safety and Health Administration (OSHA) requires that all potentially harmful substances have a sheet on file that gives information for emergency treatment if an employee is injured with the product. This document is called the:

    a. material safety data sheet.
    b. emergency instruction information form.
    c. government format for harmful products.
    d. material information and content form.

4. When sanitizing with hot water in a manual warewashing operation, the temperature of the water in the final rinse must be maintained at:

   a. 161°F (72°C).
   b. 171°F (77°C).
   c. 181°F (83°C).
   d. 191°F (88°C).

5. Which of the following statements is **false**?

   a. Dishes should be washed in very hot water [above 171°F (77°C)] to effectively remove soil from the surface.
   b. Pre-scraping helps to remove larger food particles from dishes, which helps keep the wash water clean.
   c. The cleaning compounds used in a retail food establishment must be tailored to the individual water supply.
   d. Cleaning is a process that removes soil and prevents accumulation of food residues on equipment, utensils, and surfaces.

6. The allowable range of water temperatures for chlorine sanitizing solutions is between _____ and _____.

   a. 55°F (13°C); 120°F (49°C).
   b. 75°F (24°C); 120°F (49°C).
   c. 95°F (35°C); 140°F (60°C).
   d. 120°F (49°C); 171°F (77°C).

7. The strength of the chemical sanitizer in the third compartment of the three-compartment sink must be checked frequently because:

   a. if the chemical is too strong, it may ruin fragile dishware.
   b. the chemical strength increases over time and may leave a toxic residue on the surface of equipment and utensils.
   c. the strength of chemical sanitizers may drop off as germs are killed off and the sanitizer is diluted with rinse water.
   d. the strength of the chemical increases as germs are killed off.

8. The first step in developing a cleaning program for environmental areas is to:

   a. determine the cleaning needs.
   b. assign cleaning jobs to employees.
   c. obtain the equipment and supplies needed to implement the cleaning.
   d. conduct a training program to teach employees how to clean properly.

9. Which of the following statements is **false**?

   a. Keeping things clean is the responsibility of every person working in the food industry.

   b. Cleanliness goes beyond the removal of visible soil.

   c. A good sanitation program, if properly organized, will function successfully without the support of top management.

   d. A good sanitation program starts with a neat, clean, and properly maintained building.

10. Which of the following sequences best describes the correct way to clean and sanitize equipment and utensils in a retail food establishment?

    a. Wash, rinse, sanitize and towel dry.

    b. Pre-flush, wash, sanitize, and air-dry.

    c. Pre-flush, wash, rinse, sanitize, and air-dry.

    d. Pre-flush, rinse, sanitize, and air-dry.

11. The last step that should be taken when cleaning and sanitizing fixed equipment, such as saws and a slicer, is:

    a. Rinse all surfaces with fresh, potable water.

    b. Allow all parts to drain and air-dry.

    c. Wash parts that have been disassembled in a three-compartment sink or mechanical dishwasher.

    d. Resanitize any food-contact surface that may have been touched when reassembling the equipment.

Answers to these multiple-choice questions are available in Appendix A.

References/Suggested Readings

Code of Federal Regulations. 2008. *21 CFR 173.310—Boiler Water Additives*, U.S. Government Printing Office. Washington, DC.

Code of Federal Regulations. 2001). *21 CFR 172—Substances Generally Recognized as Safe*, U.S. Government Printing Office. Washington, DC.

Code of Federal Regulations. 2008. *21 CFR 184—Direct Food Substances Affirmed as Generally Recognized as Safe.* U.S. Government Printing Office. Washington, DC.

Code of Federal Regulations. 2008. *21 CFR 186—Indirect Food Substances Affirmed as Generally Recognized as Safe.* U.S. Government Printing Office. Washington, DC.

Food and Drug Administration. 2009. *2009 Food Code*. U.S. Public Health Service. Washington, DC.

Suggested Web Sites

All QA Products
www.allqa.com

Bowerman Marketing Group
www.ebowerman.com

Champion Industries
www.championindustries.com

Chemstar
www.chemstarcorp.com

Duke Manufacturing Company
www.dukemfg.com

Ecolab
www.ecolab.com

Hobart Corporation
www.hobartcorp.com

Johnson Diversey
www.johnsondiversey.com

Paper Thermometer Company
www.mv.com/ipusers/paperthermometer

The Soap and Detergent Association
www.sdahq.org

Steritech Group, Inc.
www.steritech.com

NSF International
www.nsf.org

Underwriters Laboratories, Inc.
www.ul.com

The Food Marketing Institute
www.fmi.org

Gateway to Government Food Safety Information
www.foodsafety.gov

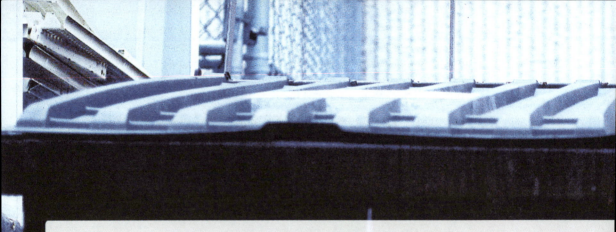

Learn How To:

- Describe how the visual appearance of a retail food establishment can affect a customer's opinion about the cleanliness and sanitation of the operation.

- Identify the equipment and supplies that must be provided in a properly equipped restroom facility.

- Identify the main components of a properly equipped handwashing station.

- Explain how conveniently located handwashing sinks contribute to good personal hygiene.

- Identify the types of plumbing hazards that can have a negative effect on public health.

- Identify some types of pests and common signs of pest infestation that may be found in retail food establishments.

- Describe how integrated pest management (IPM) is used to control pests in retail food establishments.

- Explain how proper disposal and storage of garbage and refuse help prevent contamination and pest problems in a retail food establishment.

CHAPTER 7

Environmental Sanitation and Maintenance

Bulk Food Storage and Display Bins Serve More Than Customers

The local food market is known for exotic ingredients, fresh produce, and hard-to-find items and enjoys a high volume of business. It uses a lot of self-service display bins for rice, beans, peppers, and other dried foods. Customers scoop up the amounts of these products they wish to purchase and place them into plastic bags. The foods are often spilled as they are put into the plastic bags, and the areas around the bins are difficult to keep clean. There are bins of candy and dried fruits displayed and dispensed in the same manner in the aisle next to the dried vegetables.

The company, hired to provide cleaning and general maintenance of the establishment, reported to the manager it had seen signs of rodent and insect infestation. Rub marks had been seen along the walls behind the display bins, and rodent droppings had been seen near the bins and in the storeroom. Cockroach egg cases had been found near the raisin and candy containers.

The manager called the pest control operator (PCO) who was under contract with the facility and asked for an immediate visit. In the meantime, the local inspector arrived to conduct a routine survey of the facility. Evidence of pest infestation was noticed, and the infraction was checked on the inspection form. Following the inspection, the PCO and the market manager held a meeting. What measures should they take for the pest problem at the establishment?

Essential Terms

Air gap	Garbage
Backflow	Integrated pest management (IPM)
Coving	Refuse
Cross connection	Vacuum breaker

Condition of the Establishment

The exterior of the facility must be free of litter and debris that could attract and harbor pests and ruin the appearance of the facility. Grass and weeds should be regularly mowed to eliminate harborage areas for insects, rodents, and other pests. Walking and driving surfaces should be constructed of concrete, asphalt, gravel, or similar materials to facilitate maintenance and control dust. These surfaces should also be properly graded to prevent rainwater from pooling and standing on parking lots and sidewalks. To attract customers, the exterior of the building should be clean and attractive and make a good impression.

A pleasant facility attracts customers.

Proper Water Supply and Sewage Disposal System

An adequate water supply and proper sewage disposal are vital to the sanitation of retail food establishments. The water source and ability to meet hot water generation needs should be sufficient to meet the demands of the retail food establishment. Drinking water for retail food establishments must be obtained from an approved source. Most establishments will be connected to a public water system. However, when a private well or other nonpublic water system is used, it must be constructed, maintained, and operated according to the water quality requirements of the jurisdiction. Wells must be located and constructed in a manner that will protect them from sewage and other sources of contamination. Periodic sampling is required to monitor the safety of the water and to detect any change in water quality.

To render the water safe, a drinking water system must be flushed and disinfected before being placed into service. The *Food Code* prescribes that a

> According to the *Food Code*, water from a nonpublic water system must be sampled and tested at least annually and as required by state water quality regulations.

drinking water system must be flushed after construction, repair, or modification and after an emergency situation, such as flood, that may introduce contaminants to the system.

A reservoir used to supply water to a device, such as a produce mister, must be maintained in accordance with the manufacturer's specifications. The reservoir must be cleaned at least once a week in accordance with manufacturer's specifications or according to the following procedures, whichever is more stringent:

1. Drain and completely disassemble the water and aerosol contact parts.

2. Brush-clean the reservoir, aerosol tubing, and discharge nozzles with a suitable detergent solution.

3. Flush the complete system with water to remove the detergent solution and particle accumulation.

4. Rinse by immersing, spraying, or swabbing the reservoir, aerosol tubing, and discharge nozzles with at least 50 ppm hypochlorite solution.

Proper disposal of sewage greatly reduces the risk of fecal contamination of food and water. The FDA *Food Code* requires sewage from retail food establishments to be disposed through an approved facility that is:

- A public sewage treatment plant, or:
- An individual sewage disposal system that is sized, constructed, maintained, and operated according to rules and regulations of the jurisdiction.

> **The use of nonpotable water sources in retail food establishments must be approved by the regulatory authority in the jurisdiction and may only be used for nonculinary purposes, such as air handling systems, cooling systems, and fire protection.**

Condition of Building

The cleanliness and attractiveness customers view upon entering the building influence their overall shopping experience. Entrance doors should be self-closing to discourage flying insects. Clearly mark the doors for entrance and exit to prevent accidents between those entering and leaving the establishment.

The entrance area to a retail food establishment creates a lasting impression.

Floors, Walls, and Ceilings

Consider the specific needs of the different departments when selecting materials for floors, walls, and ceilings. Some criteria that should be used for all departments are:

- Sanitation
- Safety
- Durability
- Comfort
- Cost.

Materials used for floors, walls, and ceilings in food preparation areas, storerooms (including dry storage areas and walk-in refrigerators), warewashing areas, and restrooms must be:

- Smooth
- Nonabsorbent
- Easy to clean
- Resistant to damage and deterioration.

Proper construction, repair, and cleaning of floors, walls, and ceilings are important elements of an effective sanitation program.

Floors

The *Food Code* prohibits the use of carpeting in:

- Food preparation areas
- Walk-in refrigerators

- Warewashing areas
- Toilet room areas where handwashing lavatories, toilets, and urinals are located
- Refuse storage rooms or other areas subject to moisture.

> **Coving** is a curved sealed edge between the floor and wall that eliminates sharp corners or gaps that would make cleaning difficult and ineffective.

Floors graded to drains are needed in retail food establishments where water-flush methods are used for cleaning. In addition, the floor and wall must be coved and sealed. **Coving** is a curved sealed edge between the floor and wall that eliminates sharp corners or gaps that would make cleaning difficult and ineffective. When cleaning methods other than water flushing are used for cleaning floors, the floor and wall juncture must be coved with a gap of no more than 1/32 inch (1 mm) between the floor and wall and sealed.

Use mats and other forms of anti-slip floor coverings where necessary to

Anti-slip mats help prevent falls.

protect employees from slips and falls. These devices should also be impervious, nonabsorbent, and easy to clean.

Walls and Ceilings

Walls and ceilings in food production and warewashing areas must be made of a light colored material to enhance the artificial lighting in these areas. This will make soil and dirt easier to see and will help employees know when they have done an effective job cleaning a surface. Walls and wall coverings should be constructed of materials such as ceramic tile, stainless steel, or fiberglass when used in areas cleaned frequently.

Ceilings should be constructed of nonporous, easily cleanable materials. Studs, rafters, joists, or pipes must not be exposed in walk-in refrigeration units, food preparation and warewashing areas, and toilet rooms.

> **Light fixtures, ventilation system components, and other attachments to walls and ceilings must be easy to clean and maintained in good repair.**

Restroom Sanitation

Toilet facilities near work areas promote good personal hygiene, reduce lost productivity, and permit closer supervision of employees. Toilet rooms in retail food establishments must be completely enclosed and provided with tight-fitting and self-closing doors.

Materials used in the construction of toilet rooms and toilet fixtures must be durable and easily cleanable. The floors, walls, and fixtures in toilet areas must be clean and well maintained. Supply toilet tissue at each toilet. Provide easy-to-clean containers for waste materials and have at least one covered container in toilet rooms used by women.

> **Employee restrooms must be conveniently located and accessible to employees during all hours of operation.**

Handwashing Sinks

Food employees must know when and how to wash their hands. Refer to Chapter 3 for details on the proper way to wash your hands. Conveniently located and properly equipped hand-washing sinks are key factors in getting employees to wash their hands. Hand-washing sinks should be conveniently located

> **Poor sanitation in toilet areas can spread disease. Never store food or items associated with food handling in restroom areas.**

in or near areas where food is prepared or handled and in warewashing areas. Handwashing sinks must also be located in or adjacent to restrooms. The number of handwashing sinks required and their installation are usually set by local health or plumbing codes.

A handwashing sink must be equipped with:

- Hot and cold running water under pressure
- A supply of soap
- A way to dry hands without contaminating them (i.e., paper towels or hot-air dryer)
- A waste receptacle
- A handwashing poster or sign

A handwashing sink must be able to provide water at a temperature of at least 100°F (38°C) through a mixing valve or combination faucet. If a self-closing, slow-closing, or metering faucet is used, it must provide a flow of water for at least 15 seconds without the need to be reactivated.

Each handwashing sink must be equipped with a dispenser containing liquid or powdered soap. The use of bar soap is frequently discouraged by regulatory agencies because bar soap can become contaminated with germs and soil.

Handwashing station

Individual disposable towels and mechanical hot-air dryers are the preferred hand drying devices. Most local health departments do not allow retractable cloth towel dispenser systems because there are too many possibilities for contamination. Common cloth towels, used multiple times by employees to dry their hands, are also prohibited. A sign or poster that notifies food employees to wash their hands must be clearly visible at all handwashing sinks used by food workers.

> **Handwashing sinks should be clean and well maintained and never be used for purposes other than handwashing.**
>
> **Sinks used for preparing produce and warewashing must not be used for handwashing.**

Plumbing Hazards in Retail Food Establishments

A properly designed and installed plumbing system is very important to food sanitation. The *Food Code* includes many different components within the definition of a plumbing system. In particular, it identifies the:

- Water supply and distribution pipes
- Plumbing fixtures and traps
- Soil, waste, and vent pipes
- Sanitary and storm sewers
- Building drains, including their respective connections and devices within the building and at the site.

Numerous outbreaks of gastroenteritis, dysentery, typhoid fever, and chemical poisonings have been traced to cross connections and other types of plumbing hazards in retail food establishments. The plumbing system in a retail food establishment must be maintained in good repair. When repairs to the plumbing system are required, they must be completed in accordance with applicable local ordinances and state regulations.

Cross Connections

A **cross connection** may be either direct or indirect. A direct cross connection occurs when a potable water system is directly connected to a drain, sewer, non-potable water supply, or other source of contamination. In indirect cross connection, the source of contamination (sewage, chemicals, etc.) may be blown across, sucked into, or diverted into a safe water supply.

> **A cross connection is any physical link through which contaminants from drains, sewers, or waste pipes can enter a potable (safe to drink) water supply.**

Backflow

Backflow occurs most frequently under two conditions:

1. Backpressure where contamination is forced into a potable water system through a connection that has a higher pressure than the water system.

> **Backflow is the backward flow of contaminated water into a potable water supply.**

2. Backsiphonage occurs when there is reduced pressure or a vacuum formed in the water system. This might be caused by a water main break, the shutdown of a portion of the system for repairs, or heavy water use during a fire.

Methods and Devices to Prevent Backflow

In the event of water pressure drop... backsiphonage occurs.

Backsiphonage

The plumbing system in a retail food establishment must be designed, constructed, and installed according to the plumbing code in the local jurisdiction. A properly designed and installed plumbing system will keep food, equipment, and utensils from becoming contaminated with disease-causing microorganisms found in sewage and other pollutants. Cross connections and backflow can be prevented using devices such as **air gaps**, **vacuum breakers**, and check valves.

Devices to Prevent Cross Connections and Backflow	
Device	**Key Features**
Air gap (illustration showing opening of faucet, air gap 2D, flood rim, and air gap at drain)	• The most dependable backflow prevention device • Vertical air space separates potable and non-potable systems • Distance must be at least 2 times the diameter of the supply pipe (2D), but never less than 1 inch (25 mm).

(continued)

Devices to Prevent Cross Connections and Backflow (continued)

Device	Key Features
Atmospheric vacuum breaker 	• Atmospheric vent used in combination with a check valve • Valve's air inlet closes when the potable water flows in the normal direction, but as water ceases to flow the air inlet opens, thus interrupting the possible backsiphonage effect.
Pressure type vacuum breaker 	• Designed for use under continuous supply pressure, but not effective under backpressure • Use only where non-pressure vacuum breakers cannot be used.
Dual check valve 	• Two internally loaded, independently operating check valves that may be used as protection for all direct connections through which foreign materials might enter a potable water system.

(continued)

Devices to Prevent Cross Connections and Backflow (continued)

Device	Key Features
Reduced pressure principle backflow preventers 	• Used on all direct connections that may be subject to backpressure or backsiphonage • Used when there is a possibility of contamination by material that is a health hazard.

Backflow Prevention Devices on Carbonators

Carbonators on soft drink dispensers form carbonic acid by mixing carbon dioxide with water. The carbonic acid is then mixed with the syrups to produce the soft drinks. If the carbon dioxide backs up into a copper water line, the carbonic acid will dissolve some of the copper. The water containing the dissolved copper will then be used in dispensing soft drinks, and the first few customers receiving the drinks are likely to suffer the symptoms of copper poisoning. An air gap or a vented backflow prevention device meeting American Society of Sanitary Engineering (ASSE) Standard No. 1022 must be installed upstream from a carbonating device and downstream from any copper in the water supply line to reduce incidences of copper poisoning.

Backflow preventer on a carbonator

Grease Traps

Retail food establishments that produce large amounts of grease from a meat department and similar operations should be equipped with a grease trap. These devices remove liquid grease and fats after they have hardened and become separated from the waste water. Grease traps are especially important when the retail food establishment is connected to a septic system or other type of onsite wastewater treatment and disposal system. A grease trap must be properly located for easily accessible cleaning.

Failure to properly clean and maintain grease traps can result in the harborage of pests and/or the failure of the facility's sewage system.

External grease trap recessed underground

Garbage and Refuse Sanitation

Proper storage and disposal of **garbage** and **refuse** are required at retail food establishments to protect food and equipment from contamination. Insects, rodents, and other pests are also less likely to be attracted to these establishments when garbage and refuse are properly managed. Effective waste management requires:

- Proper handling and short-term storage of the materials inside the operation
- Proper storage of the waste outside the building until it is picked up by a commercial refuse disposal company.

Garbage is the term applied to food wastes that cannot be recycled.

Refuse is trash, rubbish, and other types of solid waste not disposed of through the sewage system.

Inside Storage

Waste containers must be provided in all departments and other areas in a retail food establishment where refuse is produced or discarded. Containers used to collect garbage and refuse must be:

- Durable
- Cleanable
- Insect and rodent proof
- Leak proof
- Nonabsorbent
- Covered with a tight-fitting lid when not in use.

Plastic bags and wet strength paper bags are frequently used to line waste containers. Do not place waste containers in locations where they might create a public health nuisance.

Waste storage container with a plastic liner

Refuse storage rooms and containers must be cleaned as part of the establishment's routine cleaning program. Keeping the area clean is your best defense against pests. When cleaning this equipment, be careful not to contaminate food, equipment, utensils, linens, or single-service and single-use articles. Wastewater produced while cleaning the equipment and receptacles is considered to be sewage. It must be disposed of through an approved sanitary sewage system or other system constructed, maintained, and operated according to law.

Outside Storage

A retail food establishment should also have an outside storage area and enclosure to hold refuse, recyclables, and returnables awaiting pickup. An outdoor storage surface should be durable, cleanable, and maintained in good repair. Dumpsters and storage areas must be covered with tight-fit-

> **Dirty equipment, containers, and waste facilities attract insects and rodents.**

ting lids, doors, or covers to discourage insects, rodents, and other types of pests.

Outside garbage and refuse station

Refuse and garbage should be removed from the site as often as necessary to prevent objectionable odors and avoid conditions that attract or harbor insects and rodents.

Outdoor storage areas must be kept clean and free of litter. Suitable cleaning equipment and supplies must be available to clean the equipment and receptacles. Refuse storage equipment and receptacles must have drains, and drain plugs must be in place.

Compactors and other equipment for refuse, recyclables, and returnables must be installed to minimize the accumulation of debris. Always make sure you clean under and around these units to prevent insect and rodent harborage.

Some retail food establishments may provide redeeming machines for recyclables or returnables. According to the *Food Code*, a redeeming machine may be located in the packaged food storage area or consumer area of a retail food establishment if food, equipment, utensils and linens, and single-service and single-use articles are not subject to contamination from the machine and a public health nuisance is not created.

Trash bailer

Pest Control

Every retail food establishment should have a pest control program. The targets of this program are insects and rodents that can spread disease and damage food. These pests carry disease-causing microorganisms in and on their bodies and can transfer them to food and food-contact surfaces. Pests also destroy millions of dollars of food each year by eating it or by contaminating it with urine and feces.

The key element of a successful pest control program is prevention. However, no single measure will effectively prevent or control insects and rodents in retail food establishments. It takes a combination of three separate activities to keep pests in check. You must:

1. Prevent entry of insects and rodents into the establishment.
2. Eliminate food, water, and places where insects and rodents can hide.
3. Implement an integrated pest management (IPM) program to control insect and rodent pests that enter the establishment.

Prevent pests from invading your establishment.

Insects

What insects lack in size, they more than make up for in numbers. Insects may spread diseases, contaminate food, destroy property, or be nuisances in retail food establishments. Insects need water, food, and a breeding place in order to survive. The best method of insect control is keeping them out of the establishment coupled with good sanitation and an IPM when needed.

Insects Common to Retail Food Establishments

Flies

Common Types:	- Houseflies - Blowflies - Fruit flies. 
Common Problems:	- When a fly walks over filth, material sticks to its body and leg hairs, which contaminates food when a fly walks over it; the fly vomits on solid food to soften it before eating, spreading bacteria to food and food-contact surfaces - Blowflies are attracted by odors in food establishments - Fruit flies are attracted by decaying fruit.
Control Methods:	- Eliminate the insect's food supply; store food, garbage, and other wastes in fly-tight containers; regularly clean kitchen, dining, toilet, and waste storage facilities. - Equip windows, doors, and loading and unloading areas with tight-fitting screens or air curtains. - Insect electrocuting devices must be installed so dead insects and insect parts cannot fall on food and food-contact surfaces. Non-electrocuting systems, using glue traps and pheromone attractants, are allowed in areas of the establishment where electrocuting devices are not. - Chemical insecticides may be applied by a professional pest control operator as a supplement to proper food-handling practices and a clean establishment.

(continued)

Insects Common to Retail Food Establishments		(continued)
Cockroaches		
Common Types:	• German cockroach 	
Common Problems:	• Carry bacteria on their hairy legs and body as well as in their intestinal tract • Commonly hide in cracks and crevices under and behind equipment and facilities.	
Control Methods:	• Maintain good housekeeping indoors and outside; eliminate hiding places by picking up unwanted materials; fill cracks and crevices in floors and walls and around equipment; doors and windows should be tight-fitting and protected by screening, air curtains, or other effective means • Check incoming food and supplies for signs of infestation such as egg cases and live roaches; store food in containers that are insect proof and have tight-fitting lids • Keep floors, tables, walls and equipment clean and free of food wastes • Residual insecticides and baits can be used when a serious infestation exists.	

(continued)

Insects Common to Retail Food Establishments (continued)

Moths and beetles

- Indian meal moth
- Saw-toothed grain beetle
- Flour weevil
- Rice weevil.

- These insects feed on corn, rice, wheat, flour, beans, sugar, meal, and cereals
- These insects create problems of wasted food and nuisance rather than disease.

- Inspect incoming products for signs of infestation
- Use FIFO system of stock rotation; store opened packages or bags of food in covered containers
- Clean shelves and floors frequently
- Keep dry food storage areas cool
- Residual insecticides and pheromone traps are available to control these pests.

Rodents

Rodents are known to carry microorganisms that can cause a number of human diseases including salmonellosis, plague, and murine typhus. Rodents also consume and damage large quantities of foods each year. Rats typically carry their food back to their nest rather than eat it where it is found.

Domestic rodents in the United States include the *Norway rat*, the *roof rat*, and the *house mouse*. The Norway rat is also known as the brown rat, sewer rat, and wharf rat and is the one most commonly found in the United States.

The *Norway rat* hides in burrows in the ground around buildings, and in sewers. Norway rats will eat almost any food but prefer garbage, meat, fish, and cereal. They stay close to food and water, and their range of travel is usually no more than 100 to 150 feet.

The *roof rat* generally harbors in the upper floors of buildings but is sometimes found in sewers. Roof rats prefer vegetables, fruits, cereal, and grain for food. The range of travel for the roof rat is also about 100 to 150 feet.

House mouse
(Courtesy of Bell Laboratories, Inc.)

The *house mouse* is the smallest of the domestic rodents. It is found primarily in and around buildings, nesting in walls, cabinets, and stored goods. The house mouse is a nibbler, and it prefers cereal and grain. Its range of travel is 10 to 30 feet.

Signs of Rodent Infestation

It is unusual to see rats or mice during the daytime since they are nocturnal. Therefore, it is necessary to look for signs of their activities. From rodent signs, you can determine the type of rodent, whether it is a new or old problem, and whether there is a light or heavy infestation.

Droppings

The presence of rat or mouse feces is one of the best indications of an infestation. Fresh droppings are usually moist, soft, and shiny, whereas old droppings become dry and hard. Norway rat droppings are the largest and have rounded ends. They look a lot like black jelly beans. Roof rat droppings are smaller and more regular in form. The droppings of the house mouse are very small and pointed at each end. They look something like dark grains of rice.

Norway Rat Droppings   Roof Rat Droppings   House Mouse Droppings

Rodent droppings

Runways and Burrows

Rats are very cautious and repeatedly use the same paths and trails. Outdoors in grass and weeds, you may see 2- to 3-inch wide paths worn down from repeated activity.

The Norway rat prefers to burrow for nesting and harborage. Burrows are found in earth banks, along walls, and under rubbish. Rat holes are about 3 inches in diameter whereas mouse holes are only about 1 inch in diameter. If a burrow is active, it will be free of cobwebs and dust. The presence of fresh food or freshly dug earth at the entrance of the burrow also indicates an active burrow.

Rub Marks

Rats prefer to stay close to walls where they can keep their highly sensitive whiskers in contact with the wall. As a rat runs along a wall, its body rubs against the wall or baseboard. The oil and filth from the rat's body are deposited on the wall and create a black mark called a rub mark. Mice do not leave rub marks that are detectable, except when the infestation is especially heavy.

Gnawings

The incisor teeth of rats grow 4 to 6 inches a year. As a result, rats have to keep these teeth filed down in order to keep them short enough to use. Gnawings in wood are fresh if they are light colored and show well-defined teeth marks.

Tracks

Tracks may be observed along rat or mouse runs both indoors and outdoors. Look for tracks in dust in little-used rooms and in mud around puddles. Rat tracks may be 1 inch long.

Miscellaneous Signs

Rodent urine stains can be seen with an ultraviolet light (black light). Rats leave a different pattern than mice. Rat and mouse hairs may be found along walls, etc. When examined under a microscope, they can be distinguished from other animal hairs.

Rodent Control

The grounds around the retail food establishment should be free of litter, waste, refuse, uncut weeds, and grass. Unused equipment, boxes, crates, pallets, and other materials should be neatly stored to eliminate places where pests might hide.

All entrances and loading and unloading areas should be equipped with self-closing doors and door flashings to prevent rodent entry into the establishment. Metal screens with holes no larger than 1/4 inch should be installed over all floor drains to prevent entry.

Effective rodent control begins with a building and grounds that will not provide a source of food, shelter, and breeding areas.

Traps are useful around retail food establishments where rodenticides are not permitted or are hazardous. Live traps can be used for collecting live rats. Check traps at least once every 24 hours. Killer or snap traps can also be used as part of a rodent control program. When using these types of traps, place them at right angles to the wall along rodent runways with the trigger side closest to the wall.

Glueboards are shallow trays that have a very sticky surface. The mouse's feet stick to the board when it walks on it, and it is caught. Glueboards should be placed next to and running parallel with the wall.

| Bait box | Bait box | Glueboard |

(Courtesy of J.T. Eaton & Company, Inc.)

Rodenticides are hazardous chemicals that can contaminate food and food-contact surfaces if not handled properly. Baits should be used outdoors to stop rodents at the outer boundaries of your property. Baits should be placed in a tamper-proof, locked bait box that will prevent children and pets from being exposed to the toxic chemicals inside. Always make certain pesticides are stored in properly labeled containers, away from food in a secure place. Dispose of containers safely and know emergency measures for treating accidental poisoning.

The use of tracking powder pesticides is prohibited in retail food establishments. These types of pesticides can be dispersed throughout the establishment and directly or indirectly contaminate food, equipment, utensils, linens, and single-service/single-use articles. This contamination could adversely affect both the safety of the food and the general environment. However, a nontoxic tracking powder such as baking soda can be temporarily used to indicate rodent infestation.

Integrated Pest Management (IPM)

Modern pest control operators use **integrated pest management (IPM)** as the primary method to control pests in retail food establishments. Chemical pesticides are used only as a last resort and only in the amount needed to support the other control measures in the IPM program and normally applied only by a Certified Pest Control Operator. If chemical pesticides are used, they must be approved for use as specified in the *Code of Federal Regulations* (40 CFR 152).

> **Integrated pest management (IPM) is a system that uses a combination of sanitation, mechanical, and chemical procedures to control pests.**

The National Pest Management Association (NPMA) recommends a five-step program for IPM:

1. Inspection.
2. Identification.
3. Sanitation.
4. Application of two or more pest management procedures.
5. Evaluation of effectiveness through follow-up inspections.

There are many benefits produced by using IPM. An IPM program is more efficient and cost effective than programs that rely exclusively on chemicals to control pests. IPM is also longer lasting and safer for you, your employees, and your customers.

Summary

Back to the Story ... *The case presented at the beginning of the chapter illustrates how pests can pose a serious challenge for retail food establishments. Pests are known to contaminate food and food-contact surfaces, and they can carry disease-causing microorganisms harmful to humans. Pests are attracted to retail food establishments by the food, water, and pleasant odors they find there. In order to keep pests under control, retail food establishments must prevent them from entering the facility, eliminate sources of food and shelter, and implement an effective sanitation program. Without these prerequisite activities in place, it would be impossible for the PCO to do his job properly.*

- ✔ Surveys of customers show cleanliness is a top consideration when choosing a place to eat or shop for food. Customer satisfaction is highest in retail food establishments that are clean and bright and where quality food products are safely handled and displayed.

- ✔ Proper construction, repair, and cleaning of floors, walls, and ceilings are important elements of an effective sanitation program. Sanitation, safety, durability, comfort, and cost are the main criteria you will use when selecting materials for floors and walls. Surfaces of floors and walls should be resistant to damage and deterioration from the water, detergents, and repeated scrubbings used to keep them clean. Walls and ceilings should be light colored to show soil and enhance the artificial lighting used in food preparation, handling, and display areas.

- ✔ Handwashing sinks must be properly equipped and conveniently located to enable food handlers to wash their hands as necessary throughout the workday.
- ✔ Clean and suitably equipped toilet facilities must be provided for employees. These facilities must be kept clean and in good repair to prevent the spread of disease and promote good personal hygiene.
- ✔ A properly designed, constructed, and installed plumbing
- ✔ system is very important to food sanitation. Air gaps and mechanical vacuum breakers are used to protect the municipal water supply. Consult a professional plumber or your local plumbing code for details about the plumbing requirements in your jurisdiction.
- ✔ Proper storage and disposal of garbage and refuse are necessary to prevent contamination of food and equipment and avoid attracting insects, rodents, and other pests to a retail food establishment. Proper facilities and receptacles must be provided inside and outside the establishment to hold refuse, recyclables, and returnables that may accumulate. Refuse and garbage should be removed from retail food establishments frequently enough to minimize the development of objectionable odors and other conditions that attract or harbor insects, rodents, and other pests.

Discussion Questions (Short Answer)

1. What are the criteria customers use when selecting a retail food establishment to shop for food?
2. How can the appearance of a retail food establishment make a positive impression on a customer?
3. Identify four characteristics that floors, walls, and ceilings should have when they are used in kitchens and warewashing areas.
4. List the primary components of a handwashing sink.
5. How does the location of handwashing sinks influence sanitation and personal hygiene?
6. How does proper refuse and garbage disposal contribute to the pest control activities of a retail food establishment?

Quiz 7 (Multiple Choice)

Choose the **best** answer for each question.

1. The most effective device for protecting the potable water system from contamination by backflow is a (an):

    a. air gap.

    b. double check valve.

    c. hose bib.

    d. vacuum breaker.

2. Coving is a (an):

    a. curved sealed edge between the floor and wall that eliminates sharp corners to make cleaning easier.

    b. anti-slip floor covering used to protect employees from slips and falls.

    c. plastic material used to seal cracks and crevices under and around equipment in a food establishment.

    d. device used to prevent backsiphonage.

3. The **best** way to encourage employees to wash their hands when needed is to:

    a. provide a separate restroom for employees and customers.

    b. provide properly equipped handwashing sinks convenient to work areas.

    c. provide hand antiseptics instead of handwashing sinks in food-preparation areas.

    d. put up a sign in the employee locker room reminding them of the importance of proper handwashing.

4. The primary responsibility of retail food establishment managers in pest control is to assure:

    a. good sanitation that will eliminate food, water, and harborage areas.

    b. pesticides are applied safely.

    c. the pest control operator they use employs integrated pest management.

    d. the parking area is kept free of litter.

5. Which of the following statements about toilet facilities is **false**?
   a. Toilet facilities must be available for all employees.
   b. Employee toilet facilities must be conveniently located and accessible to employees during all hours of operation.
   c. Separate toilet facilities should be provided for men and women.
   d. Poor sanitation in toilet facilities will influence customers' opinions about cleanliness but will not promote the spread of disease.

6. When an air gap is used, the vertical distance between the supply pipe (faucet) and the flood rim must be at least:
   a. two times the diameter of the supply pipe, but never less than 1/2 inch.
   b. two times the diameter of the supply pipe, but never less than 1 inch.
   c. three times the diameter of the supply pipe, but never less than 2 inches.
   d. four times the diameter of the supply pipe, but never less than 3 inches.

7. Which of the following statements about garbage and refuse sanitation is **false**?
   a. Proper disposal and storage of garbage and refuse are necessary to prevent contamination of food and equipment and to avoid attracting insects and rodents.
   b. A trash receptacle should be provided in each area of the retail food establishment where refuse is generated.
   c. The equipment and receptacles used to store refuse, garbage, etc., must be durable, clean, nonabsorbent, leak proof, and pest proof.
   d. Trash may be stored outdoors in plastic bags provided the bags are stored at least 15 inches off the ground.

8. You are surveying your establishment for unsafe conditions. Which one of the following situations requires corrective action?
   a. A trash receptacle with the lid off while in use.
   b. A handwashing sink with a multi-use cloth towel for hand drying.
   c. Light colored ceramic tile used for the walls of the food-preparation area.
   d. Anti-slip flooring provided in the warewashing area.

9. Backsiphonage is likely to occur if:

    a. the pressure in the potable water system drops below that of a nonpotable or contaminated water source.

    b. contamination is forced into a potable water system through a connection that has a higher pressure than the water system.

    c. pressure builds up in a sewer line due to blockage.

    d. the water seal in a kitchen trap is siphoned out.

10. What factor has the greatest influence on where people choose to eat or shop for food?

    a. Cost of the food.

    b. Nutrition of the food.

    c. Quality of service.

    d. Cleanliness of food and facilities.

Answers to the multiple-choice questions are provided in Appendix A.

References/Suggested Reading

Bennett, G, W.; J. W. Owens; and R.M. Corrigan. 1997. *Truman's Scientific Guide to Pest Management Operations, 6th ed.* Purdue University Press, West Lafayette, IN.

Code of Federal Regulations. 2009. *40 CFR 1521—Pesticide Registration and Classification Procedures.* U.S. Government Printing Office. Washington, DC.

Food and Drug Administration and Conference for Food Protection. 2000. *Food Establishment Plan Review Guide.* Washington, DC.

Kopanic, R. J.; B. W. Sheldon; and C. G. Wright. 1994. "Cockroaches as Vectors of *Salmonella:* Laboratory and Field Trials." *Journal of Food Protection*, 57(2), 125–32.

Longrèe, K.; and G. Armbruster. 1996. *Quantity Food Sanitation.* Wiley. New York, NY.

Olsen, Alan R. (1998). "Regulatory Action Criteria for Filth and Other Extraneous Materials - Review of Flies and Foodborne Enteric Diseases." *Regulatory Toxicology and Pharmacology.* Vol. 28, 199–211.

Suggested Web Sites

Actron, Inc.
http://actroninc.com

Suggested Web Sites

American Society of Sanitary Engineering
www.asse-plumbing.org

Association of Applied IPM Ecologists
www.aaie.com

B&G Equipment
www.bgequip.com

Ecolab
www.ecolab.com

EPA Office of Prevention, Pesticides, and Toxic Substances
www.epa.gov/oppts

The Food Marketing Institute
www.fmi.org

Gateway to Government Food Safety Information
www.foodsafety.gov

Hobart Corporation
www.hobartcorp.com

Insect-O-Cutor
www.insect-o-cutor.com

PestWest, USA
www.pestwest.com

National Pest Management Association
www.pestworld.org

The Orkin Company
www.orkin.com/commercial/solutions/food/qa.asp

Pest Control Services (PCO)
www.pco.ca

Pest Control Industry
www.pestweb.com

Plumbnet-Industry Resources
www.plumbnet.com/resources.html

Steritech
www.steritech.com

Do-It Yourself Pest Control
www.doyourownpestcontrol.com

Virginia Polytechnic Institute and University Pesticide Programs
www.vtpp.ext.vt.edu

Learn How To:

- Recognize how food safety management programs in retail food establishments reduce the risk of foodborne illness.

- Apply the Hazard Analysis Critical Control Point (HACCP) system as part of food safety management.

- Define Critical Control Point (CCPs) and identify critical limits (CLs) as used in the HACCP system.

- Determine the roles of managers and employees related to food safety management.

- Comply with a food recall procedure.

- Identify the need and function of product identification and product coding.

CHAPTER 8

Food Safety Management Programs

Potato Salad Encounters a Critical Control Point Violation

A large order was received from the central commissary including foods that needed to be stored under refrigeration, frozen, and in dry storage. During the storing process, some packages of potato salad were accidentally stored on a shelf in the storeroom. The potato salad needed to be kept under refrigeration.

Sometime later, an employee who was organizing the dry storage area discovered the packages that were stored out of refrigeration. The employee took the potato salad to the walk-in refrigerator and placed it under cold storage. The employee never took the temperature of the potato salad. Later, another employee pulled the potato salad from the walk-in cooler and placed it in the refrigerated display case in the deli area where it was sold to customers.

What are the potential problems from this incident? What important critical control point was ignored?

Essential Terms

Coding	Hazard Analysis Critical Control
Critical Control Point (CCP)	Point (HACCP) system
Critical Limit (CL)	Risk
Flow diagram	Standard Operating Procedures
Food Recall	(SOPs)
Good Retail Practices (GRPs)	

The Problem

The challenge of reducing the number of cases of foodborne illness has made it necessary to reevaluate our nation's food safety system. The retail food industry and food regulatory agencies must deal with:

- New hazards that cause foodborne illness
- A global food supply that carries more risks
- New techniques and equipment for processing, displaying, and serving food
- A change in eating patterns by customers including more ready-to-eat products
- An increase in the number of people who are immunocompromised and at risk for foodborne illness due to age and condition.

The size and scope of the food industry increases the workload on the Food and Drug Administration (FDA), U.S. Department of Agriculture (USDA), and state and local food regulatory agencies. The FDA identified more than 30,000 food manufacturers and 20,000 food warehouses that process and store products. Inspection of all these operations is nearly impossible. The retail and food service portion of the food industry is even larger and consists of more than one million establishments with a work force of over 15 million people.

Food safety and food quality are both major concerns for retail food establishment managers and their staff. Food safety focuses on assuring the products sold are safe to eat. Regulatory standards and guidelines related to safe food handling at retail levels are discussed in this book and in the *Food Code*. Food quality is also very important. High quality often equals high profits and returning customers. With an average profit margin of 1% to 2%, it makes good business sense to produce and sell the safest and highest quality food possible.

> **The goal of food safety management is to prevent foodborne illness.**

The Solution

Chapter 3 identifies the major risk factors related to foodborne illness. The most important factors are:

- Improper holding temperatures
- Poor personal hygiene
- Contaminated equipment
- Inadequate cooking
- Food from an unsafe source.

Food safety management programs should protect foods from the factors known to lead to foodborne illness. To ensure food safety, we need to focus on the following four keys to foodborne illness prevention:

> **Food Safety Management Programs Involve:**
>
> - Controlling time and temperature
> - Practicing good hygiene
> - Preventing cross contamination
> - Cleaning and sanitizing properly.

1. Time and temperature control.
2. Good personal hygiene practices and procedures.
3. Elimination of cross contamination.
4. An effective cleaning and sanitation program.

Food safety management programs in retail food establishments must be customized to fit company policies, the size of the establishment, and the number and types of customers served. To operate a food safety management program, you must understand the hazards that cause foodborne illness, and how these hazards can be prevented. Focus the program on elimination or control of the risk factors known to contribute to foodborne illness.

The food safety procedures in your management system must be easy for your employees to understand and implement. Management in your operation will be up to you.

Start with a Good Set of Instructions

The ability to do a job correctly depends on good instructions and properly trained employees. This holds true for all functions in a retail food establishment including marketing, purchasing, operations, and customer services. Examples include how to:

- Break down pieces of equipment for cleaning
- Stock and rotate products on shelves
- Wash hands properly
- Operate the slicer in the deli or meat department safely
- Take care of an emergency.

In retail food establishments, there are many procedures that need to be done correctly to protect the safety of foods. A detailed step-by-step form of instruction and training will help the employee do a job properly.

There are different methods the retail food industry uses for this type of information. In some cases, a book of procedures is used. In other cases, procedures are posted near work stations for easy access by employees. There are also many terms that can be used for these procedures. *Best practices* and **"Standard Operating Procedures" (SOPs)** are two terms commonly used to describe written procedures on how to perform a job. It does not matter what these procedures are called so long as they are written clearly, explained to employees, and performed correctly.

> **Best practices and Standard Operating Procedures (SOPs) are written procedures on how to perform a job.**

There are different types of SOPs that can affect the safety and quality of foods during receiving, storage, preparation, and sale.

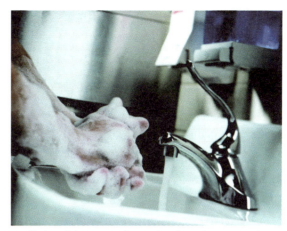

Put safety procedures in place to prevent foodborne illness.

Some examples of SOPs used by retail food establishments include:

- Good personal hygiene programs
- Cross contamination control
- Cleaning and sanitizing programs
- Pest management
- Storage practices of foods and ingredients
- Water and ice handling
- Use of chemicals.

By way of example, the Food Marketing Institute (FMI) has provided model SOPs for molluscan shellfish handling in a document titled *Molluscan Shellfish Handling for Retailers* (FMI 2009b). In this document, six important elements are indicated for each SOP including:

1. Title of the task to be completed.
2. Date the SOP was issued.
3. Area or department to use the SOP.
4. Detailed, specific actions that need to be taken to complete the task.
5. Any documentation that needs to be completed to verify the task was accomplished.
6. Approval signatures.

The following is an example of an SOP from this document specific for personal health and hygiene practices. Note the SOP contains a very specific list of instructions and includes directions for monitoring and corrective action. In this SOP, critical items are identified as those steps in the procedure most critical to food safety.

SOP for Personal Health and Hygiene

Background Notes Date Effective 6/1/09

- This procedure outlines personal health, hygiene, and handwashing requirements required for the safe handling and sale of foods.
- Employees diagnosed with a food-related illness or showing symptoms of an illness are not permitted to work with food, food-contact equipment, utensils, or surfaces.
- Employees with festering cuts, abrasions, boils, or any condition that may cause flaking or exposed skin may not have contact with food or food-contact items.

Departments: All departments

Specific Instructions

- Critical Item—Only healthy employees are permitted to handle food, food-contact equipment, and utensils. Employees that have been diagnosed with a food-related illness or are experiencing symptoms (sore throat with fever, diarrhea, vomiting, or jaundice) must immediately notify their supervisor and remove themselves from the food environment.
- Critical Item—Employees with festering cuts, abrasions, boils or any other condition that may cause flaking of exposed skin must immediately notify their supervisors and remove themselves from the food environment. An infected wound must be freshly and properly bandaged and covered with an impermeable cover (surgical glove), which will prevent contact with food or food-contact items.
- Bathe daily and have clean, well-groomed hair. Present a clean appearance.
- Wear clean, washable outer garments, clean apron, and clean shoes. Safety shoes may be necessary.
- Wear clean, effective hair restraint.
- Have clean hands and fingernails. False fingernails and nail polish are not permitted.
- Employees must avoid wearing any jewelry on hands and arms. A single, plain wedding band is allowed to be worn.
- Critical Item—All employees must wash their hands and exposed portions of their arms thoroughly:
  - Before starting work
  - When changing to new gloves
  - After using the restroom
  - Using the paper towel to contact other surfaces after handwashing
  - After eating, drinking, or using tobacco products

(continued)

SOP for Personal Health and Hygiene (continued)

- After touching their mouth or anything that has been in their mouth
- After touching their hair, nose, ears, etc.
- After handling trash, garbage, dirty utensils, or soiled equipment
- After sneezing or coughing into their hands, or using a handkerchief or disposable tissue
- After changing from raw to cooked or ready-to-eat foods
- After any absence from the work area
- Critical Item—Washing hands and exposed portions of arms is accomplished by:
  - Vigorously rubbing hands together, lathering soap, using hot water for at least 20 seconds
  - Rinsing with clean water
  - Drying with disposable paper hand towels, clean continuous dispenser towels, or air dryers
- Avoid bare hand contact with any ready-to-eat foods, including shellfish. Use single-use gloves, deli tissues, or utensils to handle product. Change single-use gloves frequently to prevent contamination. Remember gloves are not a substitute for proper hand washing.
- Remove personal items from pockets where they may fall into food, such as cigarettes, lighters, and pens.
- Employees may only eat, drink, smoke, or chew (tobacco or gum) in designated break areas.
- Employee street clothing, personal belongings, or personally owned foods and beverages should be stored in designated areas.

Monitoring

Daily: Department manager should visually observe employees for:

- Symptoms of illnesses or skin infections
- Proper handwashing practices and frequency.

Corrective Action

- Refer all employees diagnosed with a food-related illness, displaying symptoms of illnesses, or skin infection immediately to department manager.
- Refer employees to repeat handwashing procedures.

Model SOP for Personal Health and Hygiene for Molluscan Shellfish Handling (used with permission from the Food Marketing Institute—FMI, 2009)

The HACCP Approach to Food Safety

In the food industry, there are a variety of programs that can be used to manage food safety. **Hazard Analysis Critical Control Point (HACCP)** is a prevention-based program used by many segments of the food industry to assure food safety. The HACCP system can control hazards, such as disease-causing microorganisms, chemical substances, and physical objects that are common causes of foodborne illness (refer back to Chapter 2 for a detailed description of these hazards and their control).

In 1959, the National Aeronautic and Space Agency (NASA) approached the Pillsbury Company to produce food safe for astronauts to eat in zero gravity conditions in the space capsules. The project goal was to develop a system that assured nearly 100% freedom from contamination by microbial, chemical, or physical hazards. This effort resulted in the beginning of the HACCP concept for food safety management.

HACCP has been required for many years for the meat/poultry, seafood, and juice industries. Currently, HACCP is not required for retail food establishments except in a limited number of states and jurisdictions. However, many retail food establishments have implemented HACCP programs voluntarily to assure the safety and wholesomeness of the products they produce and sell.

When a HACCP program is developed, a team is chosen to discuss two fundamental questions:

1. Are there any hazards or risks associated with the ingredients, the process, or the finished food?
2. How can I make sure the identified hazards and risks are eliminated or kept at a safe level?

The Seven Principles in a HACCP System

The basic structure of a HACCP system consists of seven principles shown in the following chart. A HACCP team identifies the PHS (TCS) used and sold at the establishment. The HACCP team also discusses the different processes involved in preparing these items. After implementation of the seven principles, individuals must be trained, and the program must be evaluated to assure employees understand their roles and responsibilities related to HACCP.

The Seven Principles in a HACCP System

> **Seven Principles in a HACCP System**
> 1. Hazard analysis.
> 2. Identify the Critical Control Points (CCPs) in food preparation.
> 3. Establish critical limits (thresholds) that must be met at each identified CCP.
> 4. Establish procedures to monitor CCPs.
> 5. Establish the corrective action to be taken when monitoring indicates a critical limit has been exceeded.
> 6. Establish procedures to verify the HACCP system is working.
> 7. Establish effective record keeping that will document the HACCP system.

Principle 1—Hazard Analysis

In this first step, the team identifies hazards associated with ingredients that are received, those that may be associated with each step in the flow of food, and those important at the time of purchase or consumption by the customer. Hazards are then assessed for their risk. **Risk** indicates a level of danger based on "how likely" the hazard is to occur and "how severe" the hazard could be from a public health standpoint. Those hazards most likely to occur or pose the highest risk of disease will be addressed in the HACCP system by the HACCP team.

Principle 2—Identify Critical Control Points (CCPs)

The *Food Code* defines a **Critical Control Point (CCP)** as a point at which loss of control may result in an unacceptable health risk. A CCP can be thought of as a point in the flow of food where a preventative measure can be put into place to control the identified hazards. The team identifies areas or points in the flow of a food product that must be controlled. These are the CCPs.

Principle 3—Establish a Critical Limit (CL)

Critical Limits (CL) are the upper and lower boundaries of food safety and are set at each CCP to reduce hazards and risks to safe levels and assure the CCP is under control. Critical limits are usually based on time, temperature, pH, and moisture content of a food. When you set a critical limit, the goal is to prevent or eliminate the hazards identified during the hazard analysis portion of the program. A critical limit should be as specific as possible, such as "ground meat must be heated to an internal temperature of at least 155°F (68°C) or above for at least 15 seconds." A well-defined critical limit makes it clear and easy to determine when the limit has not been met. In retail HACCP plans, critical limits for time and temperature are most often used to keep hazards under control.

Principle 4—Monitoring CCPs

CCPs and critical limits are only effective if they are monitored during the flow of food. Monitoring includes activities, such as measuring temperature and time. Monitoring helps to assure the processes involved in the flow of food are done correctly, and the hazards are in control.

Principle 5—Take Corrective Action

Whenever the critical limit for a CCP is exceeded, something must be done to assure the food is safe. When a critical limit is not met, fix it and then determine why the problem occurred. Corrective action may include adjusting product temperature or time, or even discarding the product if necessary to assure the safety of your customers.

Principle 6—Establish Procedures to Verify the HACCP System Is Working

Once the HACCP system is in place, a designated process is used to make sure it is effective. The *Food Code* recommends three phases to verification including (1) scientific verification of CCPs and CCP limits, (2) assuring the HACCP plan is functioning effectively, and (3) repeated validation of the HACCP plan by internal or external food safety audits.

Principle 7—Establish Effective Record Keeping

This principle enforces the importance of documentation of CCPs, CCP limits, and monitoring activities. These records are the only proof the process is in control, and the retail food establishment is complying with its HACCP plan.

Retail HACCP: A Process Approach

As the food industry develops and implements HACCP programs, it makes choices between a HACCP program that is product-specific or one that is process-specific.

- A product-specific HACCP program is tailored to the production of a specific food product. When product-specific HACCP programs are used, a HACCP plan is developed for each food product produced. This approach works well, especially in food manufacturing plants, where a limited number of products are handled.
- A process-specific HACCP program is customized to the processes used to produce a particular food or group of similar foods. In the retail food industry, numerous types of PHF (TCS) are produced and sold within a single retail food establishment. It often does not make sense and is not manageable to develop a HACCP plan for each one of these food products.

Because there are such a large number of food products, the retail food industry frequently relies on process-specific HACCP programs to ensure food safety. Retail food establishments base their HACCP plans on the process, or flow of food, rather than the actual product produced. This is called a process approach to HACCP. It simplifies the procedure so HACCP plan development is manageable and so the plan requirements can be successfully implemented. For example, for hot-holding, it does not matter what type of PHF (TCS) we are monitoring. In all situations, the key is to keep the food temperature above 135°F (57°C). The product is taken into consideration only when there is a difference in temperature guidelines, such as cooking [i.e., ground meat must be cooked to at least 155°F (68°C) while poultry must be cooked to at least 165°F (74°C)].

Every process in the flow of food is created from a few basic steps. They may include:

- Receiving and storing frozen
- Thawing
- Receiving cold
- Storing cold
- Preparing cold
- Displaying cold
- Cooking

Receiving step

- Hot-holding
- Displaying hot
- Cooling
- Reheating
- Servicing and handling.

If we take the process approach, we know there are certain temperature recommendations for each of these steps. We will follow these temperature guidelines in our food safety management system.

Service and handling step

The table below shows the different areas in the flow of food and the temperature guidelines used. These guidelines provide the basis for developing safety limits for the HACCP system.

Regardless of the type of food handled and sold in a retail food establishment, the food flow is made up of a series of steps. For most of the steps in the flow of food, time and temperature controls are the same regardless of the PHF(TCS): There are a few exceptions. In receiving, eggs, molluscan shellfish, and reduced oxygen packaging (ROP) foods may be received at a temperature other than 41°F (5°C). ROP foods may also have to be held cold at a temperature other than 41°F (5°C). Safe cooking temperatures will also differ depending on the product being cooked.

Flow of Food Step	Temperature Guidelines for PHF (TCS)
Frozen Foods	
Storage	• Foods are solidly frozen when received.
Storage	• Keep all foods solidly frozen.
Thawing	• Thaw in the refrigerator at 41°F (5°C), as part of the cooking process, under cool running water, or in a microwave oven.

(continued)

Flow of Food Step	Temperature Guidelines for PHF (TCS)
Cold Foods	
Receiving	• Receive all PHF(TCS) at 41°F (5°C) or below • Whole shell eggs at 45°F (7°C) ambient temperature or below • Dairy products at 45°F (7°C) or below • Shucked shellfish at 45°F (7°C) or below • Live shellstock at 50°F (10°C) or below • ROP foods may have special temperature requirements.
Refrigerated Storage Cold-Holding Display	• Store all PHF(TCS) at 41°F (5°C) or below • ROP foods may have special temperature requirements.
Preparing Cold Foods	
	• Minimize time between 41°F (5°C) and 135°F (57°C) to less than 4 hours for PHF(TCS).
Preparing Hot Foods	
Cooking	• Cook to the safe product temperature • Poultry, stuffed meats, and stuffed pasta—165°F (74°C) or above for 15 seconds • Ground meat and pork and game animals—155°F (68°C) or above for 15 seconds • Shell eggs, meat, pork (other than roasts), and fish—145°F (63°C) or above for 15 seconds • Meat roast (rare)—130°F (54°C) for 112 minutes or 140°F (60°C) for 12 minutes • Meat roast (medium), pork roast, and ham—145°F (63°C) or above for 3 minutes

(continued)

Flow of Food Step	Temperature Guidelines for PHF (TCS)
Preparing Hot Foods (continued)	
Cooking	• All other PHF(TCS)—145°F (63°C) or above • Microwave cooking—165°F (74°C) or above for raw animal foods, covered, stirred during the cooking process, and allow to stand for 2 minutes after cooking.
Hot-holding	• Hold all PHF(TCS) at 135°F (57°C) or display above.
Cooling	• Cool all foods from 135°F (57°C) to 70°F (21°C) within 2 hours and from 135°F (57°C) to 41°F (5°C) within 6 hours [total cooling time should not exceed 6 hours from 135°F (57°C) to 41°F (5°C)].
Reheat	• Reheat all PHF(TCS) to greater than 165°F (74°C) within 2 hours.
Preparation/ handling/ service	• Restrict the amount of time PHF(TCS) are held between 41°F (5°C) and 135°F (57°C) to 4 hours or less.

Source: FDA Food Code

HACCP plans are often shown as a flow diagram. A **flow diagram** provides a visual map of the different ingredients and each of the steps involved in the handling and preparation of food. Flow diagrams may also include the CCPs included in the HACCP plan. The figure on the following page provides an example of a flow diagram for a cooked and hot-held product (rotisserie chicken). For this product, cooking and hot-holding are identified as CCPs. The critical limits for this product are cooking the chicken to an internal temperature of at least 165°F (74°C) for a minimum of 15 seconds and holding it at 135°F (57°C) or above. Cooking is important for destroying any harmful bacteria that may have been present on the raw chicken. Control of hot-holding prevents growth of harmful bacteria that may have survived cooking or that contaminated the chicken after cooking.

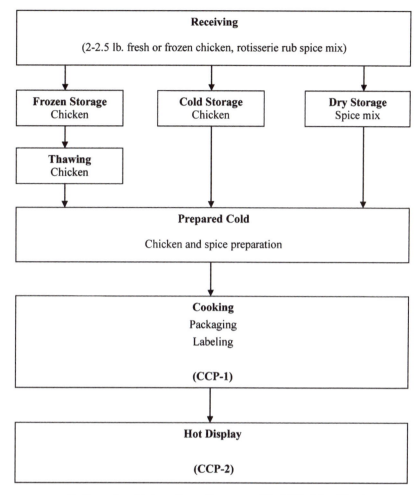

Rotisserie chicken flow diagram with CCPs identified

Food Safety Management and HACCP Requirements

A growing number of state, local, and tribal jurisdictions are starting to require retail food establishments to have a HACCP system in place. These agencies also conduct inspections of retail food establishments using HACCP principles. You may contact your local jurisdiction to obtain information about developing a HACCP system for your establishment.

The federal government requires HACCP plans and inspections for food processors that manufacture certain varieties of meat, poultry, seafood products, and unpasteurized juice products. A HACCP program is recommended when ROP foods are produced in retail food establishments.

Other Food Safety Management Programs

HACCP can be a very effective program, but it is not the cure-all for all food safety problems and in all segments of the food industry. There are many other complementary approaches that can be used.

In the food processing industry, a program called Good Manufacturing Practices (GMPs) is used as part of the food safety management program. GMPs refer to minimum sanitary and processing requirements necessary to assure the production of safe and wholesome food. GMPs include provisions for food handling related to personnel, building and facilities, equipment and utensils, and production and process controls. When implemented properly, GMPs help control the possibility of contamination from poor personal hygiene, chemicals, and physical objects. They also help assure cleaning and sanitizing procedures are done properly. There are FDA requirements for GMPs in food manufacturing operations, and they are listed in Section 21 of the *Code of Federal Regulations, Part 110*.

More recently, on-farm production of foods has adopted a new term called Good Agricultural Practices (GAPs). The goal of GAPs is to reduce the risk of contamination on farms mainly for fruit and vegetable products. Programs that use GAPs focus on farm management programs, such as personal hygiene, irrigation water, manure, and cleaning procedures for freshly harvested produce. Assuring your produce vendors adopt GAP-type programs will be very important for reducing the risk of ready-to-eat produce displayed and sold in your establishment.

Following along the same pathway, the FMI has embraced a program called **Good Retail Practices (GRPs)**. GRPs are similar to the GMPs and GAPs used in food manufacturing and food production, respectively. The main difference is GRPs focus on food safety practices for retail food distribution, preparation, display, and sale. In many retail food establishments, GRPs are considered an important and very effective way to manage food safety. GRPs can be flexible and written to enhance product quality and shelf life. Some examples of GRPs include:

- Receiving guidelines
- Storage guidelines
- Preparation guidelines

- Packaging and labeling guidelines
- Display guidelines
- Personal health and hygiene
- Employee and customer education
- Record keeping.

> **Good Retail Practices (GRPs)** focus on food safety practices for retail food distribution, preparation, display, and sale.

The FMI has published a document on sushi preparation called *FMI's Recommendations for the Safe Preparation of Sushi*. FMI 2001a. In this document, several examples of GRPs are provided. Examples of receiving and storage GRPs, respectively, from this document are provided in this example.

Examples of GRPs

Produc labeling   Display guidelines

GRP Example

A. Receiving Raw Sushi-grade Fish

All ingredients should come from approved sources. Seafood products identified as a parasite hazard in the *Seafood Hazard Guide* should be obtained from a supplier who has frozen the product throughout using one of the methods recognized in the FDA *Food Code* and identified below. If the species is identified as a histamine producer, documentation from the supplier should show temperature control from harvest through delivery was sufficient to prevent any stage of decomposition.

General Receiving Instructions:

- Check the incoming product for date code, physical condition of packaging, physical defects, insect infestation, and food quality.
- Check the temperature to assure the product is frozen solid or has remained refrigerated at 41°F (5°C) or below.
- Place ready-to-eat foods in the cooler immediately.
- Place frozen product delivery into the freezer immediately.
- Rotate delivery of the product to facilitate the first-in, first-out (FIFO) method of stock rotation.
- Obtain a letter of guarantee from the supplier stating all sushi-grade fish has been frozen at -4°F (-20°C) or below for at least seven days, or -31°F (-35°C) or below for 15 hours, or at -31°F (-35°C) until solid and stored after that at -4°F (-20°C) for at least 24 hours before it is released for distribution.
- Obtain a letter from the supplier verifying that, based on microbiological testing, the fish is high sushi-grade.
- Reject products that do not meet the above criteria.

(continued)

> **GRP Example** (continued)
>
> **B. Storage Guidelines for Raw Sushi-grade Fish**
>
> To maintain product quality once the retailer has accepted shipment:
>
> - Place product in the appropriate storage unit.
> - Equip refrigeration unit with a calibrated thermometer easily accessible for viewing.
> - Use recording devices and alarm systems.
> - Avoid cross contamination.
> - Store product in a specific, predesignated area in the refrigeration unit, away from other raw and cooked foods.
> - Keep product containers 6 inches above the floor, away from walls and ceilings, and preferably on non-wooden supports, shelving, or surfaces.
> - Use an inventory system to make sure the first product in is the first product out (FIFO).
> - Check the temperature of the refrigerator and freezer units at least twice daily to assure they are operating at 41°F (5°C) and 0°F (-18°C) or below respectively.
> - Notify store manager or person in charge immediately if improper temperatures are detected at times other than the unit's defrost times; remove food from defective unit; and place it in one that works properly.
> - Store raw foods below or away from ready-to-eat foods.
>
> GRPs for the safe preparation of sushi for storage (used with permission from the Food Marketing Institute—FMI, 2001a).

Coding and Product Identification

When monitoring is conducted, especially for time and temperature, it is important you are able to identify which product was actually measured. You need a procedure to identify the product. This is usually done with a process known as product **coding**.

Product coding will be different in almost every retail food establishment because it needs to be customized to your in-house operations. One of the more common uses of product coding is to assure foods are displayed and used on a FIFO basis and that products with an expired shelf life are discarded.

Date and source codes are printed on an item to indicate its shelf life. Date codes simplify rotation and help prevent the sale of off-quality products.

Food Recall Procedures

A retail food establishment has limited control over the food it sells. It makes good sense to assure you have checked out your supplier to determine you are receiving the best products possible. Once in the store, your job is to follow good food-handling practices to keep products safe and in good quality. On occasion, however, contaminated products may be received from food manufacturers, slaughterhouses, or farms that can present a hazard to your customers. In these situations, the company that supplied you with the contaminated product may put a **food recall** in place. When this happens, your job is to remove the contaminated product from your shelves so your customers cannot purchase it and to communicate to your customers who may have already purchased the recalled product. Another important part of your food safety management system is to develop a food recall procedure.

A food recall is the system used to protect customers from using a product that may be unsafe. There are different levels of recalls that can be issued depending on how much of a risk the product may present. Most of the time, a recall involves removing the product from retail shelves so it cannot be sold. It may also involve retrieving a product already sold or providing information to customers that have already purchased the product.

In the event of a food safety emergency or other emergencies involving security and loss prevention issues, FMI members can use the 24-hour Crisis Notification System to contact FMI staff after regular working hours.

Challenges of Food Safety Management

There are a tremendous number of challenges related to managing food safety in retail food operations. In the past decade, there has been a debate over how retail food safety programs should be developed and implmented. Like many within the food service and grocery industry, the retail food industry has a high employee turnover rate.

> **An effective food safety management program ensures the safety of the products you sell and is MANAGEABLE for you and your employees.**

There are language and cultural barriers that make food safety education difficult. The retail food industry and regulatory community do not always agree on food safety practices. Even with all these challenges, retail food safety management must be a high priority.

As you develop a food safety management program for your establishment, use the following guidelines:

- **Focus on risk**–Inspection procedures and audits for food safety management programs should focus directly on controlling risk factors that affect food safety.
- **Make it manageable**–The food management program needs to be user friendly. It should be easy to implement and manage. Food safety management programs need to be flexible and related to specific operational procedures. One size does not fit all.
- **Strengthen communication**–The retail food store industry and regulatory professionals share a common goal to protect public health by only allowing the sale of safe food. With the same goal, the food store industry and regulatory professionals should partner and work together. Education and training need to be encouraged for members of the retail food store industry and for regulators.

Summary

Back to the Story . . . If you implement a food safety management system, you can avoid situations like the one described in the story at the beginning of this chapter. In the situation with the potato salad, the time and temperature logs were not compared between departments. The potato salad was exposed to unsafe temperatures for too long a time period. Because of the exposure to unsafe time and temperature, the product should have been discarded because of the chances of bacterial growth. This type of error can be prevented when a good food safety management program is put in place and the employees are properly trained. The food safety management plan would call for monitoring the temperature and setting critical limits for storage of the potato salad. In this case, the food safety management plan would identify the appropriate corrective action (discarding the product) so customers were not put at risk.

- ✔ When a food safety management system is properly followed, it protects against many types of mishandling.
- ✔ Food safety management systems are designed to prevent foodborne illness.
- ✔ Critical limits set the range of safety, for certain conditions like time and temperature, for handling potentially hazardous products.
- ✔ Teach employees how to use the system and then monitor the application to ensure food safety.
    - ✔ Employees must be encouraged to contact their supervisor if they discover the prescribed critical limit is not being met.
    - ✔ Management must then take the steps needed to correct the problem and bring the production process under control.

Discussion Questions (Short Answer)

1. What is a HACCP system?
2. What types of foods are incorporated into the HACCP system?
3. What hazards are incorporated into the HACCP system?
4. Define Critical Control Point (CCP) and give some examples.
5. Define a critical limit (CL) and provide some examples.
6. What are SOPs? Provide some examples.
7. What are GRPs? Provide some examples.
8. Why is a procedure for food recalls important?

Quiz 8 (Multiple Choice)

Choose the **best** answer for each question:

1. A risk as used in connection with a HACCP system is:

    a. failure to meet a required critical limit for a CCP.

    b. an estimate of the likely occurrence and severity of a hazard.

    c. greatest for nonpotentially hazardous foods.

    d. lowest when complex recipes are required to produce a food item.

2. Which statement about HACCP programs is **false**?

    a. The HACCP system attempts to anticipate problems before they happen and establish procedures to reduce the risk of foodborne illness.

    b. The HACCP system targets the production of PHF (TCS) from start to finish.

    c. Records generated by the HACCP system can also be used to aid in foodborne disease investigations.

    d. A HACCP system should only be implemented by public health officials who have been certified by the FDA to conduct such programs.

3. Which of the following is an example of a common critical control point in a HACCP plan?

    a. Washing fruits and vegetables.

    b. Cooking hamburgers.

    c. Handwashing.

    d. Inspecting procedures for quality.

4. Which of the following is an example of a critical limit?

    a. Poultry and eggs are purchased from approved sources.

    b. Chicken and noodles are heated on the stove until the center of the product reaches 165°F (74°C) for 15 seconds.

    c. Only pasteurized milk is used by the establishment.

    d. The cutting board is washed and sanitized between chopping carrots and celery for the garden salad.

5. A food recall is:

    a. a procedure for removing unsafe foods from retail shelves.

    b. a process for labeling food products during preparation.

    c. only important for very large retail food operations.

    d. only important for USDA-inspected foods.

6. A hazard as used in connection with a HACCP system is:
   a. Any biological, chemical, or physical property that can cause an unacceptable risk.
   b. Any single step at which contamination could occur.
   c. An estimate of the likely occurrence of a hazard.
   d. A point at which loss of control may result in an unacceptable health risk.
7. The ultimate success of a food safety management program depends on:
   a. Eliminating all PHF (TCS) from your operation.
   b. Providing proper training and equipment for employees who are implementing the HACCP system.
   c. Having HACCP flow charts developed for every single food sold by the store.
   d. Grocery store managers having sole authority for implementing the HACCP system.

Answers to the multiple-choice questions are provided in Appendix A.

References/Suggested Readings

Bryan, Frank L. 1990. "Hazard Analysis Critical Control Point (HACCP) Systems for Retail Food and Restaurant Operations." *Journal of Food Protection* 53(11): 978–983.

Bryan, F. L. 1992. *Hazard Analysis Critical Control Point Evaluations: A Guide To Identifying Hazards and Assessing Risks Associated with Food Preparation and Storage.* World Health Organization. Geneva, Switzerland.

Bryan, F. L.; C. A. Bartleson; C. O. Cook; P. Fisher; J. J. Guzewich; B. J. Humm;, R. C. Swanson; and E. C. D. Todd. 1991. *Procedures to Implement the Hazard Analysis Critical Control Point System.* International Association of Milk, Food and Environmental Sanitarians. Ames, IA.

Corlett, D. A.; and M. D. Pierson 1992. *HACCP Principles and Applications.* Van Nostrand Reinhold. New York, NY.

Federal Register, Vol. 59, No. 149. 1994. U.S. Government Printing Office. Washington, DC.

Food and Drug Administration. 2009. *2009 Food Code*. U.S. Public Health Service. Washington, DC.

Food Marketing Institute. 2009a. *FMI's Recommendations for the Safe Preparation of Sushi*. Food Marketing Institute. Washington, DC.

Food Marketing Institute. 2009b. *Molluscan Shellfish Handling for Retailers—A Total Food Safety Management System Guide for Molluscan Shellfish*. Food Marketing Institute. Washington, DC.

LaVella, B.; and J. L. Bostic. 1994. *HACCP for Food Service—Recipe Manual and Guide.* LaVella Food Specialists. St. Louis, MO.

J. K. Lotkin. 1995. *The HACCP Food Safety Manual.* Wiley Press. New York, NY.

Pierson, M. D.; and D. A. Corlett, Jr. 1992. *HACCP Principles and Applications.* Van Nostrand Reinhold. New York, NY.

U.S. Food and Drug Administration. *Managing Food Safety: A Manual for the Voluntary Use of HACCP Principles for Operators of Food Service and Retail Establishments*. www.cfsan.fda.gov/~dms/hret2-1.html.

Food and Drug Administration. *Managing Food Safety: A Regulator's Manual for Applying HACCP Principles to Risk-based Retail and Food Service Inspections and Evaluating Voluntary Food Safety Management Systems*. www.cfsan.fda.gov/~dms/hret3toc.html.

Suggested Web Sites

Canadian Food Safety Sites Involving HACCP
 foodnet.fit.ca/safety/safety.html

International Food Information Council
 ificinfo.health.org/

NSF International
 www.nsf.org

The Food Marketing Institute
 www.fmi.org

Gateway to Government Food Safety Information
 www.foodsafety.gov

U.S. Department of Agriculture (USDA)
 www.usda.gov

Centers for Disease Control and Prevention (CDC)
 www.cdc.gov

Food and Drug Administration (FDA)
 www.fda.gov

USDA Food Safety and Inspection Service (FSIS)
www.fsis.usda.gov

USDA/FDA Food and Nutrition Information Center
www.nal.usda.gov/fnic

Partnerships for Food Safety Education
www.fightbac.org

Food and Agriculture Organization
www.fao.org

Notes

Learn How To:

- Recognize the role of federal, state, local, and tribal jurisdictions in regulating and monitoring food safety.
- Identify the areas of retail food establishments included in inspections and audits.
- Use references for federal, state, and local authorities.
- Identify organizations important to the retail food industry.
- Review procedures for crisis management due to loss of utilities.

CHAPTER 9

Food Safety Regulations and Crisis Management

Turkey Luncheon Meat Recalled for Listeria monocytogenes

"The U.S. Department of Agriculture's Food Safety and Inspection Service (FSIS) announced today that Ready-to-Go Foods is recalling over 70,000 pounds of ready-to-eat turkey luncheon meat that may be contaminated with Listeria monocytogenes. The following product is subject to recall:

16-ounce individually wrapped packages of "Deli Style Sliced Turkey." Each package bears the establishment number "P987654" inside the USDA mark of inspection and a sell-by date of June 5, 2009. Lots 845095, 845096, 845097, and 845098 are involved in the recall.

The ready-to-eat turkey product was produced on May 5, 2009, and was sent to retail establishments and institutions in the New York and Philadelphia metropolitan areas. The problem was discovered through FSIS microbiological sampling. To date, FSIS has received no reports of illnesses associated with the consumption of this product.

Consumption of food contaminated with Listeria monocytogenes *can cause listeriosis, an uncommon but potentially fatal disease. Healthy people rarely contract listeriosis. However, listeriosis can cause high fever, severe headache, neck stiffness and nausea. Listeriosis can also cause miscarriages and stillbirths, as well as serious and sometimes fatal infections in those with weakened immune systems, such as infants, the elderly and persons with HIV infection or undergoing chemotherapy."*

What could be done to prevent or minimize this type of problem?

Essential Terms

Adulteration	Inspection for wholesomeness
Centers for Disease Control and Prevention (CDC)	Misbranding
	State, local, and tribal agencies
Conference for Food Protection (CFP)	Environmental Protection Agency (EPA)
Consumer Advisory	Food and Drug Administration (FDA)
Generally Recognized As Safe (GRAS) substances	U.S. Department of Agriculture (USDA)
Grading	

State and Local Regulations

State, local, and tribal agencies responsible for enforcing food and safety requirements may be under the department of environmental health, public health, or agriculture. Jurisdiction varies from state to state. Contact your local authorities to find out what agency is in charge of food safety in your area.

Most retail food establishments will work closely with their local health department. This agency can provide you with a copy of its current food safety code. Your state and local code contains the food safety standards and regulations that would apply to your type of operation. Familiarize yourself with the key food safety provisions of the *Code*.

Permit to Operate

It is unlawful to operate a retail food establishment unless you have a valid permit issued by the regulatory authority in your area. When a permit is obtained, post it in a prominent location. Permits are generally not transferable from one person to another, from one retail food establishment to another, or from one food operation to another. If you add a partner or incorporate, these actions are considered ownership changes and may require you to apply for a new permit to operate.

Permit to operate

Retail food establishments are routinely inspected by regulatory agencies to assure they are complying with the food safety rules and regulations of the jurisdiction. Many regulatory agencies use a risk-based approach for setting inspection frequencies. Under this system, the risk a retail food establishment poses is calculated using such factors as:

- The sanitation history of the establishment
- Number of home meal replacements sold
- The amount of food preparation and handling conducted onsite
- Condition of building
- Critical violations observed.

Whenever possible, accompany the inspector during an inspection audit.

Always cooperate with inspecting personnel. Greet the inspector when he or she arrives and ask to see his or her official identification.

A routine inspection or audit normally consists of three phases:

1. A pre-inspection conference where the inspector and manager, or person in charge, review previous inspection results and discuss information relevant to the current inspection.

2. The current inspection is conducted.

3. A post-inspection conference is conducted where the results of the current inspection are reviewed and discussed with the manager or person in charge. Dates for correction of violations are negotiated, if necessary.

Most inspections will focus on:

- Foods and supplies
- Personal hygiene and employee health
- Temperatures of food and food-holding equipment
- Cleaning and sanitizing procedures
- Equipment and utensils
- Water supply and waste disposal
- Pest control and other aspects of the operation that might compromise food safety.

Historically, "critical" and "non-critical" are the terms used by inspection agencies to denote the relative risk of violations documented in retail food establishments. Examples of critical items include temperature abuse and cross contamination. When during the course of an inspection it is discovered that a critical item is "out-of-compliance", the violation must be corrected immediately. Failure to do so could result in fines and possible closure of the food establishment. When non-critical items are "out-of-compliance", they should be corrected as soon as possible and always prior to the next regularly scheduled inspection or visit.

The FDA is now recommending that retail food regulatory agencies replace the critical and non-critical risk designations with a three-tier approach "Priority", "Priority Foundation", and "Core". More information about these risk categories and their respective definitions is provided in Appendix G.

Food managers should periodically conduct self-inspections of their establishment to ensure proper sanitation and food safety. During a self-inspection, the manager should look for signs of contamination, improper food-handling practices, and other conditions that may put food safety in jeopardy.

Federal Agencies

The primary federal agencies that protect our food supply and their functions are provided in the table below.

Federal Agencies	
Name	**Primary Function or Duties**
(FDA) **Food and Drug Administration**	• Regulates the processing, manufacturing, and interstate sale of many food items, except for meat, poultry, and egg products • Sets standards with respect to composition, quality, labeling, and safety of foods and food additives • Publishes the *Food Code* • Protects the public's health by preventing the **adulteration** and **misbranding** of food • Assures food shipped in interstate commerce is safe, pure, wholesome, sanitary, and honestly packaged and labeled • Maintains a list of interstate certified shellfish shippers and a list of interstate milk shippers.
(USDA) **U.S. Department of Agriculture**	• Inspects domestic and imported meats, poultry, eggs, catfish, and processed meat and poultry products. USDA maintains a list of approved facilities for meat and poultry processing. • Conducts voluntary grading services for red meats, poultry and eggs, dairy products, and fruits and vegetables.

(continued)

Federal Agencies (continued)

Name	Primary Function or Duties
(USDC) U.S. Department of Commerce	• Develops grade standards for processed fishery products.
(NMFS) National Marine Fisheries Service	• Division of the USDC • Provides voluntary inspection service for processed fishery products • Maintains a list of approved fish processors and fishery products on a permanent basis.
(EPA) Environmental Protection Agency	• Created to prevent, control, and reduce air, land, and water pollution • Regulates the use of toxic substances (pesticides, sanitizers, and other chemicals), monitors compliance, and provides technical assistance to states. • Administers the superfund.
(CDC) Centers for Disease Control and Prevention	• Responsible for protecting public health through the prevention and control of diseases • Supports foodborne disease investigations and prepares annual summaries and statistics on outbreaks of foodborne diseases transmitted through food and water.
(OSHA) Occupational Safety and Health Administration	• Created in the U.S. Department of Labor to enforce the Occupational Safety and Health Act. It enforces health standards and regulations on safety, noise, and other workplace-related hazards
(FTC) Federal Trade Commission	• Involved in enforcing various laws regarding marketing practices and national advertising of foods and other products.

The FDA publishes the *Food Code*, which serves as a model for retail food programs regulated by federal, state, local, and tribal agencies. The *Food Code* is not a federal law or federal regulation, but is recommended for adoption by state and local, and other federal and tribal regulatory food agencies. The *Food Code* is more like a set of recommendations put forth to promote food safety and sanitation nationwide.

Other National Food Safety Related Organizations

The **Conference for Food Protection (CFP)** is a nonprofit organization that represents the major stakeholders in retail food safety. Its membership

The mission of the CFP is to promote food safety and consumer protection.

includes representatives of the food industry, government, academic community, professional organizations, and consumer groups. It meets at least every other year to identify food safety problems, make recommendations, and implement practices to ensure food safety. The CFP has no formal regulatory authority, yet over the years it has been able to effectively influence the content of model retail food laws and regulations, mostly through its biennial meetings.

Other organizations also help protect our food supply. Many of the following organizations have good information and training materials:

- The American Public Health Association (APHA)
- The Association of Food and Drug Officials (AFDO)
- The Food Marketing Institute (FMI)
- The Frozen Food Industry Coordinating Committee (FFICC)
- The Food Research Institute (FRI)
- Institute of Food Technologists (IFT)
- National Conference on Interstate Milk Shipments (NCIMS)
- International Association for Food Protection (IAFP)
- The National Environmental Health Association (NEHA)
- The National Pest Management Association (NPMA)
- The National Restaurant Association (NRA)
- NSF International (NSF)

- The National Shellfish Sanitation Program (NSSP)
- Underwriters Laboratories, Inc. (UL)
- World Health Organization (WHO).

Inspection for Wholesomeness, Grading, and Generally Recognized As Safe

Inspection for wholesomeness refers to an examination of domestic and imported meat, poultry, and egg products to assure they are wholesome and free from adulteration. These inspections are required by law and are conducted by veterinarians and technicians who work for the Food Safety and Inspection Service (FSIS) of the USDA. The USDA can also be involved with microbial testing of foods. *E. coli* O157:H7 has been declared an adulterant in raw ground beef, and no amount of these bacteria are permitted in ground beef by law. A national microbial sampling plan has been implemented to determine the prevalence of *E. coli* O157:H7 bacteria in ground beef. Under the sampling plan, USDA officials take samples of ground beef from federally inspected plants and retail food establishments and test them for *E. coli* O157:H7 bacteria. If a sample is confirmed positive for *E. coli* 0157:H7, the retail food establishment may be asked to recall the product and communicate this information to the public. It is important to develop a written procedure (i.e., SOP) for ground beef sampling and to assure measures are in place to identify different lots of ground beef.

Grading refers to the process of evaluating foods relative to specific, defined standards in order to assess its quality. Grading is a voluntary activity. However, most food processors participate in grading programs because their customers prefer to buy products that have met specific quality standards. More information on grading is provided in Chapter 4 of this book.

Substances used in foods for years and with no apparent ill effects are commonly identified as **Generally Recognized As Safe (GRAS)**. Examples of substances that fall into the GRAS category are spices, natural seasonings, flavoring materials, fruit and beverage acids, baking powder, chemicals, and drying agents. The purpose of establishing a GRAS list is to recognize the safety of basic substances without the requirement for rigorous safety testing.

Food Recall

The FDA can request a **recall of a food product** if the agency has determined a potential hazard exists. Food recalls are voluntary with the possible exception of a recall involving infant formula. In the vast majority of cases, food processors voluntarily remove products from the marketplace to keep consumers safe. However, if a firm does not agree with an FDA request for a voluntary recall, the agency may issue public press releases and proceed to seize the product in order to remove it from commerce.

There are three types of food recalls. Class I, Class II, or Class III can be issued depending on the severity of the health risk. Retail food establishments should have a policy in place to handle food recalls. Recalled foods should be promptly removed from retail shelves and cannot be sold.

Types of Food Recalls	
• Class I	Foods that may cause serious adverse health consequences.
• Class II	Foods that would result in a temporary or reversible health problem.
• Class III	Foods that are not likely to cause danger to health.

Food Labeling

Nutrition and Ingredient Labeling

The USDA and the FDA share responsibility for enforcing the Nutrition Labeling and Education Act. This law provides information on specific nutritional guidelines and defines what needs to be on a nutrition label. This label, which provides information for processed foods on protein, fat, carbohydrate, and mineral content helps customers make informed choices when selecting foods.

Although not mandatory at this time, the USDA has published guidelines for demonstrating voluntary compliance to nutritional labeling requirements. Supermarkets are encouraged to provide consumers accurate nutritional information using point-of-purchase product labels, brochures, or signage.

Retail establishments that prepare and package product in the store also must provide a

The nutrition label
www.nal.usda.gov/fnic

label for the consumer. All foods packaged in a retail food establishment must be labeled as specified in the law *(21 CFR 101—Food Labeling, and 9 CFR 317—Labeling, Marking Devices, and Containers)*. The label must include information, such as the name of the food, a list of ingredients, and the quantity of ingredients.

Food Allergen Labeling and Consumer Protection Act

Beginning January 1, 2006, the Food Allergen Labeling and Consumer Protection Act (FALCPA) mandates plain language labeling for all foods that contain one of the eight major food allergens—peanuts, eggs, milk, wheat, tree nuts, soybeans, fish, and crustacean shellfish—or a food ingredient that contains protein derived from one of these foods. The allergen labeling law does not apply to highly refined oils.

Labeling is critical when dealing with common allergens.

Allergens can be identified in either of two ways. One option is to use a "contains" statement, which means the word contains is followed by a list of all the major food allergens contained in the product. The second option is "parenthetical" listing, which means within the list of ingredients, the common or usual name of the food allergen is included in parentheses following the ingredient name. For example, printed on the label would be the words *casein (milk)*. Under this second option, a parenthetical listing is not required if the ingredient name already identifies the major allergen [i.e., *tuna gelatin (tuna)* is redundant] or if the name of the major allergen appears elsewhere, such as in the name of the product (i.e., Aunt Lily's Old-Fashioned Peanut Butter).

The person in charge (PIC) of a retail food establishment must be able to demonstrate knowledge about the eight major food allergens and the symptoms they cause. When asked by the inspector, the PIC must be able to identify the allergens and their related symptoms. The PIC should also know what actions to take if an allergic reaction occurs in his or her store. Finally, a PIC must ensure that employees are properly trained in food safety, including food allergy awareness.

Safe Food-handling Label

A safe food-handling instruction label provides helpful food-handling information for the consumer on all raw or partially precooked (not ready-to-eat) meat and poultry. The label was designed to educate the consumer for storage, preparation (including cooking), and handling of raw meat and poultry products in the home.

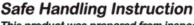

USDA safe handling instructions label
Source: www.usda.gov/agency/oc/design/art_symbols.html

Date Marking for Ready-to-eat, PHF (TCS)

Product date marking is used by retail food establishments to indicate the date or day by which refrigerated, ready-to-eat, PHF (TCS) must be consumed, sold, or discarded. New date marking provisions are now included in the *Food Code* for the following situations:

1. Retail food establishments that prepare and hold refrigerated, ready-to-eat, PHF (TCS) for more than 24 hours.

   Retail food establishment personnel must clearly mark these products to indicate the date or day by which the food must be consumed on the premises, sold, or discarded using the temperature and time combinations of 41°F (5°C) or less for a maximum of seven days.

Product label with date

The day of preparation will be counted as Day 1.

This date marking requirement does **not** apply to reduced oxygen packaged (ROP) foods prepared and held in retail food establishments. However, special handling and storage are required for ROP foods as described in Chapter 4 of this book.

2. Retail food establishments that serve and sell refrigerated, ready-to-eat, PHF (TCS) prepared and packaged by an inspected food processing plant.

If the food is to be held for more than 24 hours, the product must be clearly marked at the time the original container is first opened in a retail food establishment to indicate the date or day by which the food shall be consumed on the premises, sold, or discarded, based on the temperature and time combinations noted previously. The day the original container is first opened in the food establishment shall be counted as Day 1, and the day or date marked by the food establishment may not exceed a manufacturer's use-by date if the manufacturer determined the use-by date based on food safety.

A refrigerated, ready-to-eat, PHF (TCS) ingredient or a portion of a refrigerated, ready-to-eat, PHF (TCS) that is subsequently combined with additional ingredients or portions of food shall retain the date marking of the earliest prepared or first prepared ingredient.

The requirements described previously do **not** apply to:

1. Individual meal portions served or repackaged for sale from a bulk container upon a consumer's request.
2. Certain types of foods that pose very low or low risk of contamination and growth of *Listeria monocytogenes.* A listing of these exempted foods is provided at the end of this section.

Two examples of date marking systems that meet the criteria prescribed in the *Food Code* include:

1. Marking the date or day the food is prepared or the original container is first opened in a retail food establishment, with a procedure to discard the food on or before the last date or day by which the food must be consumed on the premises, sold, or discarded.
2. Using calendar dates, days of the week, color-coded marks, or other effective marking methods provided the marking system is disclosed to the regulatory authority upon request.

Based on the results of numerous *Listeria monocytogenes* health risk assessments and recommendations from the 2004 CFP meeting, the FDA has reevaluated its date marking rules in order to place the greatest emphasis on very high- and high-risk foods, while exempting foods that pose very low or low risk of contamination and growth of *Listeria monocytogenes*. Based on this evaluation, the FDA has determined date marking provisions do not apply to the following foods prepared and packaged by a food processing plant inspected by a regulatory authority:

1. Deli salads, such as ham salad, seafood salad, chicken salad, egg salad, pasta salad, potato salad, and macaroni salad, manufactured in accordance with *21 CFR 110—Current Good Manufacturing Practice in Manufacturing.*

2. Hard cheeses containing not more than 39% moisture as defined in *21 CFR 133—Cheeses and Related Cheese Products,* such as Cheddar and Parmesan.

3. Semisoft cheeses containing more than 39% moisture, but not more than 50% moisture, as defined in *21 CFR 133—Cheeses and Related Cheese Products,* such as blue, Gorgonzola, and Monterey Jack.

4. Cultured dairy products as defined in *21 CFR 131—Milk and Cream,* such as yogurt, sour cream, and buttermilk.

5. Preserved fish products, such as pickled herring and dried or salted cod, and other acidified fish products defined in *21 CFR 114—Acidified Foods.*

6. Shelf-stable, dry fermented sausages, such as pepperoni and Genoa salami that are not labeled "keep refrigerated" as specified in *9 CFR 317—Labeling, Marking Devices, and Containers*, and that retain the original casing on the product.

7. Shelf-stable, salt-cured products such as prosciutto and Parma (ham) that are not labeled "keep refrigerated" as specified in *9 CFR 317—Labeling, Marking Devices, and Containers.*

Recent Initiatives in Food Safety

National Food Safety Initiative

From farm to table, the federal government's National Food Safety Initiative is working to reduce the incidence of foodborne illness by strengthening and improving food safety practices and policies. The initiative seeks to:

- Expand education efforts aimed at improving food handling in homes and retail outlets.
- Improve inspections and expand monitoring efforts.

- Increase research to develop new and more rapid methods to detect foodborne pathogens and to develop preventive techniques.
- Improve intergovernmental communications and coordination of responses to foodborne outbreaks. FDA, CDC, USDA, and EPA will form a new intergovernmental group to improve federal, state, and local responses to outbreaks of foodborne illnesses.
- Determine the frequency and severity of foodborne disease.
- Determine the proportion of common foodborne diseases that result from eating specific foods.
- Describe the epidemiology of new and emerging bacterial, parasitic, and viral foodborne pathogens.

The Fight BAC!™ Campaign

Fight BAC!™ logo

The Fight BAC!™ Campaign is an educational program developed by industry, government, and consumer groups to teach customers about safe food handling. The focal point of the campaign is BAC (short for bacteria), a character used to make customers aware of the invisible germs that cause foodborne illness. Even though customers cannot see, smell, or taste BAC, it and millions more germs like it are in and on food and food-contact surfaces. The Fight BAC!™ Campaign uses media and community outreach programs to teach consumers how to keep food safe from harmful bacteria through four simple steps: wash hands and surfaces often, prevent cross contamination, cook foods to proper temperature, and refrigerate foods quickly. The partners in the Fight BAC!™ Campaign use newspaper articles, public service announcements, printed brochures, and school curricula to teach consumers how to lower their risk of foodborne illness.

Project Chill Campaign

The FMI has teamed up with the Partnership for Food Safety Education to develop a national public education campaign called Project Chill. The goal of this program is to educate consumers about the dangers of listeriosis and the actions that can be taken in the home to prevent this and other foodborne diseases. A cornerstone of Project Chill is to educate consumers about the importance of keeping home refrigerators at 40°F (4.4°C) or less and using certified refrigerator thermometers to assure refrigerators are maintaining the proper temperature.

FMI is encouraging its member supermarkets to distribute educational brochures and stock certified refrigerator thermometers for sale in ready-to-eat food departments, such as delicatessens and dairy foods aisles. The message and materials provided in conjunction with Project Chill will help consumers reduce their risk of foodborne illness by assuring the refrigerator in their home is keeping foods at the proper cold temperature.

Consumer Advisory

> **The food establishment can satisfy the consumer advisory requirements by providing both a disclosure and a reminder.**

Food establishments that sell or serve raw or undercooked animal foods or ingredients for human consumption must inform their customers about the increased risk associated with eating these kinds of foods. The disclosure is used to alert consumers to the food items that either contain or may contain raw or undercooked ingredients. The reminder is a notice to the consumer to consider their health condition before consuming the identified foods, or to eat their foods fully cooked.

Disclosure is satisfied when items are described, such as oysters on the half-shell (raw oysters) and raw-egg Caesar salad, or items are asterisked to a footnote that states the items:

- Are served raw, or undercooked, or;
- Contain (or may contain) raw or undercooked ingredients.

The reminder is satisfied when the items requiring disclosure are asterisked to a footnote that states information about:

- The safety of these items, written information is available upon request
- Eating raw or undercooked meats, poultry, seafood, molluscan shellfish, or eggs, which may increase your risk of foodborne illness
- Increased risk of foodborne illness when the above products are eaten if you have certain medical conditions.

Disclosure of raw or undercooked animal-derived foods or ingredients and reminders about the risk of consuming such foods should appear at the point where the customer selects the food. Both the disclosure and the reminder need to accompany the information from which the customer makes a selection. That information could appear in many forms, such as display signage, package labels, table tents, on the menu, and consumer brochures.

Consumer advisories may be tailored to be product-specific if a food establishment either has a limited menu or offers only certain animal-derived foods in a raw or undercooked, ready-to-eat form. For example, a raw bar serving molluscan shellfish on the half shell but no other raw or undercooked animal food could elect to confine its consumer advisory to shellfish.

Crisis Management

A crisis can occur at any time. Besides natural disasters, such as fire, flood, storms, or earthquakes, retail food establishments must deal with interference in normal operations that can literally cripple production. Other types of crises that can have a significant impact on retail food operations are power outages, interruption of water and sewer service, an outbreak of foodborne illness, media investigations, and unexpected loss of personnel. How do you handle difficult situations? Develop a **crisis management plan** to handle the crisis with a problem-solving approach.

Evaluate the extent of the problem. Set priorities according to the resources that exist. Remain calm. Follow established rules and regulations as set up in codes. Identify any outside resources that can help solve the problem. Keep a record of actions and communications in case it should be needed. In all situations, be honest.

Most retail food establishments have a system of audible codes to alert employees about certain conditions through store announcements.

Water Supply Emergency Procedures

On occasion, a water utility agency will issue a boil-water order when the bacteriological quality of the water it provides does not meet the requirements of the Safe Drinking Water Act. This commonly happens when a water main breaks or when the source of the drinking water is contaminated by runoff and other sources of pollution.

To continue operating under "boil-water advisories/notices" or "interrupted water service" from all water supplies, retail food establishments must secure and use safe drinking

In emergencies, or as a temporary measure, water from contaminated or suspect sources can be disinfected by either chlorination or boiling.

water from an approved source. This can be bottled water or water hauled to the site in tank trucks. Bottled drinking water used or sold in a retail food establishment must be obtained from approved sources in accordance with the *Code of Federal Regulations* (*21 CFR 129—Processing and Bottling of Bottled Drinking Water.*)

In emergencies, or as a temporary measure, water from contaminated or suspect sources can be disinfected by either chlorination or boiling. To chlorinate water, add six drops of liquid chlorine bleach to one gallon of water and mix. Check the label on the container to make sure the active ingredient, sodium hypochlorite, is available at a concentration of 5.25%. The important things to remember when chlorinating water are:

- Wait 30 minutes after adding the chlorine before using the water for drinking or cooking purposes.
- If the six drops of bleach do not give the water a slight taste of chlorine, double the amount of chlorine until a slight taste is present. The taste of chlorine will be evidence the water is safe to drink.

Another way to purify water is to boil it. Bring the water to a full boil for at least 5 minutes. Cool and aerate the boiled water by pouring it from one clean container to another. This will reduce the flat taste caused by boiling.

- After the water emergency is officially lifted or water service resumes, these precautionary measures must be followed:
- Flush the building waterlines and clean faucet screens and waterline strainers on mechanical dishwashing machines and similar equipment.
- Flush and sanitize all water-using fixtures and appliances, such as ice machines, beverage dispensers, hot water heaters, etc.
- Clean and sanitize all fixtures, sinks, and equipment connected to waterlines.

Alternative Procedures To Minimize Water Usage

- Commercially packaged ice may be substituted for ice made on-site.
- Single-service items or disposable utensils may be substituted for reusable dishes and utensils.
- Use prepared foods from approved sources in place of complex preparation on-site.
- Restrict menu choices or hours of operation.
- Portable toilets may be utilized for sanitary purposes.

There must be water pressure before resuming operations in a retail food establishment, and the water should be sampled for bacteriological quality. The safety of water cannot be judged by color, odor, or taste. Do not hesitate to contact your local regulatory agency if you have any questions regarding appropriate operations at your establishment during water emergency orders.

Foodborne Illness Incident or Outbreak

If dealing with a suspected foodborne illness problem, cooperate with the customers and seek help from your local food regulatory agency. Work with the local regulatory agency to determine what may have caused the customer's illness. Establish the time the suspect food was purchased and eaten. If a sample of the product is still available, preserve it in a refrigerator for laboratory analysis. Ask the customer if medical attention has been sought and to save samples of any product that remains. Initiate your crisis management team members, which should include team members from your media affairs, food safety, loss prevention, and legal counsel.

If a foodborne illness is suspected, the first action is to remove all suspected product from sale.

Action Plan when Foodborne Illness Is Suspected

- Remove all affected food from the sales areas.
- Isolate it in a separate area.
- Label it so it does not become mixed with other foods.
- Do not sell any more of the suspect product.
- Listen to everything the customer says and look for clues that might explain the problem.
- Do not try to diagnose the problem or belittle the customer's complaint.
- Keep a record of the interview.
- Assure the customer you will get back to him or her after investigating the problem.
- Make sure you do contact the customer again after facts are gathered.
- Do not admit your establishment is at fault—you have no proof of that until facts are checked.

Check the Product Source

If the reported item was prepared in the store, remove it from sale immediately. If two or more persons report the same problem, consult outside resources (local health department) on how to proceed. When preparing food samples for testing, it is wise to keep a sample in your refrigerator for cross validation of laboratory results. Public health officials, insurance agents, and, if needed, an attorney can help you manage the problem.

Formal Investigations

Remove suspect items from use. Health inspectors may want to conduct an inspection at the establishment. Employees may be required to have medical examinations. Closing a facility for a period of time for cleaning may be needed. Keep in mind whatever must be done should be accomplished as quickly as possible. Cooperation to protect public health is the end goal. In the final analysis, it does not matter where the error occurred. It must be corrected and prevented from happening again.

Whatever the crisis may be, use a calm, systematic approach and evaluate actions as much as possible. Crisis management is not an easy task. It is always useful to have some kind of protocol to guide you through the event. Put together a team or committee consisting of management and employees to regularly brainstorm worst-case scenarios. Plan disaster drills to keep employees informed and trained in crisis management skills. Designate a spokesperson responsible for talking to the media, should they become involved. Keep a notebook with instructions on how to proceed in emergency situations.

Food Defense

On September 11, 2001, terrorism in the United States became a reality. In the post-9/11 era, we have become painfully aware of the physical, psychological, and economic toll that terrorism can exact upon our society. The possibility of terrorist attacks on our nation's food supply is real and must not be ignored.

Compromises to product safety, both accidental and intentional, including tampering and terrorism, pose the kind of nightmare scenario that all companies fear. A food safety crisis is not only a public relations nightmare, but it can destroy a company and its brand.

Reacting in a rational manner for food defense is extremely important to every food operation. The Food Marketing Institute (FMI) has developed guidelines to handle any suspected tampering or contamination problem in retail food establishments. There are several actions that can be used to manage these problems. These include the following:

- Monitor employees and allow only approved employees into production areas. The use of photo identification name tags helps to identify employees.
- Protect food preparation areas from anyone who is not assigned to that area.
- Review visitor policies and change rules to keep areas secure. Use sign-in and sign-out logs.
- Prohibit personal items like lunch containers, cases, purses, and other such items from processing areas. Provide storage for employee property in a separate room or locker.
- Report any unusual or suspicious activity to your supervisor or manager.
- If a suspicious problem is identified, call the Federal Bureau of Investigation (FBI) and FDA Office of Criminal Investigation. These agencies are best equipped to handle emergency situations and will advise you of the steps to follow.
- Designate a spokesperson to deal with media or other inquiries. This method assures information is managed carefully and mixed messages are avoided.

Product tampering is also a food safety concern, and many retail food establishments have developed policies and procedures to deal with such problems. Managers should teach employees to be alert and to report any unusual activity immediately. It is always better to be overly cautious than to ignore a potential incident.

FMI has a *Pre-Emergency Planning and Disaster Recovery Manual* with phone numbers and instructions on what to do in cases of emergency. For more information about this manual, you may call the FMI Publications and Video Sales Department at (202) 220-0723.

FMI can also provide assistance and information for use when implementing product recalls. For help on recalls, call the Food Safety Department at (202) 220-0661. FMI also has a document called *Measures to Improve Security in the Supermarket Industry*. For more information on store security, call the above number.

Summary

***Back to the Story . . .** As we have learned,* Listeria monocytogenes *is a dangerous foodborne pathogen that can have a very high mortality rate, and the organism can also grow in ready-to-eat processed meats during refrigerated storage and distribution. As a result, a "zero-tolerance" for* Listeria monocytogenes *has been established by USDA-FSIS for many ready-to-eat processed meat products.*

When a recall is established, the retail food establishment is responsible for initiating part of the food recall process. The retail food operator will first communicate information about affected products to all their stores providing further information about how to remove product from retail shelves, how to segregate and label removed products, and how to communicate information about the recalled products to customers. It will be important that the retail food establishment keep updated information from USDA-FSIS and for Ready-to-Go Foods about the recall, as information about recalled products can change quickly.

Recalls are a good example of the importance of effective communication between the retail food industry, federal/state/local regulatory agencies, consumers (customers), and other parts of the food industry.

For customers, there are also other sources of information that retailers can provide to help them understand the recall better. For this recall example, USDA may offer some additional helpful information. Customers with food safety questions can "Ask Karen," the FSIS virtual representative available 24 hours a day at AskKaren.gov. The toll-free USDA Meat and Poultry Hotline 1-888-MPHotline (1-888-674-6854) is available in English and Spanish and can be reached from 10 a.m. to 4 p.m. (Eastern Time) Monday through Friday. Recorded food safety messages are available 24 hours a day.

- ✔ Federal, state, and local food safety regulations are important for maintaining a safe food supply. State, local, and tribal health departments are critical when it comes to monitoring and enforcing each state or local food code. They evaluate food establishments to help ensure delivery of safe food to customers.

✓ Food establishments and regulatory agencies should work together to protect the health of customers and meet their expectations for food quality and safety.

Discussion Questions (Short Answer)

1. What are the three phases of a routine inspection?
2. What should the person in charge of a retail food establishment do during a routine inspection of his/her facility?
3. What is the purpose of the Food Allergen Labeling and Consumer Protection Act (FALCPA)?
4. Why is product date marking used by retail food establishments?
5. What is the purpose of a consumer advisory?

Quiz 9 (Multiple Choice)

Choose the **best** answer for each question.

1. The federal agency responsible for safe working conditions, such as noise and exposure to hazardous chemicals, is the:
    a. Environmental Protection Agency (EPA).
    b. Food and Drug Administration (FDA).
    c. Occupational Safety and Health Administration (OSHA).
    d. Centers for Disease Control and Prevention (CDC).
2. Which of the following regulatory agencies will have the most influence on food-handling practices for foods prepared in a retail food establishment?
    a. State and local health department or Department of Agriculture.
    b. Food and Drug Administration (FDA).
    c. U.S. Department of Agriculture (USDA).
    d. Centers for Disease Control and Prevention (CDC).
3. When an inspector from your local regulatory agency finds a critical violation of code rules, the manager and supervisor should:
    a. decide on a time to meet and discuss the problem.
    b. insist this has never caused a problem before.
    c. wait for a report to verify the problem.
    d. immediately begin to fix the problem.

4. If a customer reports a suspected foodborne illness thought to be from a product in your area, you should immediately notify the manager and

   a. wait for a decision on action to take.
   b. remove suspected product from use or sale.
   c. wait until you have two or more related complaints.
   d. notify the local health department.

5. Which federal agency prepares the model Food Code?

   a. Food and Drug Administration (FDA).
   b. U.S. Department of Agriculture (USDA).
   c. Environmental Protection Agency (EPA).
   d. Centers for Disease Control and Prevention (CDC).

6. Which federal agency is responsible for ensuring the safety of domestic meat, poultry, and egg products?

   a. Centers for Disease Control and Prevention (CDC).
   b. Environmental Protection Agency (EPA).
   c. Food and Drug Administration (FDA).
   d. U.S. Department of Agriculture (USDA).

7. Which federal agency is responsible for ensuring the safety of all foods except domestic meat, poultry, and egg products?

   a. Centers for Disease and Control and Prevention (CDC).
   b. Environmental Protection Agency (EPA).
   c. Food and Drug Administration (FDA).
   d. U.S. Department of Agriculture (USDA).

8. If the FDA determines the ingestion of a food may "cause serious adverse health consequences," a voluntary food recall may be requested. This would be an example of what kind of recall?

   a. Class I.
   b. Class II.
   c. Class III.
   d. Class IV.

9. During an inspection of a retail food establishment, the manager should:

   a. Ask to see credentials.
   b. Assist the inspector whenever possible.
   c. Discuss any violations.
   d. All of the above.

10. When a suspected foodborne illness claim is reported to an employee, what should be the first course of action?

   a. Remove all customers from the premises immediately.
   b. Call the health inspector.
   c. Locate the food manager and assure the suspect food is removed.
   d. Contact the CDC.

11. Responsibilities of a food manager include:

   a. Obtaining copies, understanding, and complying with rules and regulations regarding the facility.
   b. Handling retail food establishment self-inspections.
   c. Handling claims of foodborne illness.
   d. All of the above.

Answers to these multiple-choice questions are available in Appendix A.

References/Suggested Readings

Food Safety and Inspection Service. U.S. Department of Agriculture. August 2000. Washington, DC 20250-3700. www.fsis.gov/oa/pubs/dating.htm.

IFT Publication. 1992. "Government Regulation of Food Safety: Interaction of Scientific and Societal Forces." *Food Technology.* 46(1).

Labuza, T. P., and Baisier. 1992. "The Role of the Federal Government in Food Safety." *Critical Reviews in Science and Nutrition.* 31(3). 167 to 176.

National Advisory Committee on Microbiological Criteria for Foods. August 2004. "Considerations for Establishing Safety-Based Consume-By Date Labels for Refrigerated Ready-to-Eat Foods." www.fsis.usda.gov/ophs/nacmcf/2004/NACMCF_Safetybased-Date_Labels_082704.pdf.

Potter, N. N.; and J. H. Hotchkiss. 1995. *Food Science.* Chapman and Hall. New York, NY.

Suggested Web Sites

Conference for Food Protection
www.foodprotect.org

Food and Agriculture Organization
www.fao.org

Food Marketing Institute
www.fmi.org

Gateway to Government Food Safety Information
www.foodsafety.gov

U.S. Department of Agriculture (USDA)
www.usda.gov

Centers for Disease Control and Prevention (CDC)
www.cdc.gov

Environmental Protection Agency (EPA)
www.epa.gov

Food and Drug Administration (FDA)
www.fda.gov

USDA Food Safety and Inspection Service (FSIS)
www.fsis.usda.gov

USDA/FDA Food and Nutrition Information Center
www.nal.uda.gov/fnic

National Marine Fisheries Services
www.seafood.nmfs.noaa.gov

Occupational Safety and Health Administration (OSHA)
www.osha.gov

Partnerships for Food Safety Education
www.fightbac.org

World Health Organization
www.who.int

Notes

Glossary

Abrasive cleaners - cleaning compounds containing finely ground minerals used to scour articles; can scratch surfaces.

Acceptable level - within an established range of safety.

Accessible - easy to reach or enter.

Acid - a substance with a pH of less than 7.0.

Additives - natural and man-made substances added to a food for an intended purpose (such as preservatives and colors) or added unintentionally (such as pesticides and lubricants).

Adulterated - a food shall be deemed to be adulterated if it meets one of the conditions described in Section 402 of the Federal Food, Drug, and Cosmetic Act. A detailed list of conditions and exclusions associated with adulterated foods can be found at http://www.fda.gov/opacom/laws/fdcact/fdcact4.htm

Aerobe - an organism, especially a bacterium, that requires oxygen to live.

Air curtain - a window or doorway equipped with jets that force air out and across the opening to keep flying insects from entering.

Air-dry - to dry in room air after cleaning, washing, or sanitizing.

Air gap - an unobstructed, open vertical distance through air that separates an outlet of the potable water supply from a potentially contaminated source like a drain.

Alkaline - a substance that has a pH of more than 7.0.

Allergen - see food allergen and major food allergen.

Ambient - a recommended air temperature used to transport or to store perishable foods.

Anaerobe - an organism, especially a bacterium, that does not require oxygen or free oxygen to live.

Anisakiasis - disease caused by the anisakis parasite.

Anisakis **spp.** - roundworm parasite found in fish.

Aseptic processing and packaging - a method in which food is sterilized or commercially sterilized outside the can and then aseptically placed in previously sterilized containers, which are then sealed in an aseptic environment. This method may be used for liquid foods, such as concentrated milk and soups.

Asymptomatic - without obvious symptoms or indications of a disease or other medical condition, not showing symptoms because symptoms have occurred but stopped and because symptoms never became noticeable.

Bacillus cereus – sporeforming bacterium that can live with or without oxygen and causes a foodborne illness.

Backflow - flow of contaminated water into the potable supply; caused by backpressure.

Back room - a storage area for excess products kept on hand to restock the sales floor as needed.

Backsiphonage - a form of backflow that can occur when pressure in the potable water supply drops below pressure in the flow of contaminated water.

Bacteria - single-celled microscopic organisms.

Bactericide - substance that kills bacteria.

Bacterium - one microorganism.

Bagger - a retail clerk or associate who bags customers' purchases in plastic or paper bags to suit customers.

Bagging - a process of properly, carefully packing customer's purchases in plastic or paper bags to suit customers.

Bakeoff - an in-store baking process using frozen doughs and products to prepare fresh products (i.e., fresh rolls, bread, doughnuts, or other pastries).

Bale - a large bundle of cardboard that is recycled.

Baler - a device used to compact and bind corrugated cardboard into bales for recycling.

Bar code - a unique identification code on products, pallets, and coupons. The code is read by an electronic scanner for receiving, ordering, and inventory control purposes.

Bi-metallic stem thermometer - food thermometer used to measure product temperatures.

Binary fission - the process by which bacteria grow. One cell divides to form two new cells.

Biofilm - a layer of stubborn soil that develops on surfaces that are improperly cleaned or sanitized; bacteria can accumulate and grow on this surface.

Blast chiller - special refrigerated unit that quickly freezes food items.

Glossary

Bloating - a damaged, swollen processed food can or glass container, which may indicate contamination, a safety hazard.

Bloom - an indication of freshness and quality as beef turns bright red when exposed to oxygen.

Bottle returns - beverage bottles returned to a retailer for recycling.

Botulism - type of food intoxication caused by *C. botulinum.*

Box cutter - a knife-like device with a razor blade used to open boxes.

Braise - to cook meat by browning it in fat, then simmering it in a covered pan with a little liquid.

Breaking down - removing products from a case in order to clean and sanitize it; also, removing component parts of a piece of equipment, such as a slicer or a grinder, to clean and sanitize it.

Bulk produce - loose, unpackaged, fresh produce that customers select themselves.

Bulk product - unpackaged, fresh products displayed in bins in large quantities and sold by the piece or the pound, such as grains, candy, and snacks.

Calibrate - to determine and verify the scale of a measuring instrument with a standard. Thermometers used in food establishments are commonly calibrated using an ice slush method (32°F or 0°C) or a boiling point method (212°F or 100°C).

Campylobacter jejuni - a microaerophilic nonsporeforming bacterium that causes a foodborne illness.

CAP - controlled atmosphere packaging.

Case, refrigerated - a refrigerated display unit for perishable products, such as dairy products or ice cream.

Centralized prepackaging - a centralized facility that processes prepackaged perishables and ships the goods to stores.

Channel of distribution - the producers and distributors of products from a farm to the table, a path that includes a grower, producer, manufacturer, broker, wholesaler, store, and consumer.

Checker - a front-end employee who rings up, totals, and collects for a customer's order. Also known as a cashier.

Checking - the process of recording customer purchases, taking payment, making change, processing coupons, bagging, and all other functions inherent to the front-end operation.

Check out or check stand - a fixture in a supermarket where customer transactions occur and where the register, scanner, and bags are located. Also known as the front end.

Chemical sanitizers - products used on equipment and utensils after washing and rinsing to reduce the number of disease-causing microbes to safe levels.

Ciguatoxin - a toxin from reef-feeding fish that causes foodborne illness.

Clean - free of visible soil but not necessarily sanitized; surface must be cleaned before it can be sanitized.

Cleaning - removal of visible soil but not necessarily sanitized. A surface must be cleaned before it can be sanitized.

Cleaning agent - a chemical compound formulated to remove soil and dirt.

Clean-in-place (CIP) - equipment designed to be cleaned without moving, usually large or very heavy.

Clostridium botulinum **-** an anaerobic sporeforming bacterium that causes foodborne illness.

Clostridium perfringens **-** an anaerobic sporeforming bacterium that causes foodborne illness.

Code - a systematic collection of regulations, or statutes, and procedures designed to protect the public.

Coffin case or coffin freezer - a waist-high fixture used to display frozen food, with a transparent door or no door for easy access. See upright freezer.

Cold-holding - refers to the safe temperature range (less than 41°F or 5°C) for maintaining foods cold prior to service for consumption.

Cold storage - a facility that stores frozen foods and perishable items that need refrigeration or special handling.

Commingle - to combine shell stock harvested on different days or from different growing areas as identified on the tag or label, or to combine shucked shellfish from containers with different container codes or different shucking dates.

Comminuted - the resulting size of a food mass achieved by methods including chopping, flaking, grinding, or mincing.

Glossary

Commissary - A centralized food preparation facility that distributes prepared product to stores. Also a U.S. government–subsidized, nonprofit food store, operating on a military base. Operates on a nonprofit basis and sells products at cost plus a small markup.

Compactor, trash - a device used to crush dry or wet garbage. Often found in many stores in two separate units—one compactor for paper and cardboard and one for all other materials.

Conditional employee - a potential food employee to whom a job offer is made, conditional on responses to subsequent medical questions or examinations designed to identify potential food employees who may be suffering from a disease that can be transmitted through food.

Consumer - an end user of any product or service. A shopper, patron, or customer. The final link in the chain of product distribution: manufacturing, selling, wholesaling, retailing, and consuming.

Contamination - the unintended presence of harmful substances or conditions in food that can cause illness or injury to people who eat the infected food.

Controlled atmosphere packaging (CAP) - a product in a low oxygen, nitrogen rich wrap that preserves freshness.

Convenience store - a small, easy access food store with a limited assortment. Many convenience stores also sell fast-food and gasoline.

Conventional supermarket - a large, self-service, retail food store with moderate pricing and selection, and annual sales in the $2-to -$8-million range. Usually includes a meat, produce, dairy, and grocery department.

Cook-chill - a cooking and food preservation process for food service products. Food is cooked, packed, sealed, and quick chilled in a plastic pouch and stored at temperatures below 41°F (5°C).

Cooking - the act of providing sufficient heat and time to a given food to affect a change in food texture, aroma, and appearance. More importantly, cooking assures the destruction of foodborne pathogens inherent to that food.

Cooler - a refrigerated holding unit in a warehouse or store for perishables.

Cooling - the act of reducing the temperature of properly cooked food to 41°F (5°C) or below.

Cooling methods - various techniques used to promote the rapid cooling of properly cooked food to 41°F (5°C) or below. Some commonly used cooling methods include 1) placing food in shallow pans, 2) dividing large masses of food into smaller portions, 3) placing hot food in an ice water bath, 4) using cooling paddles to stir food, 5) blast chillers, 6) walk-in coolers, and, 7) adding ice as an ingredient to a condensed food.

Corrosion resistant - materials that maintain their original surface characteristics under continuous use in food service with normal use of cleaning compounds and sanitizing solutions.

Coving - a curved sealed edge between the floor and wall that makes cleaning easier and inhibits insect harborage.

Critical control point (CCP) - means a point or procedure in a specific food system where loss of control may result in an unacceptable health risk.

Critical limit - the maximum or minimum value to which a physical, biological, or chemical parameter must be controlled at a critical control point to minimize the risk that the identified food safety hazard may occur.

Cross contamination - transfer of harmful organisms between items by direct or indirect contact.

Cross connection - any physical link through which contaminants from drains, sewers, or waste pipes can enter a potable water supply.

Cryptosporidium parvum - single-cell parasites found in animal feces and contaminated water.

Cryovac - a proprietary term for vacuum packaging material, which has entered the language to mean all vacuum packaging, like "Kleenex" or "Band-Aid."

Cumulative - increasing in effect by successive additions. For example, hot food must be cooled from 135°F (57°C) to 70°F (21°C) within 2 hours; it must reach 41°F (5°C) within 6 hours to prevent bacterial growth. Therefore, the cumulative time the food is in this danger zone equals a total of 6 hours or less.

Cutting - opening or sampling a product to evaluate its appearance, flavor, quality, and/or consistency.

Cyclospora cayetanensis - a parasite that is found in contaminated water and fresh produce.

Dairy/deli case extender - an insulated container display attached to a refrigerated case that extends into an aisle to stimulate impulse buys.

Danger zone - temperatures between 41°F (5°C) and 135°F (57°C).

Date coding or marking - a date and source code printed on an item to indicate its shelf life. Date codes assist with quality control (first-in, first-out) and proper stock rotation. Date coding may also apply to affixing a "sell by" or "pull by" date on merchandise, which is on display (as in the bakery department) to prevent the sale of off-quality products.

Disinfectant - destroys harmful bacteria.

Dead man's switch - activates equipment when depressed and stops if pressure is relieved.

Deli-bake - a combination in-store bakery and deli department where equipment, floor space, and labor are shared, usually under common supervision.

Delicatessen - an in-store department with cooked foods, salads, cold cuts, and cheeses, etc.

Demo or demonstration - a product promotion in a store with samples to eat and cooking tip handouts or coupons.

Detergents - cleaning agent, which contains surfactants used with water to break down soil to make it easier to remove.

Deviation - to diverge; to go in different directions.

Digital thermometer - a battery-powered thermometer that reveals temperature in a digital numerical display.

Dock - an area to receive, load, and unload shipments.

Dressed fish - a whole scaled, cleaned fish, sold with or without the head.

Drinking water - refers to water that is safe to drink. Drinking water is traditionally known as "potable water," and it meets all criteria as specified in *40 CFR 141–National Primary Drinking Water Regulations.*

Dry grocery - nonperishable grocery products.

Dry grocery non-foods - products that are not food, such as paper products, detergents, or pet items.

Easy-to-clean - materials and design that facilitate cleaning.

Easy-to-move - on wheels, raised on legs, or otherwise designed to facilitate cleaning.

Employee - person working in or for a food establishment who engages in food preparation, service, or other assigned activity.

Enterohemorrhagic *Escherichia coli* (EHEC) - *E. coli* bacteria that produce bloody diarrhea (hemorrhagic colitis) and hemolytic uremic syndrome (HUS). EHEC are a subset of Shiga toxin-producing *E. coli* bacteria. Some examples of serotypes of EHEC include *E. coli* O157:H7 and *E. coli* O157:NM.

Equipment - the appliances: stoves, ovens, etc.; and storage containers, such as refrigerated units used in food establishments.

Ethnic foods - products that a particular ethnic (racial, national, religious, or cultural) group favor, such as Mexican, Chinese, or Kosher.

Evaluation procedures - systematically checking progress to determine if goals have been met.

Exotic produce - fruits and vegetables not grown in North America and considered exotic.

Expiration date - a manufacturer's "sell-by" date stamped on products to indicate shelf life.

Facultative anaerobe - an organism that can grow with or without free oxygen.

FATTOM - an acronym used to indicate the six conditions bacteria need for growth. These conditions are food, acid, temperature, time, oxygen, and moisture.

FIFO - acronym for first-in, first-out, used to describe stock rotation procedures of using older products first.

FMI (Food Marketing Institute) - an international trade association of independent grocers, chain stores, and wholesalers.

Food allergen - a substance in food that causes the human immune system to produce chemicals and histamines in order to protect the body. These chemicals produce allergic symptoms that affect the respiratory system, gastrointestinal tract, skin, or cardiovascular system. See major food allergen.

Food establishment - an operation that stores, prepares, packages, serves, vends, or otherwise provides food for human consumption, such as a restaurant, food market, institutional feeding location, or vending location.

Food recall - The FDA and USDA can request a recall of a food product if the agency has determined a potential hazard exists.

Foodborne disease outbreak - an incident in which two or more people experience a similar illness after ingesting a common food, and in which epidemiological analysis identifies the food as the source of the illness.

Foodborne illness - an illness caused by the consumption of a contaminated food.

Food-contact surface - any surface of equipment or any utensils that food normally touches.

Foot-candle - unit of lighting equal to the illumination one foot from a uniform light source.

Forklift - a vehicle with projecting prongs that slide under a pallet to move merchandise in a warehouse or store.

Fresh - just picked, gathered, produced, live or unprocessed, not stale food. A term associated with perimeter departments, including produce, deli, bakery, or floral; also, unfrozen.

Fungi - a group of microorganisms that includes mold and yeasts.

Giardia lamblia - single-cell parasite found in animal feces and contaminated water and causes foodborne illness.

Garbage - wet waste matter, usually food product, that cannot be recycled.

Garnish - a decoration on salads, such as sprigs of watercress, lettuce, or other colorful items.

Gastroenteritis - an inflammation of the linings of the stomach and intestines, which can cause nausea, vomiting, abdominal cramping, and diarrhea.

General merchandise (GM) - products other than food sold in supermarkets that require special buying, warehousing, and servicing. GM classes are: hardiness, softness, reading/writing lines, health and beauty care (HBC), and services.

Generally recognized as safe (GRAS) - a food safety FDA term that indicates all ingredients are approved for human consumption. (See GRAS substances.)

Germicide - a substance that kills harmful microbes and germs.

Germs - general term for microorganisms, including bacteria and viruses.

Grade - a food industry classification system or standard that indicates a quality level, such as Grade A, Prime, or Extra Fancy.

Grade standards - primarily standards of quality to help producers, wholesalers, retailers, and patrons in marketing and purchasing food products. The grade standards are not aimed at protecting the health of the consumer but rather at ensuring value received according to uniform quality standards.

GRAS substances - GRAS stands for generally recognized as safe. These are substances added to foods that have been shown to be safe based on a long history of common usage in food.

Grocery store - a retail store that sells a variety of food products, including some perishable items and general merchandise.

Grocery wholesaler - a middleman who buys food and supplies from manufacturers to resell in smaller quantities to retailers; cooperatives and voluntaries are the two major types.

HACCP - Hazard analysis critical control point.

Hand antiseptics - Antimicrobial substances that are applied to the skin to reduce the number of microbes. Hand antiseptics may be used as a topical application, a hand antiseptic solution used as a hand dip, or a hand antiseptic soap.

Handwashing - the proper cleaning of hands with soap and warm water to remove dirt, filth, and disease germs.

Handwashing sink - a lavatory or wash basin installed for use in personal hygiene and designed for the washing of the hands. Includes an automatic handwashing facility.

Harborage - shelter for pests.

Hazard - a biological, chemical, or physical agent that may cause an unacceptable consumer health risk.

Hazard analysis - to identify hazards (problems) that might be introduced into food by unsafe practices or the intended use of the product.

Hazard analysis critical control point (HACCP) - a federal guideline to ensure safe food handling and preparation from receiving to point of sale. See HACCP.

Heat-and-eat - a precooked food that requires heating before consumption.

Hepatitis A - A foodborne virus that causes foodborne illness.

Hermetic packaging - a container completely sealed by heat against the entry of bacteria, molds, yeasts, and filth as long as it remains intact.

Highly susceptible population (HSP) - persons who are more likely than other people in the general population to experience foodborne disease because they are immunocompromised, preschool-age children, or older adults and are obtaining food at a facility such as a hospital, nursing home, custodial care, or senior center.

Home meal replacement - foods prepared in a store and consumed at home or in-store, which require little or no preparation on the part of the consumer.

Hot-holding - refers to the safe temperature range of 135°F (57°C) and above to maintain properly cooked foods hot until served.

Housekeeping - operational procedures to ensure cleanliness, safety, sanitation, and maintenance for a store or warehouse.

Immunocompromised - the term used to describe individuals, such as infants, children, pregnant women, and those with weakened immune systems, for whom foodborne illness can be very severe, even life threatening.

Impermeable - does not permit passage, especially of fluids.

Individually quick frozen (IQF) - a food processing technique that freezes products in the final stage of processing. It is then wrapped and packaged for shipment.

Infection - illness caused by eating food that contains living diseasecausing microorganisms.

Infestation - presence of a large number of pests.

Injected - Manipulating meat to which a solution is introduced into the interior by processes referred to as "injecting," "pump marinating," or "stitch pumping".

Inspection for wholesomeness - an examination of domestic and imported meat, poultry, and egg products to assure they are wholesome and free from adulteration.

Integrated pest management (IPM) - a system of preventive and control measures used to control or eliminate pest infestations in food establishments.

Intoxication - illness caused by eating food that contains a harmful chemical or toxin.

Irradiation - a food preservation process that utilizes radiation to control bacteria growth and increase shelf life.

Kick plate (base) - a metal sheet, usually at the bottom of doors, for protection purposes.

Kitchenware - utensils used to prepare food.

Larva - immature stage of development of insects and parasites.

Leftovers - any food that is prepared for a particular meal and is held over for service at a future meal.

Listeria monocytogenes - A facultative microbe that causes foodborne illness.

Low temp - A refrigerator that holds products at a below-freezing temperature [32°F (0°C)] or less.

Major food allergen - milk, egg, fish (such as bass, flounder, cod), crustacean shellfish (such as crab, lobster, or shrimp), tree nuts (such as almonds, pecans, or walnuts), wheat, peanuts, and soybeans; or a food ingredient that contains protein obtained from one of these foods.

Manager - the individual present at a food service establishment who supervises employees who are responsible for the storage, preparation, display, and service of food to the public.

MAP - modified atmosphere packaging.

Measuring device - usually a thermometer that registers the temperature of products and water used for sanitizing.

Mechanically tenderized - means manipulating meat with deep penetration by processes which may be referred to as "blade tenderizing," "jaccarding," "pinning," "needling," or using blades, pins, needles or any mechanical device.

Media - newspapers, magazines, radio, and television.

Mesophile - microorganism that grows best at moderate temperatures.

Microbe - a microorganism that can cause disease. Bacteria, molds, and yeast that can grow on various food and equipment surfaces; the main cause of discoloration in meat and food poisoning.

Microorganism - bacteria, viruses, molds, and other tiny organisms that are too small to be seen with the naked eye. The organisms are also referred to as microbes because they cannot be seen without the aid of a microscope.

Misbranding - falsely or misleadingly packaged or labeled food; may contain ingredients not included on the label or does not meet national standards for that food.

Modified atmosphere packaging (MAP) - a food processing technique where foods are placed in a flexible container and the air is removed from the package. Gases may be added to help preserve the food. See MAP.

Mold - any of various fungi that spoil food and have a fuzzy appearance.

Monitoring procedures - a defined method of checking foods during receiving, storage, preparation, holding, and serving processes.

Non–food–contact surface - any area not designed to touch food.

Norovirus or **Norwalk virus** - common foodborne virus found in contaminated water, produce, seafood, and ready-to-eat foods.

Nutrition labeling - an accurate list of ingredients printed on food, beverage, and drug labels.

Occupational Safety and Health Administration (OSHA) - a federal agency that sets work place safety standards and inspects facilities for safe working conditions.

Onset time - the period between eating a contaminated food and developing symptoms of a foodborne illness.

Open dating - a date stamped or printed on the label of perishable items to indicate a pull date (a date by which the item must be sold or removed from the shelf) or pack date (the date the item was packaged). Clear, readable dates that are printed on labels.

Organically grown - an imprecise term that means a grower did not use chemicals or that a processor did not use preservatives in the product.

Ovenable - a food ready to be heated, either in an oven or microwave.

Overstock - an excessive amount of product purchased in anticipation of increased sales volume.

Over-wrap - to wrap a plastic container in cellophane to prevent tampering.

Pack date - the date on which a product was made or packaged for sale.

Palatable - having an acceptable taste and flavor.

Pallet - a standard-sized base for assembling, sorting, stacking, handling, and transporting goods as a unit. The industry standard is GPCspec- 4-way entry, 48 inches x 40 inches hardwood pallets.

Parasite - an animal or plant that lives in or on another and from whose body it obtains nourishment.

Parts per million (ppm) - unit of measure for water hardness and chemical sanitizing solution concentrations.

Pasteurization - a low-heat treatment used to destroy disease-causing organisms and/or extend the shelf life of a product by destroying organisms and enzymes that cause spoilage.

Pathogenic - capable of causing disease; harmful; any disease-causing agent.

Perishables - foods requiring refrigeration or special handling because they spoil easily, such as meat, seafood, produce, deli, bakery, and dairy.

Personal hygiene - health habits including bathing, washing hair, wearing clean clothing, and proper handwashing.

Pest control operator - licensed individual or certified technician who provides pest control services.

pH - the symbol that describes the acidity or alkalinity of a substance, such as food.

Physical hazard - particles or fragments of items not supposed to be in foods.

Point of sale (POS) - the place in a retail store where products are scanned through the register system, data is collected, and sales are tendered. POS also describes sales data generated by checkout scanners.

Point of purchase - the locations within a retail store where a customer purchases products.

Potable water - water that is safe to drink. Also known as drinking water.

Potentially hazardous food (time/temperature control for safety food) - a food that requires time/temperature control for safety (TCS) to limit the growth of pathogenic microorganism or toxin formation. Potentially hazardous food (time/temperature control for safety food) [PHF (TCS)] includes an animal food that is raw or heat-treated; a plant food that is heat-treated or consists of raw seed sprouts, cut melons, cut tomatoes, cut leafy greens, or garlic-in-oil mixtures that are not modified in a way that results in mixtures that do not support pathogenic microorganism growth or toxin formation. A food that because of the interaction of it's A_w and pH values is designated as Product Assessment required (PA) should be considered a PHF (TCS) until further study proves otherwise.

Pounds per square inch (psi) - amount of pressure per square inch.

Premises - physical environment of the food establishment; grounds, interior, and exterior of building(s).

Preventive measures - procedures that keep foods from becoming contaminated.

Proof box - a piece of equipment in which heat and humidity are controlled in order for dough to rise in preparation for baking.

Psychrophiles - microorganisms that grow best at cold temperatures.

Pull date - the date by which a product must be either sold or pulled from a shelf.

Quaternary ammonium - a chemical sanitizing compound that is relatively safe for skin contact and is generally noncorrosive; effective in both acid and alkaline solutions.

Ratite - a flightless bird, such as an emu, ostrich, or rhea.

Reach-in case - a refrigerated display case with a self-service door used for perishable products.

Ready-to-eat foods - products that are in a form that is edible without washing, cooking, or additional preparation by the food establishment or the patron.

Receiver - an authorized associate of a warehouse or retail store who receives and checks deliveries for condition and accurate amount. The first handler of the delivery receipt or invoice.

Receiving - a door or dock of a warehouse or store designated for receiving merchandise from a supplier. The procedure for physically and legally accepting a shipment of product.

Receiving clerk - see receiver.

Receiving log - the record or listing of products received with appropriate entries.

Reclaimed goods - Unsalable product at the time of delivery that is returned to a wholesaler/vendor for reclamation.

Reconstitute - to combine dehydrated foods with water or other liquids to bring back to its original state; example, addition of water to powdered milk. **Refuse** - trash, rubbish, waste.

Reheating - the act of providing sufficient heat [at least 165°F or (74°C)] within a 2-hour time period to ensure the destruction of any foodborne pathogens that may be present in that cooked and cooled food.

Re-service - the transfer of food that is unused and returned by a consumer after being served or sold and in the possession of the consumer, to another person.

Returns - unsold, damaged, or defective merchandise sent to a supplier or distributor for credit or refund.

Rework - perishables: to crisp or trim a product that looks case-worn, grocery: to re-affix labels. To refine a category or shelf set.

Re-wraps - products that are removed, reconditioned (if salable), and displayed with limited sell-by dates.

Risk - the chance of injury, damage, or loss.

Rotation - a shelf-stocking procedure that ensures first-in, first-out by pulling older stock forward and placing newer stock at the back during restocking.

Rotavirus - viral infection associated with sewage, contaminated food and poor handwashing, and found especially in infants and children.

Rotisserie - a rotating grill with an electrically turned spit that cooks meats.

Safety cutter - a case cutter used to open cases of product.

Salmonella **spp.** - facultative anaerobe that causes foodborne illness.

Salvage - product containers/shippers (bales, pallets, containers) that must be returned or recycled to defray operational costs.

Sanitary - healthful and hygienic. The number of harmful microorganisms and other contaminants have been reduced to safe levels.

Sanitation - maintenance of conditions that are clean and promote good health.

Sanitizer - approved substance or method to use when sanitizing.

Sanitizing - application of an agent that reduces microbes to safe levels.

Scombrotoxin - seafood toxin originating from histamine producing bacteria.

Sealed - closed tightly.

Segregation - locating general merchandise products (GM) in a well-defined area of a store rather than in aisles next to or across from food products.

Selectivity - chemical sanitizers, especially quats, may kill only certain organisms and not others.

Sensitive ingredient - an ingredient that is prone to support bacterial growth.

Shelf life - time period a product can be expected to maintain maximum quality and freshness.

Shelf stable - a processed food product that remains safe to eat without refrigeration.

Shell fish - an aquatic animal. Molluscan shellfish include clams, oysters, mussels, squid, octopus, and scallops. Crustacean shellfish include crabs, lobster, and shrimp.

Shellstock - raw, in-shell molluscan shellfish.

Shiga toxin-producing *Escherichia coli* - any *E. coli* capable of producing Shiga toxins (also called verocytotoxins or "Shiga-like" toxins). This includes, but is not limited to, *E. coli* reported as serotype O157:H7, O157:NM, and O157:H.

Shigella **spp.** - facultative anaerobic bacteria that cause foodborne illness.

Shucking - a process of opening shellfish and removing the animal from the shell, such as oysters, clams, mussels, etc.

Silicate - salt or ester derived from silica; a hard, glassy material found in sand.

Single-use articles - items intended for one use and then discarded, such as paper cups or plastic eating utensils.

Slacking - the process used to moderate the temperature of a food, such as allowing a food to gradually increase from -10°F (-23°C) to 25°F (-4°C) in preparation for deep-fat frying or to facilitate even heat penetration during the cooking or reheating of a previously block-frozen food, such as spinach.

Sneeze guard - a clear, solid barrier that partially covers food in self-service areas to keep customers from coughing, sneezing, or projecting droplets of saliva directly onto food.

Soil - dirt and filth.

Sous vide - a European food-packaging technique in which a prepared product is placed in individual pouches, cooked under a vacuum, and quickly chilled. Products are frozen or refrigerated until used.

Splash contact surfaces - areas that are easy to clean and designed to catch splashed substances in work areas.

Spoilage - significant food deterioration, usually caused by bacteria and enzymes, that produces a noticeable change in the taste, odor, or appearance of the product.

Spoils - goods that cannot be sold for which a retailer receives a credit from a supplier. Also called stales.

Spore - the inactive or dormant state of some rod-shaped bacteria.

Standard of identity - Food and Drug Administration (FDA) standards for food composition.

Standard operating procedures - a comprehensive book of a company's policies and procedures. Also called SOPs.

Staphlococcus aureus - facultative anaerobic bacterium that produces a heat stable toxin as it grows on food.

Stationary equipment - equipment that is permanently fastened to the floor, table, or counter top.

Sulfites - preservatives used to maintain freshness and color of fresh fruits and vegetables; subject to state regulations.

Supermarket - a conventional grocery store, but not a warehouse club or mass merchant, with annual sales of $2 million or more per store.

Supplier - a generic term for wholesalers, who sell to and supply retailers directly and indirectly (i.e., manufacturer, vendor, broker, reseller).

Surfactant - chemical agent in detergent that reduces the surface tension, allowing the detergent to penetrate and soak soil loose; wetting agent.

Swells - unsalable items with expanded containers or lids signifying faulty food handling, processing, or sealing.

Tableware - plates, cups, bowls, etc.

Task analysis - examining a job task to determine what it takes to do the job.

Temperature abuse - allowing foods to remain in the temperature danger zone [41°F (5°C) and 135°F (57°C)] for an unacceptable period of time.

Temperature danger zone - temperatures between 41°F (5°C) and 135°F (57°C) at which bacteria grow best.

Test kit - device that accurately measures the concentration of sanitizing solutions to assure they are at proper levels.

Thermocouple - a temperature-measuring device that consists of two different types of metals, joined together at one end. When the junction of the two metals is heated or cooled, a voltage is created that can be correlated back to the temperature. Thermocouples are the preferred temperature-measuring devices for use with all foods.

Trichinella spiralis - Foodborne roundworm that causes a foodborne infection.

Unsalables - products unworthy of sale (i.e., damaged, out of date, spoiled).

Upright freezer - an upright refrigerated display unit with doors used for merchandising frozen foods.

USDA Grade - U.S. Department of Agriculture grades that relate to a specified quality of product. Grade denotes quality and USDA denotes product inspected for wholesomeness.

U.S. grade stamp - signifies that a product is clean, safe, and wholesome, and has been produced in an acceptable establishment, with the appropriate equipment, under the supervision of federal inspectors. It also indicates the product is of a specific grade.

U.S. Department of Agriculture (USDA) - a federal agency that oversees food production and inspection. The USDA establishes grade standards for commodities, conducts agricultural research and makes results available, administers food programs (i.e., food stamps), and distributes food.

U.S. Department of Commerce (USDC) - a federal agency that oversees trade and competition. The USDC establishes grade standards for seafood commodities, conducts agricultural research, and makes results available.

Utensil - a food-contact implement or container used in the storage, preparation, transportation, dispensing, sale, or service of food, such as kitchenware or tableware that is multi-use, single-service, or single-use; gloves used in contact with food; temperature-sensing probes of food temperature-measuring devices; and probe-type price or identification tags used in contact with food.

Vacuum breaker - designed for use under a continuous supply of pressure. Spring-loaded device to operate after extended periods of hydrostatic pressure.

Vacuum packaging - a packaging process in which air is removed from a package as it is sealed.

Vegetative state - the active state of a bacterium in which the cell takes in nourishment, grows, and produces wastes.

Ventilation - air circulation that removes smoke, odors, moisture, and grease-laden vapors from a room and replaces them with fresh air.

Verification - to prove to be true by evidence, usually a record of times and temperatures of food from receiving to serving or vending.

Vibrio **ssp.** - group of three organisms (*Vibrio* cholera, *Vibrio* parahaemolyticus, *Vibrio* vulnificus) found in raw or improperly cooked fish and shellfish that can cause foodborne illness.

Viruses - any of a group of infectious microorganisms that reproduce only in living cells. They cause diseases, such as mumps and Hepatitis A, and can be transmitted through food.

Warewashing - the cleaning and sanitizing of utensils and food-contact surfaces of equipment.

Water activity (A_w) - a measure of the free moisture in a food. Pure water has a water activity of 1.0, and potentially hazardous foods have a water activity of 0.85 and higher.

Waxing - applying an edible wax to some fruits and vegetables to help maintain a fresh, bright appearance and to preserve product quality.

Wetting agent - a substance that breaks down the soil to allow water and soap or detergent to liquefy and remove dirt and grease.

Whole-muscle, intact beef - whole-muscle beef that is not injected, mechanically tenderized, reconstructed, or scored and marinated, from which beef steaks may be cut.

Wholesome - something that is favorable to or promotes health.

Yeast - type of fungus that is not known to cause illness when present in foods but can cause damage to food products and will change taste; useful in making products, such as bread and beer.

Appendix A

Answers to End-of-Chapter Quizzes

Chapter 1 Answers
Quiz 1.1 Multiple Choice

1) d
2) a
3) d
4) c
5) d
6) d
7) b
8) d
9) c

Quiz 1.2 True/False

1) False
2) False
3) True
4) True
5) True

Chapter 2 Answers
Quiz 2

1) c
2) b
3) a
4) d
5) b
6) c
7) b
8) d
9) b
10) c
11) a

Chapter 3 Answers
Quiz 3

1) c
2) b
3) a
4) b
5) a
6) a
7) d
8) b
9) d
10) d
11) d
12) c

Chapter 4 Answers
Quiz 4

1) b
2) d
3) a
4) d
5) c
6) b
7) d
8) c
9) a
10) c
11) b
12) c
13) d
14) c
15) d
16) c
17) b

Chapter 5 Answers
Quiz 5

1) c
2) d
3) a
4) b
5) d
6) c
7) a
8) d
9) d
10) c
11) b
12) d
13) a

Chapter 6 Answers
Quiz 6

1) a
2) b
3) a
4) b
5) a
6) a
7) c
8) a
9) c
10) c
11) d

Chapter 7 Answers
Quiz 7

1) a
2) a
3) b
4) a
5) c
6) b
7) d
8) b
9) a
10) d

Chapter 8 Answers
Quiz 8

1) b
2) d
3) b
4) b
5) a
6) a
7) b

Chapter 9 Answers
Quiz 9

1) c
2) a
3) d
4) b
5) a
6) d
7) c
8) a
9) d
10) c
11) d

Appendix B

The Process for Determining Potentially Hazardous Food (Time/Temperature Control for Safety Food [PHF (TCS)])

The information appearing below was taken from pages 320 and 321 of "Annex 3—Public Health Reasons/Administrative Guidelines" of the 2009 *Food Code*. Additional information about PHF (TCS) and how to use the decision tree and tables presented in Annex 3 of the *Food Code* to determine if an item is a PHF (TCS) can be found at the following Web site: www.fda.gov/Food/FoodSafety/RetailFoodProtection/FoodCode/FoodCode2009/ucm189170.htm

Instructions for Using the Decision Tree and Table A and Table B:

1. Does the operator want to hold the food without using time or temperature control?

    a. No—Continue holding the food at ? 41°F (5°C) or ?135°F (57°C) for safety and/or quality.

    b. Yes—Continue using the decision tree to identify which table to use to determine whether time/temperature control for safety (TCS) is required.

2. Is the food heat-treated?

    a. No—The food is either raw, partially cooked (not cooked to the temperature specified in section 3-401.11 of the *Food Code*) or treated with some method other than heat. Proceed to step 3.

    b. Yes—If the food is heat-treated to the required temperature for that food as specified under section 3-401.11 of the *Food Code*, vegetative cells will be destroyed although spores will survive. Proceed to step 4.

3. Is the food treated using some other method?

    a. No —The food is raw or has only received a partial cook allowing vegetative cells and spores to survive. Proceed to step 6.

    b. Yes—If a method other than heat is used to destroy pathogens, such as irradiation, high-pressure processing, pulsed light, ultrasound, inductive heating, or ozonation, the effectiveness of the process needs to be validated by inoculation studies or other means. Proceed to step 5.

4. Is it packaged to prevent recontamination?

   a. No—Recontamination of the product can occur after heat treatment because it is not packaged. Proceed to step 6.

   b. Yes—If the food is packaged immediately after heat treatment to prevent recontamination, higher ranges of pH and/or A_w can be tolerated because sporeforming bacteria are the only microbial hazard. Proceed to step 7.

5. Further product assessment or vendor documentation required.

   a. The vendor of this product may be able to supply documentation that inoculation studies indicate the food can be safely held without TCS.

   b. Food prepared or processed using new technologies may be held without time/temperature control provided the effectiveness of the use of such technologies is based on a validated inoculation study.

6. Using the food's known pH and/or A_w values, position the food in the appropriate table.

   a. Choose the column under "pH values" that contains the pH value of the food in question.

   b. Choose the row under "A_w values" that contains the A_w value of the food in question.

   c. Note where the row and column intersect to identify whether the food is "non-PHF/non-TCS food" and therefore does not require time/temperature control, or whether further product assessment (PA) is required. Other factors, such as redox potential, competitive microorganisms, salt content, or processing methods may allow the product to be held without time/temperature control, but an inoculation study is required.

7. Use **Table A** for foods that are heat-treated and packaged **OR** use **Table B** for foods that are not heat-treated or heat-treated but not packaged.

8. Determine if the item is non-PHF/non-TCS or needs further product assessment (PA).

The Process for Determining PHF (TCS)

Table A Interaction of pH and A_w for control of spores in food heat-treated to destroy vegetative cells and subsequently packaged

A_w values	pH values		
	4.6 or less	>4.6 – 5.6	>5.6
≤0.92	non-PHF*/non-TCS food**	non-PHF/non-TCS food	non-PHF/non-TCS food
> 0.92 – 0.95	non-PHF/non-TCS food	non-PHF/non-TCS food	PA***
> 0.95	non-PHF/non-TCS food	PA	PA

* PHF means Potentially Hazardous Food
** TCS food means Time/Temperature Control for Safety Food
*** PA means Product Assessment required

Table B Interaction of pH and A_w for control of vegetative cells and spores in food not heat-treated or heat-treated but not packaged

A_w values	pH values			
	< 4.2	4.2 – 4.6	> 4.6 – 5.0	> 5.0
< 0.88	non-PHF*/non-TCS food**	non-PHF/non-TCS food	non-PHF/non-TCS food	non-PHF/non-TCS food
0.88 – 0.90	non-PHF/non-TCS food	non-PHF/non-TCS food	non-PHF/non-TCS food	PA***
>0.90 – 0.92	non-PHF/non-TCS food	non-PHF/non-TCS food	PA	PA
>0.92	non-PHF/non-TCS food	PA	PA	PA

* PHF means Potentially Hazardous Food
** TCS food means Time/Temperature Control for Safety Food
*** PA means Product Assessment required

Before using Tables A and B in determining whether a food requires TCS, answers to the following questions should be considered:

- Is the intent to hold the food without using time or temperature control?
  - If the answer is no, no further action is required. The decision tree presented at the beginning of the Appendix is not neededto determine if the item is a PHF (TCS).
- Is the food raw or is the food heat-treated?
- Does the food already require TCS according to the definition of PHF (TCS)?
- Does a product history with sound scientific rationale exist indicating a safe history of use?
- Is the food processed and packaged so that it no longer requires TCS, such as ultrahigh temperature (UHT) creamers or shelfstable canned goods?
- What is the pH and A_w of the food in question using an independent laboratory and Association of Official Analytical Chemists (AOAC) methods of analysis?

A food designated as meeting PA, in either Table A or B should be considered PHF until further study proves otherwise. The PA means that based on the food's pH and A_w and whether it was raw or heat-treated or packaged, it has to be considered PHF until inoculation studies or some other acceptable evidence shows that the food is a PHF (TCS) or not. The *Food Code* requires a variance request to be sent in advance to the regulatory authority with the evidence that the food does not require TCS.

Appendix C

Summary of Agents That Cause Foodborne Illness

CAUSATIVE AGENT (*Sporeforming bacteria)	TYPE OF ILLNESS	SYMPTOMS ONSET	COMMON FOODS	PREVENTION
Anisakis spp.	Parasitic infection	Coughing, vomiting 1 hr to 2 weeks	Raw or undercooked seafood, especially bottom-feeding fish	Cook fish to the proper temperature throughout; freeze to meet 2009 FDA *Food Code* specifications.
*Bacillus cereus	Bacterial intoxication or toxin-mediated infection	(1) Diarrhea, abdominal cramps (8 to 16 hrs) (2) Vomiting type, vomiting, diarrhea, abdominal cramps (30 minutes to 6 hrs)	(1) Diarrhea type: meats, milk, vegetables (2) Vomiting type: rice, starchy foods; grains and cereals	Properly heat, cool, and reheat foods.
Campylobacter jejuni	Bacterial infection	Watery, bloody diarrhea (2 to 5 days)	Raw chicken, raw milk, raw meat	Properly handle and cook foods; avoid cross contamination.
Ciguatoxin	Fish toxin, originating from toxic algae of tropical waters	Vertigo, hot/cold flashes, diarrhea, vomiting (15 minutes to 24 hrs)	Marine finfish including grouper, barracuda, snappers, jacks, mackerel, triggerfish, reef fish	Purchase fish from a reputable supplier; cooking WILL NOT inactivate the toxin.

CAUSATIVE AGENT (*Sporeforming bacteria)	TYPE OF ILLNESS	SYMPTOMS ONSET	COMMON FOODS	PREVENTION
*Clostridium botulinum	Bacterial intoxication	Dizziness, double vision, difficulty in breathing and swallowing, headache (12 to 36 hrs)	Improperly canned foods, vacuum-packed refrigerated foods, cooked foods in anaerobic mass	Properly heat process anaerobically packed foods; DO NOT use home canned foods.
*Clostridium perfringens	Bacterial toxin-mediated infection	Intense abdominal pains and severe diarrhea (8 to 22 hrs)	Spices, gravy, improperly cooled foods (especially meats and gravy dishes)	Properly cook, cool, and reheat foods.
Cryptosporidium parvum	Parasitic infection	Severe watery diarrhea within (1 week of ingestion)	Contaminated water, food contaminated by infected food workers	Use potable water supply; practice good personal hygiene and handwashing.
Cyclospora cayetanensis	Parasitic infection	Watery and explosive diarrhea, loss of appetite, bloating (1 week)	Water, strawberries, raspberries, and raw vegetables	Good sanitation; reputable supplier
Food allergens	An allergic reaction usually involving the skin, mouth, digestive tract, or airways	Skin: hives, rashes, and itching Mouth: swelling and itching of the lips and tongue Digestive tract: vomiting and diarrhea Airways: difficulty breathing, wheezing	Foods that contain: milk, soybeans, egg, wheat, nuts and peanuts, fish, and shellfish	Packaged and prepared foods must be properly labeled if they contain common food allergens so sensitive people can avoid them.
Giardia lamblia	Parasitic infection	Diarrhea within 1 week of contact	Contaminated water	Potable water supply; good personal hygiene and handwashing

Summary of Agents That Cause Foodborne Illness

CAUSATIVE AGENT (*Sporeforming bacteria)	TYPE OF ILLNESS	SYMPTOMS ONSET	COMMON FOODS	PREVENTION
Hepatitis A virus	Viral infection	Fever, nausea, vomiting, abdominal pain, fatigue, swelling of the liver, jaundice (15 to 50 days)	Foods that are prepared with human contact, contaminated water	Wash hands and practice good personal hygiene; avoid raw seafood.
Listeria monocytogenes	Bacterial infection	(1) Healthy adult: flu-like symptoms (2) Highly susceptible population: septicemia, meningitis, encephalitis, birth defects (1 day to 3 weeks)	Raw milk, dairy items, raw meats, refrigerated ready-to-eat foods, processed ready-to-eat meats, such as hot dogs, raw vegetables, and seafood	Properly store and cook foods; avoid cross contamination; rotate processed refrigerated foods using FIFO to assure timely use.
Mycotoxins	Intoxication	(1) Acute onset: hemorrhage, fluid buildup, possible death (2) Chronic: cancer from small does over time	Moldy grains: corn, corn products, peanuts, pecans, walnuts, and milk	Purchase food from a reputable supplier; keep grains and nuts dry; protect products from humidity.
Norovirus (Norwalk-like virus)	Viral infection	Vomiting, diarrhea, abdominal pain, headache, and low-grade fever; (onset 24 to 48 hrs)	Sewage, contaminated water, contaminated salad ingredients, raw clams, oysters	Use potable water; cook all shellfish handle food properly; meet time temperature guidelines for PHF.
Rotavirus	Viral infection	Diarrhea (especially in infants and children), vomiting, low-grade fever, (1 to 3 days onset; lasts 4 to 8 days)	Sewage, contaminated water, contaminated salad ingredients, raw seafood	Good personal hygiene and handwashing; proper food-handling practices

CAUSATIVE AGENT (*Sporeforming bacteria)	TYPE OF ILLNESS	SYMPTOMS ONSET	COMMON FOODS	PREVENTION
Salmonella spp.	Bacterial infection	Nausea, fever, vomiting, abdominal cramps, diarrhea (6 to 48 hrs)	Raw meats, raw poultry, eggs, milk, dairy products	Properly cook foods; avoid cross contamination.
Scombrotoxin	Seafood toxin originating from histamine producing bacteria	Dizziness, burning feeling in the mouth, facial rash or hives, peppery taste in mouth, headache, itching, teary eyes, runny nose (1 to 30 minutes)	Tuna, mahi-mahi, bluefish, sardines, mackerel, anchovies, amberjack, abalone	Purchase fish from a reputable supplier; store fish at low temperatures to prevent growth of histamine producing bacteria; toxin IS NOT inactivated by cooking.
Shellfish toxins: PSP, DSP, DAP, NSP	Intoxication	Numbness of lips, tongue, arms, legs, neck; lack of muscle coordination (10 to 60 minutes)	Contaminated mussels, clams, oysters, scallops	Purchase from a reputable supplier.
Shiga toxin-producing *Escherichia coli*	Bacterial infection or toxin-mediated infection	Bloody diarrhea followed by kidney failure and hemolytic uremic syndrome (HUS) in severe cases (12 to 72 hrs)	Undercooked hamburger, raw milk, unpasteurized apple cider, lettuce, and spinach	Practice good food sanitation; handwashing; properly handle and cook foods.

Summary of Agents That Cause Foodborne Illness

CAUSATIVE AGENT (*Sporeforming bacteria)	TYPE OF ILLNESS	SYMPTOMS ONSET	COMMON FOODS	PREVENTION
Shigella spp.	Bacterial infection	Bacillary dysentery, diarrhea, fever, abdominal cramps, dehydration (1 to 7 days)	Foods that are prepared with human contact: salads, raw vegetables, milk, dairy products, raw poultry, non-potable water, ready-to-eat meat	Wash hands and practice good personal hygiene; properly cook foods.
Staphylococcus aureus	Bacterial intoxication	Nausea, vomiting, abdominal cramps, headaches (2 to 6 hrs)	Foods that are prepared with human contact, cooked or processed foods	Wash hands and practice good personal hygiene; cooking WILL NOT inactivate the toxin.
Toxoplasma gondii	Parasitic infection	Mild cases of the disease involve swollen lymph glands, fever, headache, and muscle aches. Severe cases may result in damage to the eye or the brain. (10 to 13 days)	Raw meats, raw vegetables, and fruit	Good sanitation; reputable supplier; proper cooking
Trichinella spiralis	Parasitic infection from a nematode worm	Nausea, vomiting, diarrhea, sweating, muscle soreness (2 to 28 days)	Primarily undercooked wild game meats (bear, walrus) and undercooked pork	Cook foods to the proper temperature throughout.
Vibrio spp.	Bacterial infection	Headache, fever, chills, diarrhea, vomiting, severe electrolyte loss, gastroenteritis (2 to 48 hrs)	Raw or improperly cooked fish and shellfish	Practice good sanitation, properly cook foods, avoid serving raw seafood.

Notes

Appendix D

Multi-tiered, Risk-based Employee Health System

The *Food Code* recommends that retail food establishments implement a risk-based employee health system that will reduce the likelihood that the "Big Five" pathogens—Norovirus, *Salmonella* Typhi, Enterohemorrhagic or Shiga toxin-producing *Escherichia coli*, Hepatitis A Virus, and *Shigella* spp.—will be transmitted from infected food workers into food. These agents are known to be readily transmissible via food that has been contaminated by ill food workers and, therefore, are the primary focus of the "Employee Health" section of the *Food Code*.

The *Food Code* recommends a multi-tiered, risk-based system that balances a food employee's need to work and earn a living with an acceptable health risk for the public. It assures removal of infected food workers when they are most likely to transmit a pathogen to food items and provides guidance on when ill food employees can safely return to work.

Four levels of illness or potential illness have been identified by the FDA as follows:

- **Level 1 involves food employees who have specific symptoms (i.e., vomiting, diarrhea, jaundice) while in the work place.** These symptoms are known to be commonly associated with the agents most likely to be transmitted from infected food workers through contamination of food. The first level also relates to employees who have been diagnosed with typhoid fever or an infection with Hepatitis A Virus (within 14 days of symptoms). The first level poses the highest potential risk to public health. **The most significant degree of restriction and exclusion applies to the first level of food employee illness.** Infected food employees in Level 1 are likely to be excreting high levels of an infectious pathogen, increasing the chance of transmission to food products and placing the public at higher risk.

- **Level 2 relates to employees who have been diagnosed with a specific agent of concern, but who are not currently exhibiting symptoms of disease.** Food employees in Level 2 are still likely to be carrying the infectious agent, but they are less likely to spread the agent into food. However, these employees diagnosed with one of the agents of concern still pose an elevated threat to public health. For this reason, there are a series of exclusions if the employee works in a facility serving highly susceptible populations (HSP) and restrictions (for non-HSP facilities) may be greater, depending on the agent involved.

- **Level 3 relates to employees who are diagnosed with a specific agent but never develop any gastrointestinal symptoms.** These food employees are typically identified during a foodborne illness outbreak investigation through microbiological testing. The *Food Code* provides restriction or exclusion guidelines of infected employees who are identified through microbiological testing as carrying a listed pathogen, but are otherwise asymptomatic and clinically well. The exclusion or restriction guidelines are applied until the identified food employees no longer present a risk for foodborne pathogen transmission.
- **Level 4 relates to those individuals who are clinically well but who may have been exposed to a listed pathogen and are within the normal incubation period for the disease.** For example, a food employee may have attended a function at which he/she ate food that was associated with an outbreak of shigellosis, but the employee remains well. Such individuals present a lower risk to public health than someone who is either symptomatic or who has a definitive diagnosis. However, they present a level of risk to public health that is greater than if they had not had the exposure. The recommendation in the *Food Code* is to restrict food employees who have had a potential exposure based on the incubation times (time between exposure and the onset of symptoms) of the various agents. As a further protection to public health, it is recommended that such exposed food employees pay particular attention to personal hygiene and report the onset of any symptoms.

This tiered approach links the degree of exclusion and restriction to the degree of risk that an infected food worker will transmit an agent of concern through food. It seeks to strike a balance between protecting public health and meeting the needs of the food employee and employer.

Below is the specific information from the *Food Code* regarding reportable diseases and activities; exclusions and restrictions; and removal, adjustment, or retention of exclusions and restrictions.

2-2 Employee Health

Subpart

> **2-201 Responsibilities of Permit Holder, Person in Charge, Food Employees, and Conditional Employees.**

Responsibilities and Reporting Symptoms and Diagnosis	**2-201.11 Responsibility of Permit Holder, Person in Charge, and Conditional Employees**
	(A) The permit holder shall require food employees and conditional employees to report to the person in charge information about their health and activities as they relate to diseases that are transmissible through food. A food employee or conditional employee shall report the information in a manner that allows the person in charge to reduce the risk of foodborne disease transmission, including providing necessary additional information, such as the date of onset of symptoms and an illness, or of a diagnosis without symptoms, if the food employee or conditional employee:

Reportable *symptoms*	(1) Has any of the following symptoms:
	   (a) Vomiting,
	   (b) Diarrhea,
	   (c) Jaundice,
	   (d) Sore throat with fever, or;
	   (e) A lesion containing pus, such as a boil or infected wound that is open or draining and is:
	      (i) On the hands or wrists, *unless an impermeable cover, such as a finger cot or stall protects the lesion and a single-use glove is worn over the impermeable cover,*
	      (ii) On exposed portions of the arms, *unless the lesion is protected by an impermeable cover,* or;
	      (iii) On other parts of the body, *unless the lesion is covered by a dry, durable, tight-fitting bandage.*

Reportable *diagnosis*	(2) Has an illness diagnosed by a health practitioner due to:
	   (a) Norovirus,
	   (b) Hepatitis A Virus,
	   (c) *Shigella* spp.
	   (d) Enterohemorrhagic or Shiga toxin-producing *Escherichia coli*, or;
	   (e) *Salmonella* Typhi.

Reportable *past illness*	(3) Had a previous illness, diagnosed by a health practitioner, within the past 3 months due to *Salmonella* Typhi, without having received antibiotic therapy, as determined by a health practitioner.

Reportable *history of exposure*	(4) Has been exposed to, or is the suspected source of, a confirmed disease outbreak, because the food employee or conditional employee consumed or prepared food implicated in the outbreak, or consumed food at an event prepared by a person who is infected or ill with:
	   (a) Norovirus within the past 48 hours of the last exposure,
	   (b) Enterohemorrhagic or Shiga toxin-producing *Escherichia coli*, or *Shigella* spp. within the past 3 days of the last exposure,
	   (c) *Salmonella* Typhi within the past 14 days of the last exposure, or;
	   (d) Hepatitis A Virus within the past 30 days of the last exposure.

(Continued)

Responsibilities and Reporting Symptoms and Diagnosis	2-201.11 Responsibility of Permit Holder, Person in Charge, and Conditional Employees (Continued)

Reportable *history of exposure*	(5) Has been exposed by attending or working in a setting where there is a history of confirmed disease outbreak, or living in the same household as, and has knowledge about, an individual who works or attends a setting where there is a confirmed disease outbreak, or living in the same household as, and has knowledge about, an individual diagnosed with an illness caused by:
	  (a) Norovirus within the past 48 hours of the last exposure,
	  (b) Enterohemorrhagic or Shiga toxin-producing *Escherichia coli*, or *Shigella* spp. within the past 3 days of the last exposure,
	  (c) *Salmonella* Typhi within the past 14 days of the last exposure, or;
	  (d) Hepatitis A Virus within the past 30 days of the last exposure.

Responsibility of person in charge to *notify the regulatory authority*	(B) The person in charge shall notify the regulatory authority when a food employee is: (1) Jaundiced, or; (2) Diagnosed with an illness due to a pathogen as specified under Subparagraphs (A)(2)(a)—(e) of this section.
Responsibility of the person in charge to *prohibit a conditional employee from becoming a food employee*	(C) The person in charge shall assure that a conditional employee: (1) Who exhibits or reports a symptom, or who reports a diagnosed illness as specified under subparagraphs (A)(1)–(3) of this section, is prohibited from becoming a food employee until the conditional employee meets the criteria for the specific symptoms or diagnosed illness as specified under § 2-201.13, and; (2) Who will work as a food employee in a food establishment that serves a highly susceptible population and reports a history of exposure as specified under subparagraphs (A)(4)–(5), is prohibited from becoming a food employee until the conditional employee meets the criteria as specified under ¶ 2-201.13(I).
Responsibility of the person in charge to *exclude or restrict*	(D) The person in charge shall assure that a food employee who exhibits or reports a symptom, or who reports a diagnosed illness or a history of exposure as specified under subparagraphs (A)(1)–(5) of this section is: (1) Excluded as specified under ¶¶ 2-201.12 (A)–(C), and subparagraphs (D)(1), (E)(1), (F)(1), or (G)(1) and in compliance with the provisions specified under ¶¶ 2-201.13(A)–(G), or; (2) Restricted as specified under subparagraphs 2-201.12(D)(2), (E)(2), (F)(2), (G)(2), or ¶¶ 2-201.12(H) or (I) and in compliance with the provisions specified under ¶¶ 2-201.13(D)–(I).

(Continued)

Responsibilities and Reporting Symptoms and Diagnosis	**2-201.11 Responsibility of Permit Holder, Person in Charge, and Conditional Employees** (Continued)
Responsibility of food employees and conditional employees to *report*	(E) A food employee or conditional employee shall report to the person in charge of the information as specified under ¶ (A) of this section.
Responsibility of food employees to *comply*	(F) A food employee shall: (1) Comply with an exclusion as specified under ¶¶ 2-201.12(A)-(C) and subparagraphs 2-201.12(D)(1), (E)(1), (F)(1), or (G)(1) and with the provisions specified under ¶¶ 2-201.13(A)-(G); or (2) Comply with a restriction as specified under subparagraphs 2-201.12(D)(2), (E)(2), (F)(2), (G)(2), or ¶¶ 2-201.12(H) or (I) and comply with the provisions specified under ¶¶ 2-201.13(D)-(I).
Conditions of Exclusion and Restriction	**2-201.12 Exclusions and Restrictions**
	The person in charge shall exclude or restrict a food employee from a food establishment in accordance with the following:
Symptomatic with **vomiting or diarrhea**	(A) *Except when the symptom is from a noninfectious condition,* exclude a food employee if the food employee is: (1) Symptomatic with vomiting or diarrhea, or; (2) Symptomatic with vomiting or diarrhea and diagnosed with an infection from norovirus, *Shigella* spp., or Enterohemorrhagic or Shiga toxin-producing *E. coli*.
Jaundiced or diagnosed with **Hepatitis A infection**	(B) Exclude a food employee who is: (1) Jaundiced and the onset of jaundice occurred within the last 7 calendar days, *unless the food employee provides to the person in charge written medical documentation from a health practitioner specifying that the jaundice is not caused by Hepatitis A Virus or other fecal-orally transmitted infection,* (2) Diagnosed with an infection from Hepatitis A Virus within 14 calendar days from the onset of any illness symptoms, or within 7 calendar days of the onset of jaundice, or; (3) Diagnosed with an infection from Hepatitis A Virus without developing symptoms.

(Continued)

Conditions of Exclusion and Restriction	2-201.12 Exclusions and Restrictions (Continued)
Diagnosed or reported previous infection due to **S. Typhi**	(C) Exclude a food employee who is diagnosed with an infection from *Salmonella* Typhi, or reports a previous infection with *Salmonella* Typhi within the past 3 months as specified under subparagraph 2-201.11(A)(3).
Diagnosed with an asymptomatic infection from **norovirus**	(D) If a food employee is diagnosed with an infection from norovirus and is asymptomatic: (1) Exclude the food employee who works in a food establishment serving a highly susceptible population, or; (2) Restrict the food employee who works in a food establishment not serving a highly susceptible population.
Diagnosed with ***Shigella* spp.** infection and asymptomatic	(E) If a food employee is diagnosed with an infection from *Shigella* spp. and is asymptomatic: (1) Exclude the food employee who works in a food establishment serving a highly susceptible population, or; (2) Restrict the food employee who works in a food establishment not serving a highly susceptible population.
Diagnosed with **EHEC or STEC** and asymptomatic	(F) If a food employee is diagnosed with an infection from Enterohemorrhagic or Shiga toxin-producing *E. coli*, and is asymptomatic: (1) Exclude the food employee who works in a food establishment serving a highly susceptible population, or; (2) Restrict the food employee who works in a food establishment not serving a highly susceptible population.
Symptomatic with **sore throat with fever**	(G) If a food employee is ill with symptoms of acute onset of sore throat with fever: (1) Exclude the food employee who works in a food establishment serving a highly susceptible population, or; (2) Restrict the food employee who works in a food establishment not serving a highly susceptible population.
Symptomatic with **uncovered infected wound or pustular boil**	(H) If a food employee is infected with a skin lesion containing pus, such as a boil or infected wound, that is open or draining and not properly covered as specified under subparagraph 2-201.11(A)(1)(e), restrict the food employee.
Exposed to foodborne pathogen and works in food establishment serving HSP	(I) If a food employee is exposed to a foodborne pathogen as specified under subparagraphs 2-201.11(A)(4) or (5), restrict the food employee who works in a food establishment serving a highly susceptible population.

Multi-tiered, Risk-based Employee Health System

Managing Exclusions and Restrictions	2-201.13 Removal, Adjustment, or Retention of Exclusions and Restrictions
	The person in charge may remove, adjust, or retain the exclusion or restriction of a food employee according to the following conditions:
	(A) *Except when a food employee is diagnosed with an infection from* Hepatitis A Virus *or Salmonella* Typhi:
Removing exclusion for food employee who was symptomatic and not diagnosed	(1) Reinstate a food employee who was excluded as specified under subparagraph 2-201.12(A)(1) if the food employee: (a) Is asymptomatic for at least 24 hours, or; (b) Provides to the person in charge written medical documentation from a health practitioner that states the symptom is from a noninfectious condition.
Norovirus diagnosis	(2) If a food employee was diagnosed with an infection from norovirus and excluded as specified under subparagraph 2-201.12(A)(2):
Adjusting exclusion for food employee who was symptomatic and is now asymptomatic	(a) Restrict the food employee, who is asymptomatic for at least 24 hours and works in a food establishment not serving a highly susceptible population, until the conditions for reinstatement as specified under subparagraphs (D)(1) or (2) of this section are met, or;
Retaining exclusion for food employee who was asymptomatic and is now asymptomatic and works in food establishment serving HSP	(b) Retain the exclusion for the food employee, who is asymptomatic for at least 24 hours and works in a food establishment that serves a highly susceptible population, until the conditions for reinstatement as specified under subparagraphs (D)(1) or (2) of this section are met.
Shigella **spp. diagnosis**	(3) If a food employee was diagnosed with an infection from *Shigella* spp. and excluded as specified under subparagraph 2-201.12(A)(2):
Adjusting exclusion for food employee who was symptomatic and is now asymptomatic	(a) Restrict the food employee, who is asymptomatic for at least 24 hours and works in a food establishment not serving a highly susceptible population, until the conditions for reinstatement as specified under subparagraphs (E)(1) or (2) of this section are met, or;
Retaining exclusion for food employee who was asymptomatic and is now asymptomatic	(b) Retain the exclusion for the food employee, who is asymptomatic for at least 24 hours and works in a food establishment that serves a highly susceptible population, until the conditions for reinstatement as specified under subparagraphs (E)(1) or (2), diagnosis or (E)(1), and (3)(a) of this section are met.

(Continued)

Managing Exclusions and Restrictions	2-201.13 Removal, Adjustment, or Retention of Exclusions and Restrictions (Continued)
EHEC or STEC diagnosis Adjusting exclusion for food employee who was symptomatic and is now asymptomatic Retaining exclusion for food employee who was symptomatic and is now asymptomatic and works in food establishment serving HSP	(4) If a food employee was diagnosed with an infection from Enterohemorrhagic or Shiga toxin-producing *Escherichia coli* and excluded as specified under subparagraph 2-201.12(A)(2): (a) Restrict the food employee, who is asymptomatic for at least 24 hours and works in a food establishment not serving a highly susceptible population, until the conditions for reinstatement as specified under subparagraphs (F)(1) or (2) of this section are met, or; (b) Retain the exclusion for the food employee, who is asymptomatic for at least 24 hours and works in a food establishment that serves a highly susceptible population, until the conditions for reinstatement as specified under subparagraphs (F)(1) or (2) are met
Hepatitis A Virus or jaundice diagnosis—removing exclusions	(B) Reinstate a food employee who was excluded as specified under ¶ 2-201.12(B) if the person in charge obtains approval from the regulatory authority and one of the following conditions is met; (1) The food employee has been jaundiced for more than 7 calendar days, (2) The anicteric food employee has been symptomatic with symptoms other than jaundice for more than 14 calendar days, or; (3) The food employee provides to the person in charge written medical documentation from a health practitioner stating the food employee is free of a Hepatitis A Virus infection.
***S*. Typhi diagnosis—removing exclusions**	(C) Reinstate a food employee who was excluded as specified under ¶ 2-201.12(C) if: (1) The person in charge obtains approval from the regulatory authority, and; (2) The food employee provides to the person in charge written medical documentation from a health practitioner that states the food employee is free from *S*. Typhi infection.

(Continued)

Managing Exclusions and Restrictions	2-201.13 Removal, Adjustment, or Retention of Exclusions and Restrictions (Continued)
Norovirus diagnosis— removing exclusion or restriction	(D) Reinstate a food employee who was excluded as specified under subparagraphs 2-201.12(A)(2) or (D)(1) who was RESTRICTED under subparagraph 2-201.12(D)(2) if the person in charge obtains approval from the regulatory authority and one of the following conditions is met: (1) The excluded or restricted food employee provides to the person in charge written medical documentation from a health practitioner stating that the food employee is free of a norovirus infection, (2) The food employee was excluded or restricted after symptoms of vomiting or diarrhea resolved, and more than 48 hours have passed since the food employee became asymptomatic, or; (3) The food employee was excluded or restricted and did not develop symptoms and more than 48 hours have passed since the food employee was diagnosed.

***Shigella* spp. diagnosis— removing exclusion or restriction**	(E) Reinstate a food employee who was excluded as specified under subparagraphs 2-201.12(A)(2) or (E)(1) or who was restricted under subparagraph 2-201.12(E)(2) if the person in charge obtains approval from the regulatory authority and one of the following conditions is met:
	
	(1) The excluded or restricted food employee provides to the person in charge written medical documentation from a health practitioner stating that the food employee is free of a *Shigella* spp. infection based on test results showing two consecutive negative stool specimen cultures that are taken:
	  (a) Not earlier than 48 hours after discontinuance of antibiotics, and
	  (b) At least 24 hours apart,
	
	(2) The food employee was excluded or restricted after symptoms of vomiting or diarrhea resolved, and more than 7 calendar days have passed since the food employee became asymptomatic, or;
	
	(3) The food employee was excluded or restricted and did not develop symptoms and more than 7 calendar days have passed since the food employee was diagnosed.

(Continued)

Managing Exclusions and Restrictions	2-201.13 Removal, Adjustment, or Retention of Exclusions and Restrictions (Continued)

EHEC or STEC diagnosis— removing exclusion or restriction	(F) Reinstate a food employee who was excluded or restricted as specified under subparagraphs 2-201.12(A)(2) or (F)(1) or who was restricted under subparagraph 2-201.12(F)(2) if the person in charge obtains approval from the regulatory authority and one of the following conditions is met:
	
	(1) The excluded or restricted food employee provides to the person in charge written medical documentation from a health practitioner stating that the food employee is free of an infection from Enterohemorrhagic or Shiga toxin-producing *Escherichia coli* based on test results that show two consecutive negative stool specimen cultures that are taken:
	    (a) Not earlier than 48 hours after discontinuance of antibiotics; and
	    (b) At least 24 hours apart,
	(2) The food employee was excluded or restricted after symptoms of vomiting or diarrhea resolved and more than 7 calendar days have passed since the food employee became asymptomatic, or;
	(3) The food employee was excluded or restricted and did not develop symptoms, and more than 7 days have passed since the food employee was diagnosed.

Sore throat with fever— removing Exclusion or restriction	(G) Reinstate a food employee who was excluded or restricted as specified under subparagraphs 2-201.12(G)(1) or (2) if the food employee provides to the person in charge written medical documentation from a health practitioner stating the food employee meets one of the following conditions: (1) Has received antibiotic therapy for *Streptococcus pyogenes* infection for more than 24 hours, (2) Has at least one negative throat specimen culture for *Streptococcus pyogenes* infection, or; (3) Is otherwise determined by a health practitioner to be free of a *Streptococcus pyogenes* infection.

(Continued)

Managing Exclusions and Restrictions	2-201.13 Removal, Adjustment, or Retention of Exclusions and Restrictions (Continued)
Uncovered infected wound or pustular boil—removing restriction	(H) Reinstate a food employee who was restricted as specified under ¶ 2-201.12(H) if the skin, infected wound, cut, or pustular boil is properly covered with one of the following: (1) An impermeable cover such as a finger cot or stall and a single-use glove over the impermeable cover if the infected wound or pustular boil is on the hand, finger, or wrist, (2) An impermeable cover on the arm if the infected wound or pustular boil is on the arm, or; (3) A dry, durable, tight-fitting bandage if the infected wound or pustular boil is on another part of the body.
Exposure to foodborne pathogen and works in food establishment serving HSP— removing restriction	(I) Reinstate a food employee who was restricted as specified under ¶ 2-201.12(I) and was exposed to one of the following pathogens as specified under subparagraph 2-201.11(A)(4) or (5):
Norovirus	(1) Norovirus and one of the following conditions is met: (a) More than 48 hours have passed since the last day the food employee was potentially exposed, or; (b) More than 48 hours have passed since the food employee's household contact became asymptomatic.
***Shigella* spp., EHEC, or STEC**	(2) *Shigella* spp. or Enterohemorrhagic or Shiga toxin-producing *Escherichia coli* and one of the following conditions is met: (a) More than 3 calendar days have passed since the last day the food employee was potentially exposed, or; (b) More than 3 calendar days have passed since the food employee's household contact became asymptomatic.
***S.* Typhi**	(3) *S.* Typhi and one of the following conditions is met: (a) More than 14 calendar days have passed since the last day the food employee was potentially exposed, or; (b) More than 14 calendar days have passed since the food employee's household contact became asymptomatic.

(Continued)

Managing Exclusions and Restrictions	2-201.13 Removal, Adjustment, or Retention of Exclusions and Restrictions (Continued)

Hepatitis A Virus	(4) Hepatitis A Virus and one of the following conditions is met:
	  (a) The food employee is immune to Hepatitis A Virus infection because of a prior illness from Hepatitis A Virus,;
	  (b) The food employee is immune to Hepatitis A Virus infection because of vaccination against Hepatitis A Virus,
	  (c) The food employee is immune to Hepatitis A Virus infection because of IgG administration,
	  (d) More than 30 calendar days have passed since the last day the food employee was potentially exposed,
	  (e) More than 30 calendar days have passed since the food employee's household contact became jaundiced, or;
	  (f) The food employee does not use an alternative procedure that allows bare hand contact with ready-to-eat food until at least 30 days after the potential exposure, as specified in subparagraphs (I)(4)(d) and (e) of this section, and the food employee receives additional training about:
	    (i) Hepatitis A symptoms and preventing the transmission of infection,
	    (ii) Proper handwashing procedures, and;
	    (iii) Protecting ready-to-eat food from contamination introduced by bare hand contact.

Appendix E

Conversion Table for Fahrenheit and Celsius for Common Temperatures Used in Food Establishments

°F	°C	°F	°C
212	100	85	30
200	93	75	24
194	90	70	21
190	88	68	20
180	82	55	13
171	77	50	10
165	74	45	7
160	71	41	5
155	68	38	3
150	66	36	2
145	63	34	1
140	60	32	0
135	57	30	-1
130	54	28	-2
120	49	0	-18
110	43	-4	-20
100	38	-31	-35

Notes

Appendix F

Areas of Knowledge Deemed Important for the Person in Charge

Paragraph 2-102.11 (C) of the current *Food Code* identifies the following areas of knowledge as being important for the person in charge of a retail food operation:

1. Describing the relationship between the prevention of foodborne disease and the personal hygiene of a food employee,
2. Explaining the responsibility of the person in charge for preventing the transmission of foodborne disease by a food employee who has a disease or medical condition that may cause foodborne disease,
3. Describing the symptoms associated with the diseases that are transmissible through food,
4. Explaining the significance of the relationship between maintaining the time and temperature of PHF (TCS) and the prevention of foodborne illness,
5. Explaining the hazards involved in the consumption of raw or undercooked meat, poultry, eggs, and fish,
6. Stating the required food temperatures and times for safe cooking of PHF (TCS) including meat, poultry, eggs, and fish,
7. Stating the required temperatures and times for the safe refrigerated storage, hot-holding, cooling, and reheating of PHF (TCS),
8. Describing the relationship between the prevention of foodborne illness and the management and control of the following:
    a. Cross contamination,
    b. Hand contact with ready-to-eat foods,
    c. Handwashing,
    d. Maintaining the food establishment in a clean condition and in good repair,
9. Describing foods identified as major food allergens and the symptoms that a major food allergen could cause in a sensitive individual who has an allergic reaction, and ensuring that employees are properly trained in food safety, including food allergy awareness, as it relates to their assigned duties,

10. Explaining the relationship between food safety and providing equipment that is:
    a. Sufficient in number and capacity, and;
    b. Properly designed, constructed, located, installed, operated, maintained, and cleaned;
11. Explaining correct procedures for cleaning and sanitizing utensils and food-contact surfaces of equipment,
12. Identifying the source of water used and measures taken to assure that it remains protected from contamination such as providing protection from backflow and precluding the creation of cross connections,
13. Identifying poisonous or toxic materials in the food establishment and the procedures necessary to assure that they are safely stored, dispensed, used, and disposed of according to law,
14. Identifying critical control points in the operation from purchasing through sale or service that when not controlled may contribute to the transmission of foodborne illness and explaining steps taken to assure that the points are controlled in accordance with the requirements of this Code,
15. Explaining the details of how the person in charge and food employees comply with the HACCP plan if a plan is required by the law, this Code, or an agreement between the regulatory authority and the food establishment,
16. Explaining the responsibilities, rights, and authorities assigned by this Code to the:
    a. Food employee,
    b. Conditional employee,
    c. Person in charge,
    d. Regulatory authority, and;
17. Explaining how the person in charge, food employees, and conditional employees comply with reporting responsibilities and exclusion or restriction of food employees.

Appendix G

New Risk Designations for *Food Code* Provisions

The FDA has created a new three-tier system to designate *Food Code* provisions in terms of their relationship to the risk factors most likely to contribute to foodborne illness and the public health interventions and good retail practices that result in safer food and protect the consumer. "Priority," "Priority Foundation" and "Core" were the terms chosen to describe the relationship of the *Food Code* provisions to preventing, eliminating or reducing to an acceptable level, hazards associated with foodborne illness. The definitions for these three risk designations are as follows:

- **Priority** - means a provision in the *Food Code* whose application contributes directly to the elimination, prevention or reduction to an acceptable level of hazards associated with foodborne illness or injury and there isn't another provision that more directly controls the hazard.

  Priority items include those provisions in the *Food Code* which have a quantifiable measure or critical limit to show control of the hazard such as cooking, reheating, cooling, and handwashing. A "Priority Item" is denoted in the Code with the superscript letter ^{P}. When considering if a provision in the Code is a priority item, you should ask "Is there a measurable critical limit?" and "Do other provisions in the Code more directly control the hazard?"

- **Priority Foundation** - means a provision in the Code whose application supports, facilitates, or enables the active managerial control of one or more priority items.

  Priority foundation includes the purposeful incorporation of specific actions, equipment or procedures by industry management to attain control of factors that contribute to foodborne illness or injury such as personnel training, infrastructure or necessary equipment, HACCP plans, documentation or record keeping, and labeling. "Priority Foundation Item" is denoted in the *Food Code* with the superscript letters ^{PF}.

- **Core** - means a provision in the *Food Code* that is not designated as a Priority item or a Priority Foundation item. Core items include an item that usually relates to general sanitation, operational controls, sanitation standard operating procedures (SSOPs), facilities or structures, equipment design, or general maintenance.

Notes

Index

A

A_w, 36–37
Abrasive cleaning, 199–200
Abrasives, 203
Acid detergent, 202
Acidic, 34
ADA, 97
Added man-made chemicals, 65-66
Adulterated food, 119
Aerobic, 36
Aflatoxin, 65
Air conditioning, 186
Air gap, 242
Alkaline, 34
Alkaline detergent, 202
Allergies, 60–61, 196, 226, 300,344
Ambient display equipment, 178–179
Americans with Disabilities Act (ADA), 97
Anaerobic, 36
Anaphylaxis, 60
Anisakis spp., 55–56, 343
Answers to end-of-chapter quizzes, 337–338
Anti-slip mats, 238
Areas of knowledge, person in charge, 363–364
Aseptic processing and packaging, 122
Aspergillus spp., 65
Atmospheric vacuum breaker, 243

B

Bacillus cereus, 43, 343
Backflow, 241–244
Backsiphonage, 242
Bacteria, 29–37
    acidity, 34
    defined, 29
    food, 33
    foodborne illness, 40–52
    growth, phases of, 31
    how destroyed/controlled, 29
    moisture, 36–37
    non-sporeforming, 46–52
    oxygen, 36
    pathogenic, 31
    spoilage, 31
    sporeforming, 41–42, 43–45
    temperature, 35
    time, 35
Bacterial growth, 31, 32
Bagging, 149
Bait box, 255
Band saw, 177
Beetles, 251
Best practices, 266
Bi-metal thermometer, 80, 82
Big Five pathogens, 349. *See also* individual pathogens
Binary fission, 31, 32
Biological hazards, 28–29, 41
Boil water advisories, 306
Boiling point method, 83
Bottled drinking water, 306–307
Bucket and brush method, 220
Built-in thermometer, 81
Butter, 122

C

Calibrating a thermometer, 82–83
Campylobacter jejuni, 46
CAP, 115
Carbonators, 244
CCP, 271
CDC, 75, 328
Ceilings, 223, 237–239
Celsius-fahrenheit conversion table, 361
Centers for Disease Control and Prevention (CDC), 76, 296
Certification, 15–17

Certified Food Protection Manager, 15–17, 363–364. *See also* Person In Charge
CFP, 297
Changing trends in food consumption, 7
Check valve, 243
Checkout counter, 149–150
Cheese, 122
Chemical hazards, 29, 59–65
   added man-made chemicals, 65
   ciguatoxin, 62
   employee medication, 66
   food allergens, 60–61
   histamine, 63
   scombrotoxin, 63
   shellfish toxins, 63–64
Chemical sanitizing, 208–212
Chemical storage, 132–133
Chemical test strips, 210
Children's menu, 142
Chlorinating water, 306–308
Chlorine, 208–211
Chopper, 176
Ciguatoxin, 62, 343
Clean-in-place (CIP), 199, 220–221
Cleaning agents, 198, 202–203
Cleaning and sanitizing, 12, 100, 194–231. *See also* Environmental sanitation and maintenance
   abrasive cleaning, 199–200
   ceilings, 223
   chemical sanitizing, 208–212
   clean-in-place (CIP), 199, 220–221
   cleaning agents, 202–203
   cleaning equipment, 221–226
   cleaning frequency, 203–205
   factors to consider, 200–201
   fixed equipment cleaning, 218–222
   floors, 223–224
   general principles, 196–198
   heat sanitizing, 206–208
   manual warewashing, 216–218
   mechanical warewashing, 213–216
   removal of food participles, 198
   rinsing, 200
   soaking, 198, 199
   spray methods, 199
   walls, 219
Clostridium botulinum, 45, 344
Clostridium perfringens, 44, 344
Cockroaches, 250
Cod worm, 56
Code of Federal Regulations (CFR), 99
Coding, 281
Cold food holding, 88
Cold-holding, 139–141
Cold storage, 128–130
Compactor, 247
Conference for Food Protection (CFP), 297
Construction materials, 166–169
Consumer advisory, 305–306
Contains statement (allergens), 300
Contamination, 8–9, 97–100
Controlled atmosphere packaging (CAP), 115
Convection oven, 170
Conversion table (fahrenheit-celsius), 387
Convenience store, 5
Cook-chill, 115, 170
Cooking, 141–143
Cooking hot foods, 86
Cooking temperatures/times, 86
Cooling, 143–144
Coving, 238
Crisis management, 306–308
Critical control point (CCP), 271
Critical limits, 271–272
Cross connections, 241
Cross contamination, 97–98
Crustacean shellfish tank, 179
Crustaceans, 123
Cryptosporidium parvum, 58, 344
Cyclospora cayentanensis, 56–57, 344

D

DAP, 64, 346
Date marking, 301–303
Deck, 170

Definitions (glossary), 317–336
Degreasers, 203
Delivery vehicles, 109
Dented cans, 113
Design, layout, and facilities, 162–163
Detergent, 202, 203
Detergent sanitizers, 203
Determining food quality, 109–110
Dial-face metal stem type (bi-metal) thermometer, 80, 82
Diarrhetic shellfish poisoning (DSP), 64, 346
Digital thermometer, 80
Dinoflagellates, 64
Direct cross connection, 241
Discarding food, 147
Disclosure (consumer advisory), 305–306
Disease-causing bacteria, 31–37. *See also* Bacteria
Dishwashing machines, 181–183
Display case/tanks, 174, 178–180
Disposable gloves, 93–94
Domoic acid poisoning (DAP), 64, 346
Dry milk, 122
Dry storage, 131
DSP, 64, 346
Dual check valve, 243

E

E. coli, 47–48
Education and training, 13
Eggs, 120–121, 134
Emergency procedures. *See* Food safety regulations and crisis management
Employee health system, 349–359
Employee medication, 66
End-of-chapter quizzes, answers, 337–338
Environmental Protection Agency (EPA), 296
Environmental sanitation and maintenance, 232–261. *See also* Cleaning and sanitizing
ceilings, 238–239
exterior of building, 234–235
floors, 237–238
garbage, 245–247
hand washing sinks, 239–240
pest control, 2473–256
plumbing, 241–245
restrooms, 239
sewage disposal, 236
walls, 237, 238
water supply, 235–236
EPA, 296
Equipment, 160–193. *See also* Facilities, equipment and utensils
ambient display, 178–179
chopper, 176
cleaning, 224–226
construction materials, 166–169
cook-chill, 174–175
grinder, 176
hot-holding, 175
ice machine, 177–178
live seafood display tanks, 179–180
low-temperature storage equipment, 171–172
mixers, 176
oven, 169–170
rapid-chill system, 174–175
refrigeration unit, 171–173
saws, 176
selection, 165
single-source/single-use articles, 180
size and design, 165–166
slicers, 176
tenderizers, 176
warewashing, 181–183
Escherichia coli, 47–48
Exterior of building, 234–235

F

F-A-T-T-O-M, 33
FAAN, 61
Facilities, equipment and utensils, 160–193
equipment. *See* Equipment
HVAC system, 186–187

installation, 183
layout/design, 186–187
lighting, 184–186
maintenance and replacement, 184
regulatory considerations, 163–164
work centers, 164
Facultative anaerobic, 36
Fahrenheit-celsius conversion table, 361
FALCPA, 300
FDA, 295–296
FDA Food Allergen Labeling Act, 60
FDA Food Code, 15, 296
Federal agencies, 295–296
Federal Trade Commission (FTC), 286
FIFO, 128
Fight BAC! Campaign, 304
Finfish, 62
First-in, first-out (FIFO), 128
Fish, 123–125, 135
Fish tank, 180
Fixed equipment cleaning, 218–222
Flies, 249
Floor drains, 223
Floor mounted equipment, 166
Floors, 223–224
Flow diagram, 276–277
Fluid milk, 122
FMI's Recommendations for the Safe Preparation of Sushi, 279
Food, 33
Food Allergen Labeling and Consumer Protection Act (FALCPA), 60, 300
Food allergens, 60–61, 300, 344
Food Allergy and Anaphylaxis Network (FAAN), 61
Food allergy awareness poster, 60-61
Food and Drug Administration (FDA), 295
Food Code, 88
Food-contact surfaces, 167
Food defense, 309–310
Food establishment, 5
Food flow diagram, 111
Food handling, 143–147

Food industry, 15
Food labeling, 299–303
Food labels, 117, 153
Food manager certification, 16–17
Food Marketing Institute (FMI), 6
Food packaging, 112–117
Food preparation, 136
Food preservation, 86–87
Food product flow, 10–11, 106–159
  bagging, 149–150
  checkout counter, 149–150
  cold-holding, 139–141
  cooking, 141–143
  cooling, 143–144
  determining food quality, 109–110
  discarding food, 147
  eggs, 120–121
  fish, 123–125
  food handling, 146–147
  food preparation, 136
  frozen foods, 127
  fruit and vegetables, 125–126
  game animals, 120
  home meal replacement, 152–153
  hot-holding, 145–146
  ingredient substitution, 136–137
  inspecting delivery vehicles, 109
  juice, 126–127
  measuring temperatures, 110
  milk products, 122
  mobile food facilities, 150–151
  packaging, 112–117
  poultry, 119–120
  process approach to HACCP, 273–277
  receiving, 111–112
  reconditioning food, 147
  red meat products, 118–119
  refilling returnable containers, 147–148
  reheating, 145–146
  self-service bar, 148–149
  storage of food, 128–136
  temperature abuse, 137
  temporary facilities, 150–151

thawing food, 137–138
vegetables, 125–126
vending machines, 151–152
Food recall, 282, 298–299
Food safety management program, 261–289
  challenges, 283
  coding, 281, 282
  food recall, 282
  GAPs, 278
  GMPs, 278
  GRPs, 278–279
  guidelines, 283
  HACCP system, 270–278
  instructions, 266–269
  product identification, 281
  SOPs, 266–269
  what to focus on, 265
Food safety regulations and crisis management, 290–316
  consumer advisory, 305–306
  crisis mangement, 306-308
  date marking, 301–303
  federal agencies, 295–296
  Fight BAC! Campaign, 304
  foodborne illness incident or outbreak, 308–310
  food defense, 309–310
  food recall, 298, 299
  grading, 298
  GRAS, 298
  inspection/audit, 293–294
  inspection for wholesomeness, 297–298
  labeling, 299–303
  National Food Safety Initiative, 303–304
  other organizations, 297
  permit to operate, 293
  Project Chill, 304–305
  state and local regulations, 293
  suspected foodborne illness procedure, 308–309
  tampering, 309
  terrorism, 309

water supply emergency procedures, 306–308
Food temperature-measuring device, 79. *See also* Thermometer
Foodborne disease outbreak, 8, 308–309
Foodborne hazards. *See* Hazards to food safety
Foodborne illness
  causative agents, 343–347
  classification, 27
  cleanliness. *See* Cleaning and sanitizing operations
  contamination, 97–100
  cross contamination, 97–98
  defined, 5
  disposable gloves, 93–95
  foodborne hazards. *See* Hazards to food safety
  handwashing, 90–93
  no "bare" hands policy, 92–93
  onset time, 28
  outbreak, 8, 308–309
  outer clothing and apparel, 95
  personal health, 96
  personal hygiene, 95
  risk factors, 265
  suspected outbreak, 308–309
  symptoms, 27
    time and temperature abuse, 78–89. *See also* Time and temperature abuse
Foodborne parasites, 55–58
Four Rs (food allergy), 61
Freezer, 171–173
Freezer storage, 130
Frozen, ready-to-eat foods, 140
Frozen foods, 83–85, 127
Fruits and vegetables, 125–126, 133
FTC, 296
Fungi, 59

G

Game animals, 120
GAPs, 278

Garbage, 245–247
Generally recognized as safe (GRAS), 215, 330
Germs, 10
Giardia lamblia, 345
Glossary, 317–336
Gloves, 93–94
GMPs, 278
Good agricultural practices (GAPs), 278
Good manufacturing practices (GMPs), 278
Good retail practices (GRPs), 278–281
Government regulations. *See* Food safety regulations
Grade standards, 118
Grading, 118, 298
GRAS, 215, 298
Grease traps, 245
Grinder, 176
GRPs, 278–281

H

HACCP system, 11–12, 270–277
    flow diagram, 276–277
    process approach, 273–277
    regulatory requirements, 277–278
    seven principles, 210–272
Hand washing sinks, 239–240
Handwashing, 90–93
Hard water, 197
Hazard analysis critical control point. *See* HACCP system
Hazards to food safety, 24–73, 343–347
    bacteria. *See* Bacteria
    biological hazards, 28–29, 41
    causative agents, 343–347
    chemical hazards. *See* Chemical hazards
    fungi, 59
    parasites, 55–58
    physical hazards, 29, 66–67
    potentially hazardous foods [PHF(TCS)], 37–40
    ready-to-eat foods, 40
    virus, 52–54
Heat sanitizing, 206–208

Heat-sensitive label, 207
Hepatitis A Information Guide, 54
Hepatitis A virus, 53, 54, 345
Hermetic packaging, 113
Herring worm, 56
Histamine, 63
Holding thermometer, 207–208
Home canned food, 108
Home meal replacement, 152–153
Hood systems, 271
Hot-holding, 145–146
Hot-holding equipment, 175
Hot-holding temperatures/times, 83
House mouse, 252
Hurdle technology, 39
HVAC system, 186–187

I

Ice machine, 177–178
Ice point method, 83
Immunocompromised, 28
In-place sanitizer, 221
Indirect cross connection, 241
Infection, 27
Infectious hepatitis, 54
Infrared thermometer, 81
Ingredient substitution, 136–137
Insects, 248–251
Inspecting delivery vehicles, 109
Inspection/audit, 293–294
Inspection for wholesomeness, 118, 297–298
Installation, 183
Instructions, 267–269
Integrated pest management (IPM), 255–256
Intoxication, 27
Iodine, 209, 211
Iodophors, 211
IPM, 100, 255–256
Irradiation, 117

J

Juice, 126–127

K

Kitchenware, 181
Knowledge requirements, person in charge, 363–364

L

Label warnings, 117, 127
Labeling, 299–303
Lighting, 184–186
Listeria monocytogenes, 48, 345
Live seafood display tanks, 175–176, 220
Local regulations, 293–294
Low-temperature dishwashers, 183
Low-temperature storage equipment, 171–174
Luncheon meats, 140

M

Maintenance and replacement, 184
Manager certification examinations, 16
Manual warewashing, 177–178, 216–218
MAP, 112, 113, 134
Material safety and data sheet (MSDS), 225–226
Maximum registering thermometer, 79, 208
Meal solutions (home meal replacement), 152–153
Measures to Improve Security in the Supermarket Industry, 275
Meat/meat products, 118–119, 133–134
Mechanical warewashing, 178–179, 213–216
Mechanically tenderized, 142
Metal cans, 113
Metals, 167
Microbes, 10
Microbial growth barriers, 116
Microorganisms, 10
Microwave, 170
Milk/milk products, 122, 135
Misting system, 220
Mixer, 176
Mobile food facilities, 150–151

Modified atmosphere packaging (MAP), 114, 115, 136
Moisture, 36–37
Mold, 59, 65
Molluscan shellfish, 123–125
Molluscan Shellfish Handling for Retailers, 267
Molluscan shellfish tank, 179–180
Moths, 251
MSDS, 225–226
Multi-tank hot water sanitizers, 214
Multi-tiered, risk-based employee health 349–359
Mushrooms, 65
Mycotoxins, 59, 65, 345

N

National Food Safety Initiative, 303
National Marin Fisheries Service (NMFS), 295
Natural toxins, 62
Neurotoxic shellfish poisoning (NSP), 64, 346
New Risk Designations for Food Code, 365
NMFS, 295
No "bare" hands policy, 92–93
Non-food contact surfaces, 167
Non-sporeforming bacteria, 42, 46–52
Norovirus, 54
Norwalk virus, 54, 345
Norway rat, 252
NSP, 64, 346
Nutrition label, 299
Nutrition Labeling and Education Act, 299

O

Occupational Safety and Health Administration (OSHA), 225, 296
Outer clothing and apparel, 95
Oven, 169–170

P

Packaging, 112–117
Paralytic shellfish poisoning (PSP), 64, 346
Parasites, 55–58

Parenthetical listing (allergens), 300
Pasteurization, 122
Pathogenic bacteria, 31
Permit to operate, 293
Person in charge, knowledge requirements, 363–364
Personal health, 96–97, 268–269
Personal hygiene, 95, 268–269
Pest control, 247–256
Pesticides, 65
pH, 34, 210
PHF(TCS), 38–40, 339–342
Physical hazards, 29, 65–66
Plastic, 167, 168
Plumbing, 241–245
Post-inspection conference, 294
Potable water, 197
Potentially hazardous foods [PHF(TCS)], 37–40, 339–342
Poultry, 119–120, 134
Pre-Emergency Planning and Disaster Recovery Manual, 310
Pre-flushing, 198
Pre-inspection conference, 294
Prepackaged foods, 139–141
Prepared salads, 139–140
Preserving food, 86–87
Pressure type vacuum breaker, 243
Preventing temperature abuse, 85–87
Process approach to HACCP, 273–274
Process-specific HACCP program, 273
Produce misting system, 220
Product coding, 281
Product date marking, 301–303
Product identification, 281
Product-specific HACCP program, 273
Product tampering, 310
Professional organizations, 297
Project Chill, 304
PSP, 64, 346

Q

Quaternary ammonium compounds (quats), 209, 211–212
Quizzes, answers, 337–338

R

Radura, 117
Range, 169
Rapid-chill system, 174–171
Rats, 251–255
Reach-in refrigeration, 172–173
Ready-to-eat foods, 40
Recall of food product, 282, 298–299
Receiving, 111–112
Receiving and storing (temperature), 86
Reconditioning food, 147
Red meat products, 118–119
Reduced oxygen packaging (ROP), 112–117
Reduced pressure principle backflow preventers, 244
Refilling returnable containers, 147–148
Refrigerated display cases, 139–140
Refrigerated foods, 86–87
Refrigerated storage, 129–130
Refrigeration unit, 171–174
Refuse, 245–247
Regulations. *See* Food safety regulations
Reheating, 145–146
Reheating temperatures/times, 86–87
Reminder (consumer advisory), 305
Replacement of equipment, 184
Restrooms, 239
Retail food establishment, 5
Retail food manager, 6
Retail food safety management. *See* Food safety management program
Returnable containers, 147–148
Rinsing, 200
Risk, 271
Risk-based employee health system, 349–359
Rodent, 251–255
Rodenticides, 255
Roof rat, 252

ROP packaging, 112–117
Rotavirus, 346
Rotisserie, 170
Rotisserie chicken flow diagram, 277
Routine inspection/audit, 294
RTE (ready-to-eat) foods, 40
Rusty cans, 113

S

Safe food-handling instruction label, 300–301
Safe load line, 140
Salmonella spp., 48–50, 346
Sanitary, 12
Sanitizing. *See* Cleaning and sanitizing
Saw, 176–177
Scombrotoxin, 63, 346
Seafood, 123–125
Seafood display tanks, 175–176, 220
Self-inspection, 294
Self-service bar, 148–149
Sell-by dates, 116, 301-303
Sensory evaluation, 109-110
Sewage disposal, 236
Shelf life, 116
Shellfish, 123–125, 135
Shellfish tags, 124
Shellfish toxins, 63–64, 346
Shellstock, 124–125
Shiga-toxin-producing *E. coli*, 47–48, 346
Shigella spp., 50–51, 347
Shigellosis, 50
Signage, 240
Single-service articles, 180
Single-use articles, 180
Slicer, 176
Small batch preparation, 136
Soaking, 198, 199
Soap, 202
SOPs, 267–269
Sous vide, 114, 115, 135
Spoilage bacteria, 31

Spoilage in meat, 120
Spore, 30, 41
Sporeforming bacteria, 41–42, 43–45
Spray cleaning, 199
Spray type warewashers, 214
Stainless steel, 167
Standard operating procedures (SOPs), 267–269
Staphylococcus aureus, 51, 347
State and local regulations, 293
Steam cleaning, 207, 209
Storage of food, 128–136
Supermarket, 5
Superstore, 5
Sushi-grade fish, 280–281
Suspected foodborne illness problem, 308

T

T-Stick, 81, 207
Tableware, 181
Tampering, 310
Temperature abuse, 75. *See also* Time and temperature abuse
Temperature conversion (fahrenheit-celsius), 361
Temperature danger zone, 78, 89
Temporary food establishment (TFE), 150–151
Tenderizer, 176
Terminology (glossary), 317–336
Terrorism, 309–310
TFE, 150–151
Thawing food, 83, 86, 137–138
Thermocouple, 80
Thermometer, 80–82
Three-compartment sink, 181–182, 216–218
Time and temperature abuse, 78–87
  calibrating a thermometer, 82–83
  food preservation, 86–87
  guidelines, 86–87
  measuring food temperature, 83–85
  thawing food, 89
  thermometer, 80–82

Time as a public health control, 146
Toilet facilities, 239
Toxin-mediated infection, 27
Toxoplasma gondii, 347
Tracking powder pesticides, 255
Trash bailer, 247
Tribal agencies, 293
Trichinella spiralis, 57, 347

U

Uniform, 95
U.S. Department of Agriculture (USDA), 14, 295
U.S. Department of Commerce (USDC), 295
USDA, 295
USDC, 295
Utensils, 180. *See also* Facilities, equipment and utensils

V

Vacuum breaker, 243
Vacuum packaging, 113, 115
Vegetables, 125–126, 135
Vegetative cells, 30
Vending machines, 151–152
Ventilation system, 186–187
Vibrio cholera, 52
Vibrio parahaemolyticus, 52
Vibrio spp., 52, 347
Vibrio vulnificus, 52
Virus, 52–54

W

Walk-in refrigeration, 173
Walls, 223, 238
Warewashing, 181–183, 213–218
Waste management, 245–247
Water activity (A), 36–37
Water hardness, 193, 210
Water supply, 197, 235–236
Water supply emergency procedure, 306–307
Whole shell eggs, 134

Wholesome, 108
Wiping cloths, 221–222
Wood, 168
Work centers, 164
Work clothes, 95

Y

Yeast, 59, 65

Notes

Notes